POSITIVIST THOUGHT
IN FRANCE
DURING THE SECOND EMPIRE
1852–1870

POSITIVIST THOUGHT
IN FRANCE

DURING THE SECOND EMPIRE
1852–1870

BY

D. G. CHARLTON

OXFORD
AT THE CLARENDON PRESS
1959

Oxford University Press, Amen House, London E.C.4

GLASGOW NEW YORK TORONTO MELBOURNE WELLINGTON
BOMBAY CALCUTTA MADRAS KARACHI KUALA LUMPUR
CAPE TOWN IBADAN NAIROBI ACCRA

PREFACE

IN the course of my work on this book I have contracted many debts. Some of these are indicated by the Bibliography; others are of a more personal nature and I am happy to be able to acknowledge them here. This study is an abridged and revised version of a doctoral thesis submitted to the University of London in 1955, and my greatest obligation is to my supervisor, Professor H. J. Hunt, for his unfailingly generous and invaluable guidance, encouragement, and criticism. My warmest thanks are likewise due to Dr. R. W. Ladborough and Dr. I. D. McFarlane whose teaching first stimulated my interest and instructed me in the works of nineteenth-century French literature and thought and who have not ceased to encourage and help me; to Professor I. W. Alexander for extremely useful suggestions at an early stage in my work; and to Mr. C. B. Cox, Professor P. Mansell Jones, Professor Garnet Rees, and Dr. Colin Smith, who have read the book in its entirety and given me most helpful advice, comment, and criticism. I am also much indebted to other friends and colleagues for readily allowing me to discuss difficulties with them and to draw on their knowledge. I am no less grateful to the Librarian of the University of Hull and his staff for their help and persistence in obtaining books I wished to consult; to the Master and Fellows of Emmanuel College, Cambridge, for the financial generosity which permitted me to begin my researches; to the Cassel Trustees for their assistance in financing visits to the Paris libraries; and to the officials of the Clarendon Press for their considerate helpfulness throughout the process of publication. I wish, finally, to express my indebtedness, above all and in numerous ways (including the preparation of the Index), to my wife, and my deep gratitude to my parents, to whom this book is dedicated.

D. G. C.

Hull, 1958

CONTENTS

ABBREVIATIONS

THE following abbreviations are used in the footnotes:

R.C.C.	*Revue des cours et conférences*
R.D.M.	*Revue des Deux Mondes*
R.H.L.F.	*Revue d'histoire littéraire de la France*
R.L.C.	*Revue de littérature comparée*
R.M.M.	*Revue de métaphysique et de morale*
Rev. Philos.	*Revue philosophique de la France et de l'étranger*

Full details of publication are given for primary sources; the place and date of publication are given for secondary sources. The place of publication is Paris unless otherwise stated. Italics in quotations are those of the author cited except where otherwise stated.

I

INTRODUCTION

THE Second Empire has appeared to its later interpreters as supremely an 'age of positivism' in the history of French thought. This generalization, already prevalent in the final years of the nineteenth century, has persisted to the present day, and historians from Brunetière, Monod, Lanson, and Parodi to Thibaudet, Jasinski, Martino, and Philippe Van Tieghem in more recent years have agreed that philosophy and literature alike at this time are dominated by the positivist outlook.[1] So pervading has been this view, indeed, that at a century's distance we are almost tempted to imagine its writers still engaged, in some intellectual Valhalla, in an endless, atheistic *dîner Magny*, for ever discoursing of the virtues of science, the follies of religion, and the wickedness of priests.

The reality, inevitably, was less straightforward, and this survey of positivist thought during the Second Empire will seek not so much to repeat the historical accounts of Bréhier, Benrubi, Cresson, and others as to reveal in detail something of the ambiguities in its development.[2] Even those thinkers who seem to be the leading positivists of the age are far from consistent

---

[1] F. Brunetière, 'La Renaissance de l'idéalisme', *Discours de combat*, 1900–7, 3 vols., i. 4–5, and *L'Évolution de la poésie lyrique au dix-neuvième siècle*, 9ᵉ éd., s.d., 2 vols., ii. 114–49; G. Monod, *Les Maîtres de l'histoire — Renan, Taine, Michelet*, 1894, p. 138; G. Lanson, *Histoire de la littérature française*, 1906, p. 1014; D. Parodi, *Du positivisme à l'idéalisme — Philosophies d'hier*, 1930, *Préface*; A. Thibaudet, *Histoire de la littérature française de 1789 à nos jours*, 1936, pp. 407–9; R. Jasinski, *Histoire de la littérature française*, 1947, 2 vols., ii. 340; P. Martino, *Parnasse et symbolisme*, 7ᵉ éd., 1947, p. 32; P. Van Tieghem, *Petite histoire des grandes doctrines littéraires en France*, 1946, p. 242. Amongst many other examples cf. C. Beuchat, *Histoire du naturalisme français*, 1949, 2 vols., t. i, ch. ix, and V. Giraud, *Essai sur Taine*, 6ᵉ éd., s.d. (Hachette), pp. 67, 182–3, 185.

[2] E. Bréhier, *Histoire de la philosophie*, t. ii, *La Philosophie moderne*, 1932; I. Benrubi, *Philosophische Strömungen der Gegenwart in Frankreich*, Leipzig, 1928; A. Cresson, *Les Courants de la pensée philosophique française*, t. ii, 1927. Cf. R. B. Perry, *Philosophy of the Recent Past*, London, 1927; G. de Ruggiero, *Modern Philosophy*, translated Hannay and Collingwood, London, 1921; and J. A. Gunn, *Modern French Philosophy*, London, 1922.

B

in their loyalty; almost every writer to be discussed, in fact, is, whether consciously or not, the victim of a divided mind. They are attempting, in differing ways and to differing extents, to reconcile aspirations and convictions that are incompatible. Whilst not every symptom of their intellectual conflicts can be examined, the chapters that follow try to show the oppositions that are paramount in each particular individual.

The writers to be studied fall into three rough groups. The first comprises Comte, Renan, and Taine. All three, it will be submitted, gradually come to misrepresent the real positivist standpoint and combine it with theories that are alien to it. What they present is less positivism than a distortion of it, and these writers might be grouped together as *les faux amis de la philosophie positiviste*, were the phrase not too harsh. If this judgement appears over-severe, it must be allowed that their misconstruction of positivism is not wanton or gratuitous, nor is it altogether consciously willed. It arises from precisely those conflicts of allegiance already mentioned; and whilst others have described these thinkers as *scientistes*, this study tries to measure the full extent of the disparity between their positivist starting-point and their scientism and to uncover the motives behind it.

The second group includes those who willingly accept the positivist position but who, unlike Comte, Renan, and Taine, maintain—on balance at least—a consistent and thorough-going positivism: these thinkers, one could say, are *les vrais amis de la philosophie positiviste*. If Littré and Claude Bernard alone can be named under this heading, that perhaps indicates the confusions at this time about the issues at stake and also the difficult discipline, both intellectual and emotional, that positivism entails. Even they desert it on occasion, and Littré's philosophy is inadequate in at least one important respect. But neither is guilty of any other protracted deviation, and Littré in particular appears here as the leading defender of the true positivist position against the compromising modifications of thinkers who claim its authority for views it does not in fact support.

Having considered these writers, one has surveyed the leading philosophers of the Second Empire who, with whatever admixture of error and distortion, gave allegiance to positivism. Comte is its 'father' in this century, Littré is his most famous philosophical follower, and Taine and Renan (in Jasinski's words) are 'les deux

grands maîtres intellectuels de cette génération'.[3] One might have
included Berthelot and Scherer perhaps, but both seem to be com-
paratively minor figures in the history of philosophy, however
influential they were in other fields, the one as a chemist, the
other as a literary critic and an historian of ideas. Claude Bernard,
in contrast to Berthelot, is more than a scientist; he is also the
chief exponent at this time of the experimental method, and it is
for this reason that he is admitted whilst they are not.

Finally, however, after a brief discussion of the frequently
alleged connexion between positivism and Second Empire literature, two less-remembered writers will be considered, Louise
Ackermann and Sully Prudhomme. Both, almost alone amongst
the literary authors of the period, are explicitly indebted to
positivism and thus call for study, whereas writers betraying at
most an unacknowledged and more limited affinity of outlook
with it have had to be excluded. Their thought also has a representative interest, illustrating positivism's impact on minds
marked as much by poetic sensitivity as rational power—a theme
that, for lack of space, cannot be more fully explored. In Sully
Prudhomme's case one can go further: through all his anguish
of mind he maintains a clear-sighted fidelity to the positivist
philosophy that only Littré and Bernard can match and even
anticipates certain of its later developments: his quality as a
thinker is much higher than is commonly recognized and a full
discussion of him requires no apology.

This book concerns the debates of a hundred years ago, debates
that may sometimes, and perhaps wrongly, seem surpassed, yet
it does have a relevance to more recent thought that could lead
to misunderstanding here. The philosophy of logical positivism,
though now yielding to the rather different approach of logical
analysis, may well be thought the outstanding philosophical
movement—in Austria, Germany, America, Britain, and elsewhere—of the last fifty years. And already, despite the coolness
with which it has looked upon the history of thought, its adherents
have sought their forerunners in earlier centuries. Joergensen, for
example, cites Neurath's list of predecessors in England, France,
and Germany: 'Bacon, Hobbes, Locke, Hume, Bentham, J. S.
Mill, Spencer; Descartes, Bayle, D'Alembert, Saint-Simon, Comte,

[3] Jasinski, op. cit., ii. 341.

Poincaré; Leibniz, Bolzano, Mach.'[4] He himself adds others, and setting aside its earliest ancestors—the Sophists and Epicureans, the Nominalists of the Middle Ages and Bacon, Hobbes, and Descartes—one can broadly discern four main phases in the progress of this philosophy. First come the British empiricist thinkers from Locke onwards and their French counterparts, the *philosophes* from Bayle to Condillac and Condorcet; secondly, thinkers of the nineteenth century like Saint-Simon, Comte, Mill, Feuerbach, and Spencer; thirdly, the generation whose main achievements, especially in the study of scientific method, fall between about 1880 and 1920—Mach, Poincaré, Duhem, Russell, and others; and finally the present-day exponents of logical positivism. This is the barest sketch, but it helps to underline that our subject is related to an extensive tradition in philosophy and deals with one chapter of its fortunes in France. This work may thus serve to a small extent to clarify the ancestry of contemporary thinking.

This is no more than an incidental aim, however, and one that could easily mislead. One can reasonably ask a philosopher to remain consistent to his own theory of knowledge, but it would be unjust to expect him to conform to a more recent, maturer formulation of the same theory. It may be of interest to scrutinize past thinkers for anticipations of twentieth-century ideas, but that is not the intention here. Logical positivism may have the same starting-point as Comte and the 'verification principle' be a restatement of his definition of the 'positive' method. 'Any proposition which does not admit of being ultimately reduced to a simple enunciation of fact, special or general, can have no real or intelligible sense': that is not the earlier Ayer but Comte.[5] But the former's approach is far more linguistically conscious and presupposes all the analytical work of the intervening century. Hence this study inquires how far thinkers like Comte are true to the positivist position *as they begin by defining it*. It reviews a period of the past in relation to its own philosophical awareness and not to the insights of a later generation.

---

[4] J. Joergensen, *The Development of Logical Empiricism*, Chicago, 1951, p. 6, quoting O. Neurath, *Le Développement du cercle de Vienne et l'avenir de l'empirisme logique*, 1935, p. 58.

[5] A. Comte, *Cours de philosophie positive*, 2ᵉ éd., Baillière, 1864, 6 vols., vi. 600.

II

POSITIVISM AND
SECOND EMPIRE PHILOSOPHY

1. *The Definition of Positivism*

(a) *The positivist philosophy*

'POSITIVISM', as one of its nineteenth-century English historians remarks, is 'a hopelessly ambiguous term';[1] it is consequently all the more necessary to define it as precisely as possible. Broadly, four different usages can be distinguished. By positivism may be intended, first, 'social positivism', positivism as both a philosophy of history and a sociological theory. Secondly, though less commonly, the term may refer to 'religious positivism', the positivist Religion of Humanity established by Comte and practised in positivist Churches of Humanity throughout the world. Thirdly, positivism is sometimes used to refer to the whole body of Comte's thought, including his historical, sociological, and religious theories. Finally, it may be understood in its strict philosophical meaning, and since 'social', 'religious', and 'Comtian' 'positivism' all presuppose it and claim to be built upon it, one can say that here is its basic sense. This is the meaning intended throughout this work and the touchstone by which each writer will be judged. It is true that these different types of positivism do not develop in isolation from one another and that there are significant interactions between them: Comte, for example, misuses 'philosophical positivism' because of his overriding concern with 'social positivism'. These distinctions are nevertheless real.

'Philosophical positivism' is a theory of knowledge. It holds, in its simplest form, that, excepting knowledge of logical and mathematical systems—all of them without any necessary connexion with our observable world—science provides the model of the only kind of knowledge we can attain. All that we can know of reality is what we can observe or can legitimately deduce from what we observe. That is to say, we can only know phenomena

---

[1] R. Flint, *Anti-Theistic Theories*, Edinburgh, 1917, p. 505.

and the laws of relation and succession of phenomena, and it follows that everything we can claim to know must be capable of empirical verification. Positivism thus denies the validity of such alleged means of knowing as have been termed *a priori*, and it equally denies that we can have any knowledge about religious and metaphysical questions since these are by definition largely concerned with a realm alleged to lie behind phenomena, in a world that can never be observed. And to underline that this is not a partial definition we may quote André Lalande in his *Vocabulaire technique et critique de la philosophie*; there the doctrines of the positivist philosophy are given as the following:

que seule la connaissance des faits est féconde; que le type de la certitude est fourni par les sciences expérimentales; que l'esprit humain, dans la philosophie comme dans la science, n'évite le verbalisme ou l'erreur qu'à la condition de se tenir sans cesse au contact de l'expérience et de renoncer à tout *a priori*; enfin que le domaine des 'choses en soi' est inaccessible, et que la pensée ne peut atteindre que des relations et des lois.[2]

Lest it be thought, however, that we are calling nineteenth-century thinkers to the bar of a twentieth-century conception of the positivist viewpoint, one can emphasize that their own definitions of it were precisely the same as Lalande's. This will be apparent in succeeding chapters when the 'positivism' of each individual is clarified. But here we may anticipate by citing the definitions given by the two best-known positivists of the period, Comte and Mill. Comte described *l'état positif* by saying:

Dans l'état positif, l'esprit humain, reconnaissant l'impossibilité d'obtenir des notions absolues, renonce à chercher l'origine et la destination de l'univers et à connaître les causes intimes des phéno-mènes, pour s'attacher uniquement à découvrir, par l'usage bien combiné du raisonnement et de l'observation, leurs lois effectives, c'est-à-dire leurs relations invariables de succession et de similitude.[3]

Mill affirms the same position in describing Comte's outlook and points out that it is shared by many other thinkers, Hume, Bentham, and James Mill amongst them. Positivism's doctrines are the following:

We have no knowledge of anything but Phaenomena; and our

[2] A. Lalande, *Vocabulaire technique et critique de la philosophie*, 1951, p. 793.
[3] A. Comte, *Cours de philosophie positive*, i, 1864, pp. 9–10.

knowledge of phaenomena is relative, not absolute. We know not the essence, nor the real mode of production, of any fact, but only its relations to other facts in the way of succession or of similitude. These relations are constant; that is, always the same in the same circumstances. The constant resemblances which link phaenomena together, and the constant sequences which unite them as antecedent and consequent, are termed their laws. The laws of phaenomena are all we know respecting them. Their essential nature, and their ultimate causes, either efficient or final, are unknown and inscrutable to us.[4]

In all three definitions, one may note, there is the same underlying presupposition, explicitly declared here by Mill, an assumption which is the basis of all scientific investigation. This is the view that phenomena *are* related, that they *are* linked in terms of cause and effect. Science assumes until it has proof to the contrary, and therefore the positivist theory of knowledge assumes with it, that the world of phenomena is a determined world, a world in which, if B has constantly been observed to follow A in certain conditions, then, given exactly the same conditions, we are entitled to suppose that B will again follow A. It is not necessary here to pursue this question in its logical complexities and to discuss the problem of the validity of induction. This problem certainly preoccupied many nineteenth-century thinkers, John Stuart Mill in particular, but it is enough for present purposes to say that the operation of determinism in the world of phenomena is a working assumption of the sciences and consequently of positivism, in its nineteenth-century form at least. This working assumption may harden into the assertion that determinism is a reality, as happens in the thought of Taine, for example, and it may then be claimed that we do not merely assume but actually know that phenomena are invariably related in terms of cause and effect. But such a view goes beyond the limits of observation or verification and thereby deserts the strict positivist standpoint.

(b) The positivist état d'esprit

A derivative meaning must also be mentioned—positivism as an *état d'esprit*, as a general attitude of mind in which confidence

[4] J. S. Mill, *Auguste Comte and Positivism*, 2nd ed., London, 1866, pp. 6–8. Mill naturally adds that for Hume it is meaningless to speak of 'ultimate causes' operating 'behind' phenomena; 'cause, as he interprets it, *means* the invariable antecedent'.

in the scientific method is combined with religious and meta-physical scepticism. Parodi defines positivism in this sense by saying:

> Dédain de la métaphysique, culte du fait, de l'expérience et de la preuve, confiance sans réserve dans la science, exaltation de ses bien-faits, effort pour donner la forme de science à l'étude des faits moraux et sociaux, tel était l'état d'esprit que définit dogmatiquement Littré, qui anime les premiers écrits de Renan et de Taine. . . .[5]

This attitude was undoubtedly fostered by the spread of posi-tivist philosophy in the nineteenth century, and Parodi has given a relatively precise description of it. It has to be stressed, none the less, that such an attitude can be called 'positivist' only in so far as it follows from positivist principles. Unfortunately, other his-torians have used the concept in a far wider sense. Impersonality in art, impassibility, pessimism, objectivity, opposition to Chris-tianity, republicanism, the use of current scientific discoveries as the subject-matter of poetry—all these have been taken as evi-dence of 'positivism', even though none of them is a necessary consequence of the philosophy itself.

Such equations demand especial scrutiny, and it may be useful to take a specific illustration. Summarizing his views upon Leconte de Lisle, Martino writes:

> Tableaux des religions et des civilisations mortes, hostilité au christianisme, enthousiasme républicain et haine des autocraties, espoir d'une prochaine régénération, foi absolue en la science . . . c'est le bilan du positivisme, ou plutôt de sa philosophie populaire; ce sont aussi les thèmes favoris des Parnassiens, ceux que, entre 1850 et 1860, a magnifiés et vulgarisés Leconte de Lisle.[6]

Since he does not expand the distinction between 'positivism' and 'sa philosophie populaire', it is uncertain what he is claiming to describe. But to compare these attitudes with the corresponding tenets of the philosophy itself is to realize how misleading this résumé would be if it were taken to prove that Leconte de Lisle or the Parnassians were philosophical positivists. In regard to religious systems the positivist view is that, given the dogmas of a supernatural and of an immortal life usually embodied in them, they are based upon metaphysical doctrines about the unobserv-

---

[5] D. Parodi, *La Philosophie contemporaine en France*, 1919, p. 23.
[6] P. Martino, *Parnasse et symbolisme*, 1947, p. 38.

able: neither interest in past religions nor the belief that they were untrue is itself a sign of positivism.[7] Secondly, hostility to Christianity might be found in followers of other religions even more than in positivists. Comte, for example, is not wholly opposed to it; he admires the organization of the Catholic Church but rejects its supernatural claims. Others might attack Christianity solely on the ground of its political history and sympathies, for instance, whilst also rejecting positivism. The true mark of the positivist is opposition to Christianity in so far as it claims to know the existence of a supernatural and of an after-life and affirms the validity of non-empirical modes of knowledge. Martino's third criterion—'enthousiasme républicain et haine des autocraties'—may certainly apply to a Christian or any anti-positivist. If the positivist philosophy has a sociological consequence, it is merely through the belief that it is helpful to apply the scientific approach to the study and organization of society. Likewise, 'l'espoir d'une prochaine régénération' might well be shared by many social reformers, for example, who were not positivists. Finally, whilst it is open to doubt whether Leconte de Lisle possessed '[une] foi absolue en la science', it is assured that the characteristic view of positivism is not the infallibility of contemporary scientific theories or of any particular application of the scientific method but the assertion that empirically verified knowledge—however incomplete and hypothetical it may be—is the sole type of human knowledge.

One must also differentiate between respect for science and acceptance of the positivist position; the former, obviously enough, does not imply the latter. A writer may fully believe in the established theories of science; he may try to formulate a view of life which is compatible with those theories; he may, indeed, be a scientist—and yet not be a positivist since he does not admit that the scientific method represents man's only means of

[7] The nineteenth-century cult of *philologie*, often too closely linked with the positivist spirit, has many sources, but one widely prevalent concern is to regain the 'primitive revelation' embodied in early religions and even to formulate a new syncretist creed. Constant, Quinet, Ménard, Thalès Bernard, Laprade, and others all deeply respect 'the religious sentiment' itself and are seeking, in Quinet's words, for 'quelque débris de vérité, de révélation universelle' (*Le Génie des religions, Œuvres complètes*, t. i, 1857, p. 13). Cf. R. Schwab, *La Renaissance orientale*, 1950; C. Clerc, *Le Génie du paganisme*, 1926; and H. J. Hunt, *The Epic in Nineteenth-Century France*, Oxford, 1941, in particular for further evidence of this interest.

knowing. Such a distinction may be banal, but it helps to clear aside many considerations which are irrelevant. It allows us to agree that science greatly influences literary creation, for example, and the outlook of many writers during this period, and yet to keep an open mind as to their relationship to philosophical positivism. We are no longer tempted to identify a poet or novelist, say, as a positivist because he wishes to celebrate the inventions and discoveries of science, or because he seeks to imitate the scientific virtues of impersonality, objectivity, observation, and careful documentation and rejects the emotional and highly subjective mode of writing of his Romantic predecessors. Such an author may well be a positivist, but he is not necessarily so. The prestige of science alone in these mid-nineteenth-century years is sufficient to account for these features of his work; there is no need to invoke the shade of Comte or the positivist philosophy.

Cassagne's excellent chapter on 'L'art pour l'art et la science'[8] and other studies make it clear, moreover, that the impact of science on literature is strengthened by factors quite independent of the respect for science itself or the influence of philosophical beliefs. In particular, writers were attracted by the scientific attitude because in various ways it appealed to their personal leanings. Science was free of conventional morality and of any didactic motive; it was 'pure' in the sense in which they wished their art to be 'pure'. It was beyond the mental range of the vulgar crowd and the bourgeoisie and thus appealed to their sense of aristocratic superiority. Its objectivity and impartiality resembled their own determination to avoid sentimentality and an open display of personal feeling. Above all perhaps, and especially in the guise of *philologie*, it offered a new source of poetic inspiration and opened to the imagination a stimulating world of newly discovered facts. However fervent their admiration for science, poets like Leconte de Lisle and Ménard—in common with Flaubert or Baudelaire—still reject Ducamp's conception of a scientific poetry, and to contrast them for a moment with a writer like Zola is to realize how completely their cult of science was subordinated to their cult of art. As Cassagne remarks,

à part certains cas où la science introduite avec quelque indiscrétion s'est trouvée en excès, la devise l'art pour l'art ne s'est nullement

---

[8] A. Cassagne, *La Théorie de l'art pour l'art en France*, 1906, pp. 262–94.

changée en l'art pour la science. L'art est resté le seul but de l'artiste; la science n'a été qu'un de ses moyens.[9]

And this very equivocality in their admiration for science renders doubly misleading any deduction that they held a positivist view of life. Weinberg reports that one of the common opinions of literary critics during the years between 1840 and 1870 was that the entire approach of the realists 'results from a philosophical bias which is eminently materialistic or positivistic'.[10] More recent writers have too often asserted the same over-hasty conclusion and forgotten that evidence of a positivist standpoint must refer to intellectual beliefs and not to artistic practice, political or social sympathies, or any other non-philosophical characteristics.

The same historians have sometimes over-simplified as well the wider intellectual situation at this period: this we shall notice in looking, briefly, at the scene presented by Second Empire thought as a whole.

2. The State of Philosophy during the Second Empire

The philosophical setting in which positivist thought develops during these years is one of complexity and rich controversy. The Second Empire, even more than most periods of French philosophy, is a time when ideas are 'in the melting-pot', a time of dissension and confusion. For this numerous factors are responsible of which only the most salient need be mentioned here.

Most obvious of all is the ever-quickening pace of the 'scientific revolution'. Having rapidly recovered from the interruptions of 1789 and the Reign of Terror, the sciences were now expanding and triumphant. The foundation of the École polytechnique (1794)—nursery of generations of scientists and thinkers, including Comte and Renouvier[11]—and the reorganization of the Jardin du Roi (1793), the Académie des Sciences (1795), and the École

---

[9] Ibid., p. 294. Cf. F. Desonay, Le Rêve hellénique chez les poètes parnassiens, 1928, pp. 46, 50, for the same conclusion.

[10] B. Weinberg, French Realism—The Critical Reaction, New York, 1937, p. 193.

[11] Cf. F. A. Hayek, 'The Counter-Revolution of Science', Economica, London, N.S., viii, 1941, pp. 9 ff., 119 ff., and 281 ff. This valuable study of the growth of scientism in social thought in the earlier nineteenth century considers the École polytechnique to be 'the source of the scientistic hubris' (p. 9).

normale (1808) gave French science an impetus that never slackened throughout the century. In its first half alone physicists like Ampère, Carnot, Malus, and Fresnel, chemists like Gay-Lussac, Chevreul, J. B. Dumas, and Charles (husband of Lamartine's Elvire), physiologists like Magendie, biologists and zoologists like Lamarck, Saint-Hilaire, and Cuvier, are establishing French scientific pre-eminence, a status confirmed still more after 1850 by Berthelot, Pasteur, Claude Bernard, the Curies, Becquerel, and others. Foreign scientists like Lyell, Faraday, Darwin, or Maxwell are no less celebrated or notorious. Meanwhile, many of their discoveries are being applied in everyday life: witness the spread of industrialization, railways, gas-lighting and heating, and improved surgical and medical techniques; and less useful but equally dramatic achievements—Cuvier's reconstruction of extinct animals from unearthed fossils and bones, Le Verrier's successful prediction of the existence of a new planet, Neptune, the launching of motor-propelled balloons over Paris, for instance —all help to underline the authority and progress of science. At this time, too, the 'human sciences' are fighting to establish their place beside the natural sciences—sociology, psychology, a more scientific history, especially of previous civilizations and religions, and anthropology. The repercussions of these and other scientific novelties are numerous and complex. Science challenges—or seems to challenge—many established beliefs, and—more than ever honoured with capital letter—is endlessly discussed and related to religion, ethics, metaphysics, politics, aesthetics. Two of the most noteworthy beliefs that it engenders are particularly relevant here: first, in the reliability and fruitfulness of the scientific methods, and secondly, in the possibility—with whatever limiting conditions—of creating a 'science of man' that shall immeasurably ameliorate human life and even human nature. The task which thinkers like Comte, Renan, and Taine attempt is to work up these beliefs into a complete and more precise philosophy.

Hardly less significant to the thinkers of the day was the indirect but powerful impact of political events, of Louis-Napoléon's *coup d'état* in December 1851 and the subsequent proclamation of the Second Empire. Political reaction was revived, intellectual conservatism more firmly entrenched, and the social hopes expressed in the Revolution of 1848 were fated to frustration. In their disgust and disappointment many of the social idealists whose primary interest had been with practical action turned away from politics to immerse themselves in the arts, the sciences, or philosophy. Amongst this disheartened group of intellectuals were some of the leading thinkers of the next thirty years, men like Renouvier, Taine, Renan, Vacherot, and Ménard, and consequently, as the Second Empire begins, the philosophical debate is being enriched by the contributions of young and ardent minds all too ready to scrutinize the 'official' and established philosophy of the day, eclecticism.

Thirdly, whatever his defects as an original thinker, Victor Cousin had greatly stimulated the study of the history of philosophy, and through his influence the works of foreign thinkers were being more thoroughly appraised and more systematically translated into French.[12] The effect of this historical work is considerable in France both before and during our period, and one could hardly overestimate its value as a breeding-ground of new arguments and syntheses. Certainly it was not the scholarship of the eclectics alone that was responsible for the enthusiastic translation and exegesis of German authors, of literary writers quite as much as philosophers, and even in the field of philosophy Charles de Villers, Madame de Staël, and others had written of Kant, for example, long before Cousin and his disciples.[13] Yet the eclectics did play a notable role in diffusing knowledge about thinkers who had previously been imperfectly studied, and thereby they helped to introduce into French thought a vast store of ideas, some of which were ultimately to be turned against their own system. This interest in foreign philosophy increases throughout the Second Empire and is taken up by thinkers of the most varied philosophical complexions, as witness the neo-criticists' study of Kant, the debts of Renan and Taine to Hegel or of Ravaisson and Charles Secrétan to Schelling, to name only the most obvious examples. In the realm of translation, versions of Fichte's works had appeared in 1836, 1843, and 1845, of Schelling's

[12] The value of his influence in this historical field is stressed—and justly so— even by his critics at this time, for example by Paul Janet ('La Crise philosophique et les idées spiritualistes en France—I', R.D.M., 15 juillet 1864, p. 460) and F. Ravaisson (Rapport sur la philosophie en France au dix-neuvième siècle, 5e éd., 1904, pp. 23–25).
[13] For example, Destutt de Tracy, Degérando, A. M. Ampère, and Maine de Biran; cf. M. Vallois, La Formation de l'influence kantienne en France, s.d.

works in 1842, 1845, and 1847, and in 1851 Bénard rendered Hegel's *Philosophy of Art* of which he had already published an analysis in 1840. Véra in particular continued Bénard's work with translations of the *Logic* in 1859, *The Philosophy of Nature* in 1863–5, and *The Philosophy of Mind* in 1867, to which he added his own *Introduction à la philosophie de Hegel* in 1864. Kant also was being made available to a French-speaking public. Barni translated the *Critique of Judgement* in 1846, the *Critique of Practical Reason* in 1848, the *Foundations of the Metaphysics of Ethics* in the same year, and the *Critique of Pure Reason* (previously rendered by Tissot in 1835–6) in 1869, whilst in 1851 he published his own *Examen des Fondements de la métaphysique des mœurs et de la Critique de la raison pratique*. These works, histories of German philosophy and articles of critical commentary in such journals as the *Revue des Deux Mondes*, the *Revue de l'instruction publique*, the *Revue germanique*, the *Revue critique*, the *Revue chrétienne*, and the *Revue de Strasbourg*, all contributed to French philosophical life a fresh intellectual stimulus. Kant, Hegel, Fichte, Schelling, Herder, and Schopenhauer and, as well, such scholars as Creuzer, Burnouf, and Strauss —all these and many other German authors—Goethe, Hölderlin, Feuerbach . . . the list seems endless—were reinvigorating French thought.[14] The impact of English ideas, as expounded by such *anglicisants* as Montégut, Taine, and Milsand, is perhaps less important now than in the later years of the century, but knowledge of Mill, Carlyle, and others added to the ferment of discussion and speculation.[15]

This period also sees the breakdown of the eclectic philosophy, and that alone would suffice to make it a time of unusually strident debate. In this breakdown the factors already discussed played their part, and in particular the growing repute of the natural sciences. Philosophers no less than theologians were challenged during these mid-century years, in France as abroad, to come to terms with the new scientific theories. This, above all, is an age when Christian and other traditionalist philosophers were forced to take account of science and of the attacks delivered in its name

[14] On these German influences cf. J. M. Carré, *Les Écrivains français et le mirage allemand (1800–1940)*, 1947, and L. Reynaud, *L'Influence allemande en France au 18e et au 19e siècles*, 1922, although the latter is often heavily biased.
[15] Cf. A. C. Taylor, *Carlyle et la pensée latine*, 1937, and I. D. McFarlane, 'Joseph Milsand critique de la littérature anglaise', *R.L.C.*, xxii, 1948, pp. 200–36.

upon religion, metaphysics, and even ethics. More than most philosophies, perhaps, eclecticism was ill adapted to sustain this challenge, and it is noteworthy that even those Second Empire thinkers who were sympathetic to the spiritualist philosophy tend to dismiss Cousin as a philosophical nonentity. Thus we find Ravaisson writing of him in his famous *Rapport* (1867): 'De plus en plus on devait reconnaître . . . un orateur auquel, comme les orateurs en général, s'il faut en croire Aristote, le vraisemblable, à défaut du vrai, suffisait.'[16] Even spiritualism's most capable exponent at this time, Paul Janet, concedes that it has suffered 'un échec des plus graves', and he openly separates his position from Cousin's 'orthodox and intolerant' doctrine.[17] Secrétan, likewise, speaks of the 'sterility' of Cousin's philosophy.[18] Only isolated thinkers like Vacherot and Adolphe Franck think it worth while to defend Cousin and the old eclecticism against its antagonists.[19] And hence questions that might have seemed closed were opened once more, and a variety of theories competed to fill the vacuum left by the dispossession of the eclectics.

Nor is it only eclecticism that is crumbling. The earlier nineteenth century sees an extraordinary proliferation of metaphysical systems and religious-substitutes. Traditionalist Catholics like De Maistre, numerous social reformers from the Saint-Simonians, Comte, and Fourier to Leroux, Jean Reynaud, Cabet, and the young Karl Marx, Germans like Hegel, Fichte, or Feuerbach— all offer their vast, prophetically toned 'doctrine for the age'; the Absolute, Progress, Humanity, and Universal Harmony are only a few of the abstractions that take on apocalyptic and often semi-mystical import.[20] Bréhier claims that 1850 sees an end of men's faith in these great constructions and a revival of a more analytic, down-to-earth, and sceptical spirit.[21] Yet the metaphysical habit also persists—in Renan and Taine as well as Comte, and also in metaphysicians like Vacherot with his 'theology of the ideal',

[16] Ravaisson, op. cit., pp. 33–34.

[17] Janet, 'La Crise philosophique—I', loc. cit., p. 461; 'Le Spiritualisme français au dix-neuvième siècle', *R.D.M.*, 15 mai 1868, p. 381.

[18] C. Secrétan, *La Philosophie de la liberté*, 2e éd., 1866, p. vii.

[19] E. Vacherot, 'La Situation philosophique en France', *R.D.M.*, 15 juin 1868, pp. 951–2; and A. Franck, *Moralistes et philosophes*, 1872, pp. 429–68.

[20] Cf. A. Erdan, *La France mystique: Tableau des excentricités religieuses de ce temps*, s.d. (Coulon-Pineau), 2 vols., for an interesting but discursive contemporary account, itself rather eccentric.

[21] E. Bréhier, *Histoire de la philosophie*, t. ii, 1932, pp. 907–10.

religious syncretists like Ménard and Michelet and the many admirers of pantheism. None of these men is content to emulate Locke and be 'employed as an under-labourer in clearing the ground a little, and removing some of the rubbish that lies in the way to knowledge'. What Renan and Taine especially reveal is an uneasy alternation between the critical mood discerned by Bréhier and the metaphysical desires they inherit from their predecessors.

A final factor also deserves mention, namely, the unusual extent to which thinkers were emotionally involved in the philosophical disputes waged during these years. Religion and metaphysics in particular, we have said, are being attacked in the name of science. And to recall the problems upon which debate centred is to realize at once that this was a time when philosophers were far less concerned with (for example) the refinements of logical analysis than with the weightiest of all philosophical questions. The relation between science on the one hand and religion and metaphysics on the other, the problem of free will and determinism, the search for ethical standards to replace the Christian moral code, and, behind all these, the nature and validity of human knowledge—these were the preoccupying problems; and although they are no doubt the perennial problems of every age, they presented themselves to the thinkers of the mid-nineteenth century with unusual directness and urgency. Even more than at most periods it is the 'big questions' which have pride of place. Is religious belief compatible with scientific honesty? Is metaphysics possible or is it a futile and meaningless pursuit? Do men possess freedom of will or does it follow from the discoveries of science, especially of biology, medical science, and the new psychology, that they are rigidly determined in what they believe to be their free choices? Are there objective standards of ethical judgement or are all our moral assertions merely the expressions of subjective attitudes? What kinds of knowledge are open to us? Can we ever penetrate the mysterious realms which lie outside the range of scientific exploration? What, precisely, are the limits of this scientific exploration? These are the questions which are debated by the professional philosophers of the age, in books whose very titles—*La Crise philosophique, La Métaphysique et la science, La Science de la morale, L'Idée de Dieu et ses nouveaux critiques*, for example—reflect the importance of the issues at stake. All these thinkers, whatever their intellectual persuasion, regard philosophy as deeply relevant to the world in which men live and act. When Janet declares in a serious philosophical article that liberty and human dignity rely on the preservation of the spiritualist philosophy or Renan triumphantly claims that 'la science est donc une religion',[22] they are not untypical in their emotional tone of their whole generation. For them philosophical conclusions were still fraught with tremendous consequences, and it is not surprising that in this atmosphere, in which a general re-examination of traditional problems is under way, philosophy should present a scene of uncommon complexity.

It is all the more necessary to emphasize this complexity since the description of the Second Empire as an 'age of positivism' has tended to hide the elements of discord and division both in its philosophical speculations as a whole and in the outlook of those thinkers who are most sympathetic to positivism itself. This view has perhaps misled us on occasion into thinking of this period as a time when the opposition to positivism was largely dormant or ineffective, awaiting Lachelier, Boutroux, and, later, Bergson to awaken it from its mid-century hibernation. Yet anti-positivist currents of thought are found side by side with positivism even when the latter is most influential. The progress of philosophy in the nineteenth century is not so much a succession of pitched battles, in which now positivists and now anti-positivists are victorious and banish their opponents from the field, as a debate prolonged throughout the century. It is therefore dangerous to speak of an 'age of eclecticism' followed by an 'age of positivism' followed in turn by the 'age of the reaction against positivism' and the 'revival of idealism'. An approach like that of Thibaudet, however convenient in other ways, can only be unhelpful for a detailed study of the thought of an age. Speaking of the 'éternel dialogue humain' between 'la religion et la philosophie, ces expériences internes' and 'la science, système de l'expérience externe', he says: 'Il arrive ordinairement que, prise en bloc, chaque génération est plus ou moins déléguée à l'une des voix de ce dialogue.' Even the careful qualifications here cannot do justice to the true intricacies of a period of which he concludes: 'une sorte de matérialisme immanent formait sous cette génération

[22] Janet, 'La Crise philosophique — I', loc. cit., p. 461; and E. Renan, L'Avenir de la science, 23ᵉ éd., Calmann-Lévy, 1929, p. 108.

une assise régulière et robuste'.[23] The intellectual situation was more varied and more ambiguous than such a summary implies, and the readers of the Second Empire were solicited by opponents of positivism quite as forceful and alert as the positivist writers they attacked.

Positivism is in fact only the most immediately influential philosophical force of the age. These years see the publication of Renouvier's *Essais de critique générale* (1854–64), his *Science de la morale* (1869), and his private edition of Jules Lequier's *La Recherche d'une première vérité* (1865), Cournot's *Essai sur les fondements de nos connaissances* (1851) and his *Traité de l'enchaînement des idées* (1861), Vacherot's *La Métaphysique et la science* (1858), Ravaisson's *Rapport sur la philosophie au XIXe siècle* (1867), and the second edition of Secrétan's *La Philosophie de la liberté*, with its new preface devoted to a critique of positivism (1st ed., 1848–9; 2nd ed., 1866). They also witness a host of minor studies no less opposed to the positivist philosophy—Caro's *Le Matérialisme et la science* (1868), Paul Janet's *La Crise philosophique* (1865), and many others.

Ravaisson's report on the state of French philosophy in 1867 provides interesting evidence of the extent to which positivism was being attacked during these two decades—even when allowances have been made for the author's optimism. By 1867, he suggests,

il n'arrive pas aussi souvent qu'autrefois qu'on reste enfermé dans les sciences dont le matériel de la nature est l'objet, ... sans commerce ni avec les sciences de la vie, ni avec les beaux-arts et avec la poésie qui en fait le fond, et, en général, avec les études de l'ordre intellectuel et moral. Le matérialisme, dès lors, sous ces puissantes influences, ne subsiste guère fidèle à lui-même, mais, peu à peu modifié, altéré, se change en quelque théorie différente, plus ou moins empreinte de spiritualisme.[24]

The general tendency of thought at this time, he believes, is towards idealism, a tendency which is even illustrated by the positivists themselves. And writing of Renouvier, he maintains:

C'est à un absolu, c'est à un infini, et c'est à un absolu en possession

---

[23] A. Thibaudet, *Histoire de la littérature française de 1789 à nos jours*, 1936, pp. 407, 409. He also speaks of 'le caractère scientifique de cette génération, la marche à la positivité' (p. 404).

[24] Ravaisson, op. cit., p. 250.

de la perfection morale que tendent en définitive et que vont se terminer irrésistiblement, comme les spéculations d'Auguste Comte et de M. Herbert Spencer, comme celles de M. Taine et de M. Renan, celles de M. Renouvier.[25]

Paul Janet, writing in the following year, has become no less hopeful. He even claims that 'l'école spiritualiste est encore la plus active, la plus féconde, et je dirai même la plus progressive des écoles contemporaines'.[26] Nor is Renouvier, in his survey of French nineteenth-century philosophy, without confidence in the future: Kantian *criticisme* is admirably suited in his view to gather around it 'les esprits qui répugnent aux négations sans preuves du positivisme'.[27]

The antagonists of positivism are thus far from quiescent during these years. Christians, both Catholic and Protestant; neo-criticists like Renouvier, Cournot, Lequier, and Pillon; eclectics and spiritualists like Ravaisson, Caro, Janet, Lachelier, Saisset, and Vacherot—all these French writers, as well as the influence of foreign thinkers like Schelling, Fichte, Herder, and, more ambiguously, Kant and Hegel, uphold the tradition of anti-positivist thought.

In claiming that 'the age of positivism' is also the age of neo-criticism and a revitalized spiritualist philosophy, it is perhaps no less pertinent to question another assertion commonly advanced by historians of philosophy and literature alike. This is the view that Auguste Comte had a predominant influence upon Second Empire thinking, a view that recurs so frequently and from such authorities—Scherer, Lévy-Bruhl, Sée, Faguet, and a score of others—that one is inclined to accept their assurance.[28] It would be rash to reject it too emphatically, so hidden may be the channels of intellectual action. None the less, the impact of Comte upon the philosophy of this period seems to be more often affirmed than proven. One cannot assume that all the works after

[25] Ibid., pp. 275, 118.
[26] Janet, 'Le Spiritualisme français', loc. cit., pp. 384–5.
[27] C. Renouvier, 'De la philosophie du dix-neuvième siècle en France', *L'Année philosophique — Première Année (1867)*, 1868, p. 105.
[28] E. Scherer, *Études sur la littérature contemporaine*, t. vii, 1882, p. 342; L. Lévy-Bruhl, *The Philosophy of Auguste Comte*, translated Beaumont-Klein, London, 1903, pp. 17–18; H. Sée, *Science et philosophie de l'histoire*, 1928, pp. 83–84; E. Faguet, *Politiques et moralistes du dix-neuvième siècle*, 5e éd., 1903, 3 vols., ii. 368.

Comte which show a scientific bent or an acceptance of the scientific method must have been inspired by his philosophy;[29] on the contrary, most of them derive from a more general spirit, a spirit which informed Comte himself.

To say this is not to deny that in other fields than that of philosophy Comte may be a landmark in nineteenth-century France. His influence upon sociology, although effective for the most part in later decades of the century, was in some ways decisive. Equally, he exercised a powerful authority over those of his disciples who accepted his 'Religion of Humanity'—those 'orthodox positivists' who set up the positivist Churches—Blainville, Robinet, Laffitte, Célestin de Blignières, Audiffrent, Lombrail, Leblais, and Longchamp in France; Congreve, Harrison, Bridges, Edger in Britain; Nyström in Sweden; the Brazilian revolutionaries. Neither his sociological nor his religious importance implies a philosophical importance, however, and of contemporary thinkers only Littré, Mill, and Lewes were directly affected by him. Even here a high degree of selectiveness operated, for these are the 'heretics' who rejected the later developments of his system. 'Ce sont là [Cantecor comments] des disciples bien platoniques, qui admirent, mais ne pratiquent pas. . . .'[30] Mill himself remarks that the *Cours de philosophie positive* was largely ignored in France (in contrast to England) in the years immediately after its publication;[31] and in later years Comte's final works told heavily against his reputation. It is interesting to note how rarely Comte's philosophy is discussed at length in criticisms of positivism during the 1860's. Renouvier, for example, adopts Saint-Simon as his principal illustration of 'social positivism' and tartly dismisses later *comtisme* as 'le positivisme devenu mystère'. And when he wishes to attack 'philosophical positivism' he takes Littré as its most serious exponent.[32] The same is true of Ravaisson and of Paul Janet.[33] And although Secrétan links master and disciple as the two best representatives of positivism, it is Littré's version of Comte's philosophy

[29] This is the very marked failing of H. Grüber, *Le Positivisme depuis Comte jusqu'à nos jours*, traduit Mazoyer, 1893.

[30] G. Cantecor, *Comte*, nouv. éd., s.d., p. 167. One might add the names of Littré's collaborators, Robin, Wyrouboff, and Naquet.

[31] Mill, op. cit., p. 2.

[32] Renouvier, 'De la philosophie', loc. cit., pp. 30, 36 ff.

[33] Ravaisson, op. cit., pp. 93–96; Janet, 'La Crise philosophique — II', *R.D.M.*, 1er août 1864, pp. 721 ff.

that he discusses.[34] It seems as if for the most part Comte was influential in France only in so far as Littré accepted and popularized his beliefs; no one who has tried to read Comte's longer works will be surprised at this.[35]

Furthermore, when Comte is mentioned it is far more often by antagonists of positivism than by its adherents. It is commonly suggested that Comte deeply affected the thought of Renan and Taine. Yet what indications exist tell in the other direction. Taine, we shall see, claims to have been largely ignorant of Comte's philosophy before 1860—and by this time the main outlines of his own system were established. As to Renan, there is no reason to doubt his famous critical comment in *Souvenirs d'enfance et de jeunesse*:

... j'éprouvai une sorte d'agacement à voir la réputation exagérée d'Auguste Comte, érigé en grand homme de premier ordre pour avoir dit, en mauvais français, ce que tous les esprits scientifiques, depuis deux cents ans, ont vu aussi clairement que lui.[36]

One may perhaps hesitate before accepting the bold conclusion reached by Cantecor: 'Enfin le comtisme n'est qu'un épisode, parmi beaucoup d'autres, du développement de l'esprit positif, et on pourrait l'en supposer retranché, sans que la physionomie du siècle s'en trouvât sensiblement modifiée.'[37] This view may be false or exaggerated; but the burden of proof certainly appears to lie with those who have asserted the contrary. Quite insufficient evidence has so far been put forward to justify the claim—of especial relevance to this study—that the Second Empire is an 'age of positivism' because Comte then exercised a preponderant philosophical authority.

Nor are the intellectual divisions of this period confined to explicit oppositions between positivists and anti-positivists, conflicts between thinker and thinker. There are subtler and less obvious tensions within the minds of individual writers themselves,

[34] Secrétan, op. cit., *Préface*.
[35] There are certainly exceptions to this generalization. A noteworthy example is the very thorough 'Examen critique du positivisme' written by J. F. Astié, one of Pascal's Protestant editors (*Revue chrétienne*, 1856, pp. 156 ff., 192 ff., 336 ff., 461 ff.).
[36] E. Renan, *Souvenirs d'enfance et de jeunesse*, éd. Collection nouvelle, Calmann-Lévy, s.d., p. 219. Cf. his *Discours et conférences*, 9e éd., Calmann-Lévy, 1928, pp. 75–76. Cf. also Claude Bernard's antagonism to Comte.
[37] Cantecor, op. cit., p. 169.

and as a result it is much more difficult at this time than later to fix the true allegiance of any particular philosopher. Whereas in the later years of the century the forces making for positivism and those making against it are for the most part clearly separated, the situation before about 1870 is more indefinite. Within the work of the same writer elements of both positivism and anti-positivism can often be discerned, and in some cases it is only historical perspective and his later development that reveal the real direction of his thought. This difficulty results partly from the fact that the outlook of certain thinkers changes in emphasis with the passage of time. Thus, for example, Renouvier's *Premier essai de critique générale* is far closer to the positivist standpoint than the *Second essai* and his later works. This is the change noted by Ravaisson when he remarks that Renouvier appears to be moving away from 'le phénoménisme décidé de la première partie de ses *Essais*' and towards 'des idées moins éloignées de celles des métaphysiciens'.[38] In the thinking of other writers, positivism and anti-positivism coexist in unstable alliance. Even Ravaisson, for example, is trying to have the best of both philosophical worlds—as when he looks forward to 'la prédominance de ce qu'on pourrait appeler un réalisme ou positivisme spiritualiste'.[39] The same is true of Vacherot, whose main work, *La Métaphysique et la science*, is sub-titled *Principes de métaphysique positive*. Many anti-positivist philosophers were anxious in the face of the prestige of the sciences to give their metaphysical and ethical systems a more 'positive' or 'scientific' basis—to unite, as Vacherot puts it, spiritualism and science.[40] They seek to reconcile science and metaphysics, science and religion, hopefully differentiating between 'how' questions and 'why' questions and welcoming Spencer's notion of the 'Unknowable' as the device by which the union might be effected. Indeed, this tendency persists to the end of the century and is found, for example, in Fouillée's *Le Mouvement idéaliste* (1896) and Brunetière's *Sur les chemins de la croyance* (1905). Fouillée claims that in the philosophy of the day 'nous voyons, sous nos propres yeux, le mouvement positiviste et le mouvement idéaliste tendre vers un même but, aspirer, pour ainsi dire, aux mêmes conclusions',

---

[38] Ravaisson, op. cit., p. 117.
[39] Ibid., p. 275.
[40] Vacherot, 'La Situation philosophique', loc. cit., p. 977.

whilst Brunetière tries to demonstrate that positivism leads inevitably to a religion and a metaphysics and alleges that he has re-established metaphysics—'[une métaphysique] tout *objective*' — 'au cœur même du positivisme'.[41]

This particular study concerns only the ambiguities in positivist writers, but it would certainly be false to imply that they were alone in their attempts to serve two masters. The same efforts are found in their opponents, but from a different starting-point. They do not try to add metaphysics or religion or ethics to science, as in the case of Taine, Renan, or Comte, but try to unite science with their existing philosophy. Lenoir's comment upon Taine: 'Le philosophe me semble partagé entre deux tendances contradictoires' (between positivism and philosophical rationalism in this case) applies to them all.[42] Here our aim is to discuss the divisions in the thought of those who were sympathetic to positivism; but one could equally well consider the parallel tensions in those thinkers whose primary allegiance was to the opposite view.

[41] A. Fouillée, *Le Mouvement idéaliste et la réaction contre la science positive*, 1896, p. x; and F. Brunetière, *Sur les chemins de la croyance—Première étape: L'Utilisation du positivisme*, 1905, pp. 177, 162. On Fouillée's attempt to reconcile science and spiritualism in his other works, cf. D. Parodi, op. cit., pp. 40–48; on Brunetière, cf. J. Clark, *La Pensée de Ferdinand Brunetière*, 1954.

[42] R. Lenoir, 'L'Idéalisme de Taine', *R.M.M.*, xxiii, 1916, p. 859.

III

FROM POSITIVISM TO SCIENTISM (1)

AUGUSTE COMTE

1. *Introduction*

To inquire how far Auguste Comte is a consistent positivist may seem at first sight not unlike asking whether the Pope is a Catholic, for historians have united in proclaiming him 'the founder of positivism'. Born in 1798, he devotes his whole life from the age of nineteen when he becomes a disciple of Saint-Simon until his death in 1857 to elaborating the 'positive philosophy'. He first sketches it in various youthful *opuscules* of which the best-known is the first *Système de politique positive* (1824), but its most celebrated expression is in the *Cours de philosophie positive* (1830–42), based on lectures given privately in Paris. This is the work which influenced Littré and Mill so deeply and, after Harriet Martineau's abridged translation in 1853, other English writers like Frederic Harrison, Lewes, E. S. Beesly, and George Eliot. In later life, after a brief but intense love-affair with Clotilde de Vaux (1844–6) which made him aware of 'la prépondérance nécessaire de la vie affective', he turns more emphatically to social ethics and, especially, to the creation of a new 'religion of humanity'. Still without regular employment and living largely on the subscriptions of his disciples, Comte enters the final phase of his career—to become the high priest of the positive religion. From the little house in the rue Monsieur-le-Prince, only a few yards from the place de la Sorbonne where his statue now stands, he issues, along with a flood of archiepiscopal letters to both the faithful and the dissident, his second main group of works: *Le Calendrier positiviste* (1849), *Le Catéchisme positiviste* (1852), the second *Système de politique positive* (1851–4), and the only completed volume of the *Synthèse subjective* (1856). His most immediate—and most idiosyncratic—influence stems from these works; they inspire the foundation of positivist Churches of Humanity at places as far apart as Brazil and Newcastle upon

Tyne and they certainly establish Comte as the founder of positivism as a religion. His contributions to sociology perhaps have a lesser contemporary impact: in this period Comte finds no Durkheim, and Mill, despite all that he finds to praise, can declare that 'he has done nothing in Sociology which does not require to be done again, and better'.[1] Here, none the less, is his greatest legacy to later thinkers: all sociologists must be indebted to him for his original demarcation of their field of study and for his fruitful distinctions and generalizations. Although they have rejected much in his system, he still remains the largely undisputed father of social science.

Yet positivism as a religion or as sociology must not be confused with positivism as a theory of knowledge, and the positivist basis of Comte's philosophy is not newly created by him but restates a well-established attitude to knowledge. As Mill remarks, positivism was 'the general property of the age, however far as yet from being universally accepted even by thoughtful minds'.[2] And Littré, reminding us of Comte's acknowledged indebtedness to earlier writers, traces the positivist philosophy even in the historically conscious form the *Cours* gave to it back to Turgot, Condorcet, Kant, and Saint-Simon.[3] What is Comte's contribution to this tradition? Is the philosophical framework of his sociological and religious thought true to positivism in its epistemological sense? These questions are central to any estimate of Comte's work.

We shall be concerned throughout this chapter with Comte's divided intellectual allegiance, but it can certainly not be claimed that he is a consciously divided mind. No French philosopher exemplifies *l'esprit de système* more forcefully than he. The search for unity dominates his thought and motivates his attempts to organize the sciences, to detect the directive forces of human history, and to apply his social theory to every realm of human life—work, thought, political organization, religion, and art. It

[1] J. S. Mill, *Auguste Comte and Positivism*, London, 1866, p. 124.
[2] Ibid., p. 8.
[3] E. Littré, *Auguste Comte et la philosophie positive*, 2ᵉ éd., Hachette, 1864, pp. 38–97. H. Gouhier notes that in his early reading up to 1817, as well as Montesquieu and Condorcet, 'il fréquente alors Voltaire et Rousseau, Cabanis, Destutt de Tracy, Condillac, D'Alembert, Diderot . . .' (*La Jeunesse d'Auguste Comte et la formation du positivisme*, 1933–41, 3 vols., i. 230).

helps to explain both his masterly syntheses and many of the absurdities of the 'Religion of Humanity'; and if the *Système de politique positive* is in fact, as Mill declares, 'the completest system of spiritual and temporal despotism which ever yet emanated from a human brain, unless possibly that of Ignatius Loyola',[4] this results from Comte's abhorrence of anything less than complete unification.

It is thus an ironic stroke of fate that his most eminent disciples should have embraced one half of his teaching only to reject the other half. Littré can always call the author of the *Cours* his master, but he asserts that the doctrines of the *Système* are not deducible from the positive philosophy. 'Il a échangé la méthode objective pour la méthode subjective', he complains, and for this latter method there is no place within true positivism.[5] Mill likewise points to 'this signal anomaly in M. Comte's intellectual career': whereas the *Cours* contains 'an essentially sound view of philosophy, with a few capital errors', the later works are 'false and misleading' in a far more radical way.[6] Several of Comte's later commentators have followed Littré and Mill and alleged a fundamental division between his 'two careers'—so much so that the dispute around this question has been seen as 'le problème classique lié à l'histoire de sa philosophie'.[7]

Yet there is reason to think that the discrepancy between his earlier and later works has been exaggerated. Even Mill did not consider it complete and saw quite clearly that the views of the later books were anticipated in the *Cours*. Comte's failure to 'allow of open questions', his assertion that science must be governed by considerations of social utility, his dismissal of psychology, his desire for system and unity are all regarded by Mill as

[4] J. S. Mill, *Autobiography*, London, 1873, p. 213. In view of Mill's comparison it is interesting to note that Comte himself attacks as backward those who do not feel how superior Ignatius Loyola was in every way to Jesus Christ, and he likewise prefers to Christ 'the great', 'the incomparable Saint Paul'. Cf. H. de Lubac, *The Drama of Atheist Humanism*, translated Riley, London, 1949, in which Comte's philosophy is considered as a new and atheistic 'religion'.

[5] Littré, op. cit., pp. iv–vi.

[6] Mill, *Comte*, p. 5.

[7] Gouhier, op. cit., i. 19. Amongst those who assert a division in Comte's thought he names, as well as Littré and Mill, Wyrouboff, Robin, Seillière, and De Rouvre. Cf. also G. Cantecor, *Comte*, nouv. éd., s.d., p. 91. The majority of Comte's critics have taken the opposite view; cf. Gouhier, i. 20: this is especially true since the study by G. Dumas, *Psychologie de deux messies positivistes — Saint-Simon et Auguste Comte*, 1905.

the germs of Comte's 'later perversions'.[8] He dissents from the fourth volume of the *Cours*—the 46th lesson in particular—as much as from the *Système*: if his attack is less definite, that is because Comte's position is not yet completely declared.

Comte himself, not surprisingly, was extremely sensitive to the charge of division and often affirmed the cohesion of his entire writings. From the start, he claims, he conceived the goal of positive science as the erection of a sound philosophy capable of supplying the basis of true religion,[9] and to illustrate the homogeneity of all his work he reprints his earliest *opuscules* at the end of the later *Système*, including, most notably, his *Plan des travaux scientifiques nécessaires pour réorganiser la société* (1822). The *Système* follows logically from the *Cours*, is necessarily based upon its results and is prefigured in the concluding volume of the *Cours*, written in 1842, two years before he met Clotilde. He admits that there are differences between what he calls his two careers: feeling now replaces reason, and once the intellectual superiority of positivism over all forms of theology has been shown, moral requirements resume their rightful primacy.[10] He claims—'without affected modesty', as Lévy-Bruhl nicely puts it —to have been Aristotle in the first period; in the second he will be Saint Paul.[11] Yet differences do not imply inconsistencies, he stresses, and when he writes the introduction to the *Synthèse subjective* at the very end of his life, he asserts that this work derives from the *Système* and both from the *Cours* and that he is thus completing 'the great trilogy which will direct the spiritual reorganization of the West'.[12]

What is not clear is that Comte and the many commentators who have asserted the unity of his thought have succeeded in meeting the really damaging criticism that Littré's defection implied: that many elements in Comte's system are incompatible with positivism. And to repudiate Littré's accusation of division is also to declare that any major defect in that system is an integral

[8] Mill, *Comte*, pp. 15, 61–62, 67, 140, 62.

[9] A. Comte, *Système de politique positive*, Dalmont, 1851–4, 4 vols. [*Système*], i. 3.

[10] *Système*, i. 3–4.

[11] L. Lévy-Bruhl, *The Philosophy of Auguste Comte*, London, 1903, p. 10. Mill notes the same trait in more direct terms: 'As his thoughts grew more extravagant, his self-confidence grew more outrageous' (*Comte*, p. 130).

[12] A. Comte, *Synthèse subjective*, t. i, chez l'auteur et chez Dalmont, 1856 [*Synthèse*], p. 2.

part of it and is not confined, as Littré thought, to Comte's later years. When we reject as a witty falsification the allegation that in Comte's career the law of the three states is reversed, so that he moves from the positive through the metaphysical back to the theological state,[13] we are also led to push back in time the question of his relation to positivism. We now have to ask not so much whether the later works are consistently positivist but, more interestingly, whether the *Cours* itself is the work of a faithful positivist.

It is in fact a distraction to concentrate too much upon the appeal to emotion and the formulations of the cult of humanity in order to illustrate Comte's abandonment of positivism. Emotion is fostered and the religious practices are introduced chiefly because Comte believes they are the most effective means to the end of social cohesion that he has already postulated. When he erects 'Love' as the principle of his political system, for example, he is merely making a recommendation, philosophically speaking, that is in theory susceptible to empirical test—quite a sensible recommendation, indeed, given the end he has in mind. The same is true of the rather artificial prescriptions of the Religion of Humanity, developed in imitation of the Roman Church. One can sympathize with the dismay of Littré and Mill as they read Comte's regulations about the Great Fetich, the sacred numbers, the positivist Calendar, the routine of prayer and devotion, the hierarchy of the priesthood and the rest of the high priest's requirements. One may share Mill's view that 'an irresistible air of ridicule' surrounds the religion and feel with him that 'others may laugh, but we could far rather weep at this melancholy decadence of a great intellect'.[14] Yet the most significant respects in which Comte deserts positivism are illustrated just as distinctly in the *Cours de philosophie positive* as in the works he wrote after 1842.

2. *Comte's Positivism*

Comte's definition of the third and final stage in the progress of the human mind has rightly become a classic statement of the positivist position. Having sketched the theological and metaphy-

---

[13] Found, for example, in R. Bayer, *Épistémologie et logique depuis Kant jusqu'à nos jours*, 1954, p. 188.

[14] Mill, *Comte*, pp. 153, 199.

sical attitudes, he goes on to describe the approach which is progressively replacing them, in his view, in every department of thought.

Le caractère fondamental de la philosophie positive est de regarder tous les phénomènes comme assujettis à des *lois* naturelles invariables, dont la découverte précise et la réduction au moindre nombre possible sont le but de tous nos efforts, en considérant comme absolument inaccessible et vide de sens pour nous la recherche de ce qu'on appelle les *causes*, soit premières, soit finales.[15]

In the theological stage man seeks to know 'la nature intime des êtres, les causes premières et finales de tous les effets qui le frappent'; he aspires to 'absolute knowledge' and represents phenomena as the product of the direct action of supernatural agents. In the metaphysical stage—which is only a modified form of the theological, as Comte shrewdly remarks—there is the same illegitimate search for primary causes and absolute knowledge, but the supernatural agents are now replaced by abstractions, 'par des forces abstraites . . . conçues comme capables d'engendrer par elles-mêmes tous les phénomènes observés . . .'.[16] In the positive stage man more modestly confines himself to a 'relative knowledge', knowledge of phenomena and their relationships, and eschews the false abstraction of the metaphysician. The law of gravitation is the type of the only knowledge man can attain. It renders coherent an immense variety of phenomena and to that extent explains them. But nothing can be said as to the nature of 'weight' and 'attraction' in themselves; such questions can only be abandoned, Comte sternly adds, 'to the imagination of the theologians and the subtleties of the metaphysicians'.[17]

This is the starting-point for his most significant addition to the positivist tradition: the extension of the scientific method to the study of societies. Here again, in his discussion of sociology's aims and methods, one sees his fidelity to positivism. Social studies, he argues, are at present in their theologico-metaphysical infancy, in the same relation to a properly constituted social science as was astrology to astronomy or alchemy to chemistry. In this pre-scientific stage the state of mind which is brought to bear upon social studies is necessarily 'idéal dans la marche,

---

[15] A. Comte, *Cours de philosophie positive*, 2ᵉ éd., Baillière, 1864, 6 vols. [*Cours*], i. 16.
[16] *Cours*, i. 9.   [17] *Cours*, i. 17.

absolu dans la conception, et arbitraire dans l'application'. These are the three characteristics which a positive sociology must oppose. It must reject 'absolute ideas' and restrict itself to co-ordinating observed facts and perfecting new techniques of investigation. It must always confine itself to the relative, 'sans que l'exacte réalité puisse être jamais, en aucun genre, parfaitement dévoilée'.[18] Lastly—and most importantly for Comte—positive sociology must accurately define the limits and nature of political action. Social phenomena are, he says, 'aussi susceptibles de prévision scientifique que tous les autres phénomènes quelconques', though he soberly adds: 'entre des limites de précision d'ailleurs compatibles avec leur complication supérieure'. This predictive skill established, sociology will assume its rightful place as a fully fledged science. Elsewhere Comte gives the sociologist the right and the duty to make moral evaluations, but at this point he insists that his task is merely to understand social data and to perceive the laws which link them, 'sans admirer ni maudire les faits politiques, et en y voyant essentiellement, comme en toute autre science, de simples sujets d'observation'.[19]

Sociology resembles the other sciences in its methods as well as in its aims, even though they must take slightly different forms. Comte distinguishes four means of social investigation—observation, which is the basis of all the others, experiment, comparison, and—a method peculiar to sociology—the historical method. Experimentation might seem impossible, but it is in fact feasible in so far as we can observe what happens when some special factor interferes with the regular course of events—as occurs in times of revolution, for example. The use of comparison may be equally fruitful—comparisons between human and animal societies or, even more valuably, between coexisting human societies—just as it is in the science of biology, Comte reminds us. But above all he looks to the historical method as 'le principal artifice scientifique de la nouvelle philosophie positive'.[20] By studying the development of societies up to the present the sociologist can not only verify the laws of social statics but also reveal the laws of social dynamics: he can discern those physical, intellectual, moral, and political tendencies that have progressively become more dominant and the opposing tendencies that have gradually grown

[18] *Cours*, iv. 213–14, 216.   [19] *Cours*, iv. 226, 293.
[20] *Cours*, iv. 322.

weaker. And this analysis will finally allow him to predict the ultimate ascendancy of one set of tendencies and the decline of the other. Nor is this most important of all sociology's methods merely conjectural in Comte's view. Not only is its data taken from observations made by the sociologist or the historians on whom he relies, but its conclusions can be 'verified'. The 'laws of succession' which it advances must not contradict the established general laws of human nature; they must be such laws as our prior knowledge of man would render antecedently probable. There has been a progressive decline in the amount of food men have eaten, but to deduce that men would ultimately cease to eat at all would be false—for the reason, as Comte is careful to note, that biology has shown that all organisms require some food if they are to survive. Again, if a sociological law implied that in most men reason predominates over desire or altruism over egotism, we should know by virtue of our prior acquaintance with human nature that history had been misunderstood and that the law was false.[21]

It is noteworthy that the historical method is perfectly consistent with positivism, provided it is carefully stated, and it is certainly an advance on the methodology of Comte's predecessors. Earlier social thinkers, like Bentham in England and the *philosophes* in France, had tried to deduce a social science from the general laws of human nature. Comte insists upon the need for historical study as the foundation of sociology, and this is the emphasis which Mill welcomed most warmly, declaring that any political thinker who neglects history 'must be regarded as below the level of the age', and he adds that he was chiefly indebted to Comte for the method of 'verification' just outlined—what Mill terms 'the Inverse Deductive Method'. By means of it, 'empirical generalizations are raised into positive laws, and Sociology becomes a science'.[22]

This is strong testimony to the scientific validity of Comte's historical method, and one can also notice that at this point his claims for social science and its methods are moderate and guarded. The experimental technique is still in its infancy, he says, and its future development cannot yet be estimated. The method of comparison between men and animals is limited in

[21] *Cours*, iv, '48ᵉ Leçon'.
[22] Mill, *Comte*, p. 86, *Autobiography*, p. 210.

scope to the study of social statics and is inapplicable to social dynamics. He attaches more value to the comparison of human societies, but even here he points out 'les graves dangers scientifiques qui lui sont propres'. And again after praising the possibilities of the historical method Comte gives a warning. Despite its high intrinsic value, 'elle peut cependant . . . entraîner à de graves erreurs'; we are dealing with an extremely complex field: hence the necessity for constant verification of our hypotheses.[23] The conclusion of his 49th lesson is arresting in its reserve:

> Par la complication supérieure de ses phénomènes, aussi bien que par son essor plus récent, la science sociale devra, sans doute, toujours rester, par sa nature, plus ou moins inférieure, sous les rapports spéculatifs les plus importants, à toutes les autres sciences fondamentales.[24]

This passage does honour to Comte—although it makes his dogmatism elsewhere all the more surprising.

The same positivist standpoint is reaffirmed in the *Discours sur l'ensemble du positivisme* (1848), however overlaid now by other considerations. The true positive spirit, he repeats, consists in substituting the study of the invariable laws of phenomena for the study of their alleged causes. Comte also refutes the charges of atheism, materialism, and fatalism that had been levelled against his philosophy, and in view of later misunderstandings his assertions here are of considerable interest.[25] Atheism, he argues, is as much a metaphysical theory as is theism: neither view can be verified by observation. He himself believes that the hypothesis of an intelligent will is rather more reasonable than the atheist hypothesis—but we can have no knowledge either way. Here Comte and Mill are at one. 'The Positive mode of thought [Mill writes] is not necessarily a denial of the supernatural; it merely throws back that question to the origin of all things.' A positivist may believe in the existence of God, provided only that he accepts that the direct determining cause of every phenomenon is natural, not supernatural, and admits that this 'intelligent Governor adheres to fixed laws'.[26]

The accusation of materialism is equally misplaced, Comte

[23] *Cours*, iv. 381, 312, 316, 319, 331.
[24] *Cours*, iv. 381; cf. vi. 598–9.
[25] *Discours sur l'ensemble du positivisme*, in *Système*, i. 47–49 (on atheism), 49–54 (on materialism), and 54–55 (on fatalism).
[26] Mill, *Comte*, pp. 14–15. He incorrectly contrasts his view with Comte's.

continues, although more understandable in view of the support which many scientists have erroneously given it. Their mistake has been to transfer the assumptions of the natural sciences into the higher science of sociology: since all phenomena in the former were material, they falsely conclude that all social phenomena must also be material. Somewhat surprisingly, Comte fails to advance the far stronger argument that he has already used in his discussion of atheism: namely, that we only know phenomena and that, consequently, to class them as 'material' or 'mental', though it may sometimes be convenient, is to fall into metaphysical assertion.

He also rebuts the charge of fatalism—by drawing a very proper distinction, repeated by Mill, Littré, Bernard, and others, between a fatalist philosophy and the scientist's acceptance of the invariability of natural laws.[27] Positivism, he says, asserts that the order of Nature is subject to invariable laws in its 'primary aspects', but it also believes that all phenomena (except, perhaps, those of astronomy) can be modified by human agency in their 'secondary relations'—the more markedly so as they are more complicated. In the sociological field supremely positivism urges us to act upon the predictions made by social science. Comte is here reiterating a view that is frequently expressed in the *Cours* and that is central to his entire regulative social system: although social phenomena are not indefinitely modifiable, there are certain sources of variation—amongst them race, climate, and man's social activity.[28]

What Comte fails to say, however, is that the assumption of invariability is only a working hypothesis for the scientist. He sees that without it the search for laws and the possibility of scientific predictions would be undermined, but it was left to others, the Neo-Kantians in particular, to stress that it may be a useful hypothesis without being universally valid. Comte, in fact, is not open to admitting that chance variability is theoretically possible, even though it may seem extremely improbable. Thus he passes severe strictures on mathematical theories of chance and refers to 'le prétendu calcul des chances, que la raison

---

[27] For Mill's view cf. ibid., p. 114, where he refers to 'the prejudice which regards the doctrine of the invariability of natural laws as identical with fatalism'.

[28] *Cours*, iv. 287; cf. iv. 227.

publique flétrira bientôt comme une honteuse aberration scientifique incompatible avec toute vraie positivité'.[29] His love of order
here warps his scientific judgement, one may feel: for him the
existence of chance variations would be a flaw in an otherwise
perfect system.

In general, however, the starting-point of Comte's thought is
consistently positivist, as we have seen. From it he embarks upon
the great tasks he set himself—the enunciation and demonstration of the *loi des trois états*; his discussion of the methods of the
various sciences and his attempt to purge them of their remaining
theological and metaphysical elements; the classification of the
sciences; and his extension of the positive methods to sociology.
These achievements fully warrant the respect which he com-
manded from such thinkers as Mill, Littré, and Durkheim. Mill
speaks of his 'wonderful systematization of the philosophy of all
the antecedent sciences, from mathematics to physiology, which,
if he had done nothing else, would have stamped him . . . as one
of the principal thinkers of the age', and his survey of universal
history is hardly less admirable, he thinks.[30] Littré, if historically
less accurate, is even more fervent when he remarks: 'aujourd'hui
. . . l'on commence à regarder comme une chimère une philosophie qui n'est pas tout entière dans le relatif. Telle est l'immense
révolution mentale qui est l'œuvre de M. Comte.'[31] One may not
agree with Faguet that he is the greatest French thinker since
Descartes; that he is a seminal mind of the nineteenth century
one cannot deny.[32] And it is all the more necessary to stress this
here, since we must now concentrate on the least satisfactory parts
of his system and examine the ways in which he is unfaithful to
the positivist philosophy.

3. Comte's Divergence from Positivism. (i) His treatment and application of the scientific methods

'Science, d'où prévoyance; prévoyance, d'où action'—this is the
guiding principle of Comte's entire career.[33] In common with a
majority of his contemporaries he believes that the primary task

[29] *Cours*, vi. 560–1.
[30] Mill, *Comte*, pp. 53, 106.
[31] Littré, op. cit., p. 45.
[32] E. Faguet, *Politiques et moralistes du dix-neuvième siècle*, 1903, 3 vols.,
ii. 369.   [33] *Cours*, i. 51.

of the nineteenth century is to build a more stable social order, to remedy the political unrest bequeathed by the revolutionary and Napoleonic era. To replace the state of 'crisis' by a state of 'order' and political upheaval and schism by stability and unity is the aim of thinkers of both Right and Left at this time. On the one side, Joseph De Maistre, De Bonald, Chateaubriand, and their traditionalist adherents hold that the pre-revolutionary union of Catholic faith and the monarchy is the indispensable basis for the new organic state; on the opposite side, Fourier, Saint-Simon, and other Left-wing reformers believe that the old régime has crumbled beyond repair and that it is impossible, even if it were desirable, to return to the institutions and doctrines of the eighteenth century. But whatever the solution they advocate, all the leading thinkers of Comte's youth are convinced that their task is to create or to re-create an ordered social system. And they all agree also that this must in turn be founded upon an ordered intellectual system. Catholics and reformers alike, and Cousin and his eclectic disciples with them, believe that philosophical or religious unity is the prerequisite of social unity.

Here is the background against which Comte's work must be set. He, like them, is searching first and foremost to build the intellectual bases of the new society and beyond that to legislate for its organization. Positive sociology is to be the political direc-tor of the new state, progress is to be installed as its dynamic, and the cult of humanity is to command the religious unity of its citizens. The positive philosophy itself is to be the intellectual source of the positive polity, and thus Comte rightly points out that the two parts of his work, scientific and political, are the necessary complements of each other.[34] Without the philosophy, the polity would be arbitrary and lack intellectual authority. Con-versely, the philosophy without the polity would be sterile, for the whole end of theoretical knowledge, in Comte's view, lies in its practical application. He argues that science has always been prized chiefly as a basis of action and openly declares that the aim of his own scientific work is to discover not truth for its own sake but laws that can guide social reorganization. Indeed, he asserts the superiority of the positive over the theological and metaphy-sical philosophies less because of any epistemological advantage

[34] Cf. *Discours sur l'ensemble du positivisme*, 'Première Partie', and *Système, Préface*. Cf. also A. Comte, *Lettres à Valat (1815–1844)*, Dunod, 1870, p. 99.

than because it alone allows us to establish a sound social moral-ity.[35] And if he insists, for example, upon the proper classifica-tion of the first five sciences—mathematics, astronomy, physics, chemistry, and biology—this is because in his opinion sociology depends upon it. Nor is this emphasis confined to his later works. The title of the 1822 essay, *Plan des travaux scientifiques néces-saires pour réorganiser la société*, reprinted as the first *Système de politique positive*, indicates the perennial direction of his thought. He even asserts in the last chapter of the *Cours* that the positive philosophy takes social morality for the basis of its whole system.[36] Likewise, he thinks of religion as a basis for social organization. Whether he would admit it or not, in his preoccupation with social regeneration he is in fact faithful to his former master, Saint-Simon, and faithful throughout his entire career.

This same approach explains the greater part of his divergence from positivism, we shall see. Almost every respect in which he forsakes its principles is related, directly or indirectly, to his over-riding concern with social ethics and political reconstruction.

There are inevitable errors in Comte's treatment of the sciences and of history and unavoidable lapses from the scientific accuracy to which he laid claim, and with these he cannot reasonably be reproached. Unfortunately, he goes far beyond the limits of excusable scholarly fallibility. One cannot ignore the uncritical and therefore unscientific manner in which Comte often ap-proaches his study and applies the methods he has adopted, and here is a first illustration of his no doubt unconscious betrayal of the positivist method. His cult of 'cerebral hygiene' and the reliance he placed on phrenology, most notoriously, are not iso-lated eccentricities but symptoms of a deep-seated attitude to knowledge.

He himself stressed the need to approach the study of any field with a preconceived theory in mind. He agrees with Bacon that all knowledge must be founded upon observation of facts; but he adds a qualification which assumes ever greater significance as the *Cours* progresses.

Si, d'un côté [he remarks], toute théorie positive doit nécessairement être fondée sur des observations, il est également sensible, d'un autre

---

[35] *Cours*, vi. 633–6, 742.   [36] *Cours*, vi. 742.

côté, que, pour se livrer à l'observation, notre esprit a besoin d'une théorie quelconque.[37]

In itself this is an entirely legitimate comment: it is difficult to find any coherence amongst a welter of facts unless we have some preliminary notion of the kind of meaning and the possible general law we are seeking. But as Comte continues this comment becomes much more than a useful principle of method: it furnishes the motive for an attack upon the open-minded accumulation of facts. All isolated empirical observation is idle and radically uncertain, he submits; science can utilize only those observations which are connected, however hypothetically, with some law. With growing impatience he attacks 'empiricism'—by which he means the impartial collection of factual data without any theoretical bias. It belongs, he maintains, to the state of intellectual anarchy prior to the positive stage and constitutes as great a danger to right thinking as mysticism.[38] '. . . Aucune véritable observation n'est possible qu'autant qu'elle est primitivement dirigée et finalement interprétée par une théorie quelconque', and he adds that the contrary view is 'radicalement contraire au véritable esprit fondamental de la philosophie positive'. He admits that this approach places us in a kind of vicious circle—no observation without a prior theory, and no theory without prior observation—and he acknowledges the danger that an observer may sometimes distort facts by falsely imagining that they verify what Comte calls 'certains préjugés spéculatifs, dépourvus d'un fondement suffisant'. Nevertheless, he believes that in sociology, more than any other science, observation 'a nécessairement besoin . . . d'une intime subordination continue à l'ensemble des spéculations positives sur les lois réelles de la solidarité ou de la succession de phénomènes aussi éminemment compliqués'.[39] By the final volume of the Cours Comte has reached the bottom of this particular slippery slope and is pointing out that he has repeatedly said that sociology requires 'l'emploi capital, aussi légitime qu'étendu, des considérations à priori'.[40]

This theoretical affirmation is, hardly surprisingly, paralleled in Comte's actual practice. He has not infrequently been accused of selecting the facts which support his theories and neglecting

[37] Cours, i. 12.
[38] Cours, vi. 531, 600.
[39] Cours, iv. 300, 304, 305.
[40] Cours, vi. 670.

those which do not. So distinguished an historian as Henri Sée, for example, remarks that he fails to give the sources of his historical information and suggests that his insistence that history should move from the general to the particular is the view of a man 'qui ne s'est jamais livré personnellement à des recherches historiques'. He adds: 'Jamais Comte ne fait la critique des données historiques qu'il emploie. Il est souvent médiocrement renseigné, notamment sur l'Angleterre.'[41]

It is reflected even more clearly in the fact that the laws which he postulates often rest upon *a priori* assumptions. He affirms, for instance, that ideas govern human history, and upon this view he founds his contention that the positive philosophy offers 'la seule base solide de la réorganisation sociale'. Otherwise, indeed, the law of the three states is relevant only to the development of man's mind and not, as Comte alleges, to every aspect of human history, political, social, and economic as much as intellectual. His assertion may be correct, but it is certainly discussible and requires to be defended. Yet Comte omits any justification by means of a light, deprecating evasion.

Ce n'est pas aux lecteurs de cet ouvrage que je croirai jamais devoir prouver que les idées gouvernent et bouleversent le monde, ou, en d'autres termes, que tout le mécanisme social repose finalement sur des opinions. Ils savent surtout que la grande crise politique et morale des sociétés actuelles tient, en dernière analyse, à l'anarchie intellectuelle.[42]

Such would be Comte's refutation of Marx. And yet it is surely true that, if this assumption is false, a great deal of his system becomes irrelevant to the aim he has chiefly in mind, the reorganization of society.

Another vital assumption into which he slips is that sociology can in fact be fully scientific. This assumption is necessary to the later, legislative part of his system in particular, yet it is extremely doubtful whether it is ever adequately defended. More especially, as Mill first remarked, although Comte discusses the scientific

---

[41] H. Sée, *Science et philosophie de l'histoire*, 1928, pp. 64, 79, 80. For a similar judgement cf. G. P. Gooch, *History and Historians in the Nineteenth Century*, London, 1913, p. 585. It is not only his antagonists who make this charge; cf. J. Delvolvé, *Réflexions sur la pensée comtienne*, 1932, p. 35: 'Si son souci réel de la vérification expérimentale est médiocre, son goût de la preuve démonstrative n'a guère plus de réalité.'
[42] *Cours*, i. 40–41.

methods at length, he does not consider critically the nature of scientific proof or distinguish between the different degrees of probability which the different methods can afford.[43] It is not that he is unjustified in regarding the historical method, for instance, as scientific, but that he comes to claim a quite excessive degree of certainty for the conclusions to which it led him. We have already seen the modest reservations he makes in first discussing the methods open to sociology and that he admits that they are weak when contrasted with the procedures of the other sciences. Yet, forgetful of his own warnings, he can later claim:

notre appréciation historique de l'ensemble du passé humain con- stitue évidemment une vérification décisive de la théorie fondamen- tale d'évolution que j'ai fondée, et, qui, j'ose le dire, est désormais aussi pleinement démontrée qu'aucune autre loi essentielle de la philosophie naturelle.[44]

It is not only that he here generalizes about the whole of human history when his survey has been confined to the last 2,500 years or so of the history of western Europe—a restriction he later openly justifies as '[une] grande prescription logique'.[45] Nor is it merely that the law of the three states was announced as early as 1822 when his historical knowledge was strictly limited or that the historical evidence he does adduce falls under the suspicion of having been carefully selected to support a theory which he held for *a priori* reasons. These failings apart, there is a dispro- portion between the moderate claims he made for the methods of sociology and the certainty he now ascribes to its conclusions. The earlier confessions of difficulty and imperfection are replaced by dogmatic assurance and a mood of self-confidence in which he can affirm that the new science is founded, its methods deter- mined, and that it is distinguished by 'autant de positivité et plus de rationalité qu'aucune des sciences antérieures déjà jugées par ce Traité'.[46]

One important illustration of the same assumption is found in his attitude to the view that there are invariable natural laws in the field of human social activity. This is the keystone of Comte's belief that sociology can exercise the full predictive function of a properly constituted science—a fact he himself uses as his

[43] Mill, *Comte*, pp. 54–56.   [44] *Cours*, vi. 434.
[45] *Cours*, vi. 532.   [46] *Cours*, vi. 547.

preliminary justification for believing that the invariability hypothesis is true. We cannot, he says, escape from the chaos of prepositive society unless, to use his own term, we 'subordinate' social phenomena, like all other phenomena, to invariable natural laws. Only scientific prevision can regulate society; but if there are no invariable laws, scientific prevision is impossible.[47] In his presentation of his argument he slips quietly over the crux of his case.

Ayant déjà préalablement démontré l'existence nécessaire [necessary because prevision would be impossible without it] des lois sociologiques . . . quant à l'état statique, il serait, sans doute, inutile d'insister formellement ici sur la nécessité beaucoup mieux appréciable et bien moins contestée des lois dynamiques proprement dites.

The reality of historical movement cannot be denied, he asserts —and we may agree with him in so far as movement means no more than change. The only real controversy that can exist concerns 'la subordination constante de ces grands phénomènes dynamiques à des lois naturelles invariables', but he assures us that 'il sera facile de constater . . . que [les] modifications successives [de la société] sont toujours assujetties à un ordre déterminé . . .'.[48] Yet in fact he never demonstrates that the movement through the three stages is more than a pattern he himself is imposing upon history—and it is difficult, moreover, to see how this could possibly be done. Comte's suggestion that it could be done brings him very close to the assertion that there is a *necessary* invariability in the operation of the laws of social phenomena —and at this point he is falling into the metaphysical way of thought he condemned. The invariability hypothesis may certainly be an indispensable working assumption for the sociologist, as it is for the natural scientist. But only predictive utility can legitimize it. We can assume the invariability of the law of gravitation on our planet because thousands of predictions made in accordance with it have been justified. Even then the scientist cannot deny the theoretical possibility of chance variations. Comte, however, seeks through political action to apply the laws he announces before they have been justified in this way, and, furthermore, proceeds at once to allege that they have the

[47] *Cours*, iv. 227. Comte's standpoint is, of course, that of nineteenth-century historicism, and he slips into many of the assumptions and fallacies examined, most notably, by K. R. Popper in *The Poverty of Historicism*, London, 1957.

[48] *Cours*, iv. 265-6.

authority of properly verified scientific laws. He even claims such certainty for them that he seems to be ignoring the inevitable relativity of human knowledge. Here again there is a disproportion between his own admission that the techniques of experiment and verification are only partially applicable in sociology and the dogmatism with which he advances his laws and the social creed he bases upon them. The caution and tentativeness of the scientist yield to the arbitrary assertions of the social prophet. Even Comte's apparently modest statements that our knowledge is 'relative' are ambiguous. To say this may mean, first, that all our perceptions are conditioned by the nature of human experiencing, that our knowledge is relative—and unavoidably so—in that it can never reach the 'things in themselves' as opposed to phenomenal appearances. It may mean, secondly, that the methods and categories we employ are relative to the stage of intellectual evolution we have reached. Comte certainly held the second of these views, but it is very doubtful if he held the first: although incomplete, our knowledge is of reality itself and, he often implies, is certain.[49]

A further expression of his attitude is seen in his comments on specialized research. From the start of the *Cours* he deplores research work that neglects the relation of the part to the whole system of positive knowledge. His own historical method differs from current historical scholarship, he alleges, because it studies human development as a unified whole. He attacks 'l'irrationnel esprit de spécialité exclusive' that would reduce history to 'une vaine accumulation de monographies incohérentes'. Science must oppose 'le régime empirique d'une spécialité dispersive'.[50] Once again his approach is determined by the primacy he gives to the practical, predictive function of the sciences.

La véritable science [he writes], appréciée d'après cette prévision rationnelle qui caractérise sa principale supériorité envers la pure érudition, se compose essentiellement de lois, et non de faits, quoique ceux-ci soient indispensables à leur établissement et à leur sanction.[51]

---

[49] F. A. Hayek, pointing out that Comte accepts the 'naïve realism' view of perception, adds: 'as in almost all nineteenth-century positivism, this concept [of the object] is left exceedingly obscure' ('The Counter-Revolution of Science', *Economica*, London, N.S., viii, 1941, p. 301). C. Cantecor, op. cit., p. 67.

[50] *Cours*, i. 26–27; iv. 325–6; vi. 546.

[51] *Cours*, vi. 600.

We can certainly accept this statement of principle and sympathize with Comte's strictures on a certain kind of trivial scholarship. Unfortunately, his concern with social reorganization impels him to demand over-rapid progress from social science: the present, for Comte as for so many historicists, is a unique moment, and future action will be too late.[52] Comte is a scientist in a hurry, and his desire for quick results leads him to accept easy results. In the last resort he prefers false laws to no laws at all, as when he scorns the 'ephemeral triumphs' of scientific criticism, 'aussi faciles que désastreux, en se bornant à détruire, d'après une investigation *trop minutieuse*, les lois précédemment établies, sans aucune substitution quelconque de *nouvelles règles*'. In this complaint Comte's real motive as a social scientist is revealed. He seeks rules for social action rather than truth about social phenomena, and when he remarks in the *Discours sur l'ensemble du positivisme* that the intellect's proper function is as servant of the social sympathies, he is making explicit a point of view assumed throughout his work.[53] Passion for truth in itself, he here asserts, is an expression of intense egotism; and although this overt declaration is new, the disdain for truth in itself is equally clear in the earlier works and is reflected in the hasty and incautious syntheses he has already advanced. The later writings merely establish as principles the practices and assumptions adopted in the earlier.

Mill remarks that 'the *fons errorum* in M. Comte's later speculations is [his] inordinate demand for "unity" and "systematization"'.[54] This demand is also the source of much that is arbitrary in the *Cours* itself and helps to explain at least a part of the unscientific attitude and procedure that have just been sketched. His search for unity derives partly from his own mental make-up and partly from his belief that only a complete and authoritative system could provide a foundation for the organic society of the future. But whatever its origin, it leads him to diverge from the positivist principles from which he began.

'It is one of M. Comte's mistakes that he never allows of open questions', Mill suggests in another context.[55] Probabilities and

---

[52] R. V. Sampson well remarks of such thinkers: 'The illusion that the present occupies a special, if not unique place of honour at the banquet of history, is one that dies hard' (*Progress in the Age of Reason*, London, 1956, p. 159).

[53] *Cours*, vi. 639 (my italics), and *Système*, i. 15–17.

[54] Mill, *Comte*, p. 141.   [55] Ibid., pp. 14–15.

uncertainties are anathema to him; he is therefore determined to resolve every problem once and for all. Nor is it only his major theories which reveal this *esprit de système*—the reduction of history to a few dominant laws; the strictly authoritarian organi- zation of the positive society and of the Religion of Humanity; and the dogmatism of his code of social morality. It is the same desire for completeness that leads him to assert without any fac- tual evidence that the positive stage is the final stage in man's development.[56] Yet again, combined with his utilitarian notion of science, it prompts him to propose that scientific research in the new society shall be controlled and co-ordinated in accordance with the demands of social order. And its influence is no less clear at more minor points in his thinking; two examples may perhaps suffice to illustrate a practice that is very common in Comte. He considers the hierarchy of importance of the six sciences and concludes that sociology is of the greatest value. It is instructive to note the terms in which he begins his discussion of the question.

Une véritable unité philosophique exigeant certainement l'entière prépondérance normale de l'un des éléments spéculatifs sur tous les autres, la question principale se réduit donc ici à déterminer directe- ment quel [which of the six fundamental points of view] est celui qui doit finalement prévaloir. . . .[57]

It is neither an examination of facts nor considerations of utility which lead to this hierarchical classification, but Comte's own desire for systematization.[58] Again, in the second *leçon* of the *Cours*, in speaking of the classification of the sciences, he declares, with appropriate reserve:

quelque naturelle que puisse être une telle classification, elle renferme toujours nécessairement quelque chose, sinon d'arbitraire, du moins d'artificiel, de manière à présenter une imperfection véritable.

There are 720 different possible arrangements, he points out, yet he goes on at once to postulate that there is 'un seul ordre vrai- ment rationnel'—which he then establishes.[59] Nor is he merely

---

[56] Cf. *Cours*, vi. 437.   [57] *Cours*, vi. 553.
[58] A very minor but characteristic example of his love of systematization (and of his preoccupation with social utility) is found in his declaration that men's sympathetic feelings towards their fellows should be extended to include 'tous les êtres sensibles qui nous sont subordonnés, proportionnellement d'ailleurs à leur dignité animale et à leur utilité sociale' (*Cours*, vi. 744).
[59] *Cours*, i. 60, 67.

asserting that one order of classification will be more useful to the scientist than the remaining 719 others, but that there is one correct order; and here, just as in his treatment of the invaria-bility hypothesis, he is slipping into a metaphysical way of thought.

In all these respects Comte abuses the scientific method and claims for his own beliefs and hypotheses a certainty that is far from justified by the facts he adduces. He not only abuses the method, moreover; ultimately, he is led to redefine it in terms that afford a greater justification for his malpractices. Perhaps nothing more arrestingly reveals his movement away from posi-tivism than the definition of the term 'positive' he advances in the first chapter of the *Discours sur l'ensemble du positivisme*. He alleges here that the true positive spirit is nothing other than generalized good sense directed to a social purpose and marked by an explicit 'organic' tendency, and that it includes within itself all the highest attributes of human wisdom, with the sole excep-tion for the moment of the moral insights of the heart. 'Positive' is thus construed as meaning relative, organic, precise, certain, useful, and real.[60] As Cantecor says of this greatly enlarged definition:

il [Comte] substitue insensiblement à la tradition de Galilée, de Des-cartes ou de Newton une conception de l'attitude scientifique qui lui est exclusivement personnelle et qu'il ne laisse pas de présenter comme une donnée de l'histoire et comme l'expression de l'esprit moderne.[61]

Social utility replaces truth as the goal of science, and it is a short step from this to asserting that their usefulness is the criterion by which laws and ideas are to be endowed with a scientific status.

4. Comte's Divergence from Positivism. (ii) The transition from social science to social ethics

Comte not only seeks to establish sociology as a science capable of predicting future social developments. He also makes a transi-tion to social ethics by maintaining that certain of these develop-ments are morally desirable—particularly the trends towards greater positivity and altruism that he foresees—and that we

[60] *Système*, i. 57–58.　　　[61] Cantecor, op. cit., pp. 88–89.

ought to assist and hasten them. 'L'amour pour principe, l'ordre pour base, et le progrès pour but': such is the slogan of his later works. A law of progress guides and dominates men, who are only its instruments, sweeping them along to their 'true providence'; and once we become conscious of this progression instead of being blindly impelled by it, we can make it the basis for a new scientific ethical code. This we shall enforce in the new positive society and thereby speed the consummation of the purposes of history. Such is the view he makes explicit in the later *Système de politique positive* when he modifies his earlier classification of the sciences by adding a seventh science, *la morale*, whose principle is 'Vivre pour autrui'. It is present, too, when he tries to replace 'revealed religion' by his 'proven religion', the cult of humanity, based first on a new deity whose existence (unlike that of a supernatural God) cannot be doubted in his judgement, based secondly on a 'proven' moral creed. Indeed, the ethic of his religious and social systems alike rests upon the jump he makes from the sociological prediction that 'this is most likely to happen' to the ethical claim that 'this happening is morally desirable'. And if this be invalid, his ethic loses its allegedly scientific foundation and becomes no more than a private assertion of belief.

The transition is seen at three turning-points of his thought in particular. First, he argues that we ought to assist the advance of the human mind into the complete positive state because this advance is part of the evolutionary process; strangely enough, he thinks this a more potent reason than the fact that the positive approach gives us verified knowledge, although he naturally stresses this fact. Writing of the law of the three states he says:

> Or, l'usage graduel de cette grande loi nous a finalement conduits à déterminer, à l'abri de tout arbitraire, la tendance générale de la civilisation actuelle, en marquant, avec une précision rigoureuse, le pas déjà atteint par l'évolution fondamentale; d'où résulte aussitôt l'indication nécessaire de la direction qu'il faut imprimer au mouvement systématique, afin de le faire exactement converger avec le mouvement spontané.[62]

The jump is here openly made.

It is seen again in his assertions that positivism can establish a new social morality, that it provides the only sane basis for social

---

[62] *Cours*, vi. 435.

reorganization and that morality in the future society will be immovably founded upon it.[63] Of social science and its functions he writes:

> Conduisant enfin, de même que toute autre science réelle . . . à l'exacte prévision systématique des événements qui doivent résulter, soit d'une situation donnée soit d'un ensemble donné d'antécédents, la science politique fournit directement aussi à l'art politique . . . l'indispensable détermination préalable des diverses tendances spontanées qu'il doit seconder. . . .[64]

Since evolution is moving irresistibly in a certain direction, all action counter to it will be 'nulle ou éphémère, et dès lors dangereuse'.

A similar leap into ethical judgement is seen in his interpretation of progress.[65] Although he does not equate it with increasing happiness in the manner of the utilitarians but with the continuous development of human nature, and although he tends to avoid the ethically toned term 'progress' in favour of the more neutral term 'development' (exactly like Hegel, who used the term 'Entwicklung'), Comte nevertheless asserts that there has been a progressive amelioration, particularly of morals. He declares, 'de la manière la plus explicite', 'que cette amélioration continue, ce progrès constant, me semble aussi irrécusables que le développement même d'où ils dérivent . . .'. This progress is visible in the external realm—in the conquests of the sciences and the arts, in the improvements in the physical conditions of man's life, in the more effective organization of society, and in the increase in the world's population. It is found also in the psychological realm. There has been 'une certaine amélioration graduelle et fort lente de la nature humaine'—in accordance, Comte thinks, with the Lamarckian theory of the inheritance of acquired characteristics. Man's intellectual powers have increased, and there is also 'une prépondérance croissante des plus nobles penchants de notre nature'. Improvement is thus a fact. And he goes even further and maintains that at each stage of man's development, the social state has been as 'perfect' as conditions allowed. Perhaps no other of his views suggests more definitely Comte's closeness to the assertion of his eighteenth-century predecessors that Nature is good.

[63] Cours, i. 40; vi. 464 ff.   [64] Cours, iv. 294.
[65] Cours, iv. 273–9.

He tries to justify his leap from science to ethics by relying upon the analogy of medicine. In referring to social disturbances, for example, he claims: 'Ces perturbations quelconques constituent, pour l'organisme social, l'analogue exact des maladies proprement dites de l'organisme individuel.'[66] The sociologist is the doctor of society; having diagnosed a social malady, he gives his prescriptions. Unfortunately, Comte omits any discussion of the limits of this analogy, even though it is so vital to his religious and legislative systems.

Two comments are especially pertinent. First, the moral justification of individual medicine itself involves a jump—from an analysis of the nature of sound health to the ethical assertion that sound health is desirable. In practice, most of us agree on this (although certain religious sects do not), and the philosophical jump is therefore of no importance. If we ask to what extent the same is true of social good health, we may all agree that law and order are desirable—and that the existence of a police force is therefore morally justified. But we are very far from agreeing upon many other matters of social organization; upon these the analogy with medicine breaks down. Secondly, we are apt to overlook the cases in individual medicine in which the doctor has an ethical decision to make. In a child-birth, for example, he may have to save either mother or child, being unable to save both. This may be an isolated case for the doctor, but for the sociologist and politician the art of government involves a constant compromise between a variety of interests—the claims of law and order, the claims of personal freedom, and the like. Here again, Comte's analogy fails to bear the weight he is placing upon it. It can only be sustained by neglecting the conflict of interests in society and affirming that society is a single, coherent unit in which no division is possible and that the individual is a 'pure abstraction'. Comte, significantly, does not hesitate to make these assertions; and had he not already presupposed them, indeed, it is doubtful whether the analogy would have impressed him so deeply. In a page which admirably summarizes the double function of sociology as science and as political director he declares:

cette science nouvelle . . . représente nécessairement, d'une manière directe et continue, la masse de l'espèce humaine, soit actuelle, soit

66 *Cours*, iv. 309; cf. iv. 233–4, 291.

passée, soit même future, comme constituant, à tous égards, et de plus
en plus . . . une immense et éternelle unité sociale, dont les divers
organes, individuels ou nationaux, unis sans cesse par une intime et
universelle solidarité, concourent inévitablement . . . à l'évolution
fondamentale de l'humanité, conception vraiment capitale et toute
moderne, qui doit devenir ultérieurement la principale base rationnelle de la morale positive.[67]

The underlying assumption of Comte's political and religious
creed—and of political and religious authoritarianism in general
—was never more uncompromisingly stated than in this passage.
There follows from it with irresistible logic Comte's later aboli-
tion of any distinction between the public and private functions
of individuals; 'dans toute société vraiment constituée [he adds],
chaque membre peut et doit être envisagé comme un véritable
fonctionnaire public'. He postulates 'la nécessité permanente
d'une certaine discipline systématique naturellement incompatible avec le caractère purement individuel'; 'la subordination
sociale' is to be the natural basis of the new society.[68]

We are not primarily concerned with these specific political
recommendations, however, no matter how unsavoury they may
seem to be, but with the philosophical form of his argument.
Summarized, this is that scientific study demonstrates that the
evolution of humanity is towards the triumph of altruism over
individual egotism, that the direction of this evolution is good,
and that therefore we ought to follow and assist this trend. The
weakness of his position is, first, that his interpretation of the
direction of evolution is in fact arbitrary and not derived from
a comprehensive and unbiased study of facts, and, secondly, that
in any case it does not follow that we ought to accept this trend
as our criterion of moral value. Further, in his attempt to make
the transition from a descriptive science of society to a prescrip-
tive moral philosophy for society, he is led to introduce into his
system a metaphysical abstraction as gross as those of the metaphysicians he attacked and to elevate it to the status of a self-
existing entity—namely, 'le Grand Être', humanity.[69] Comte's

[67] Cours, iv. 293-4.
[68] Cours, vi. 482-9.
[69] Comte has also been accused of giving independent reality to other abstractions like l'état and la famille; cf. E. Caird, The Social Philosophy and Religion
of Comte, Glasgow, 1893, p. 66, and Faguet, op. cit., ii. 358-9.

real standpoint is very well summed up by a contemporary sociologist, Ginsberg, when he writes:

> Comte's fundamental law is . . . ethical rather than sociological. It
> indicates the goal to which humanity ought to be moving; it does
> not describe the course which humanity has in fact steadily followed
> and which it must necessarily continue to follow in the future.[70]

5. Conclusion

The philosophical apostasy of which Littré accused his master
is far from confined, as he thought, to Comte's later works: its
essential features are found as clearly in the *Cours de philosophie
positive*, even if in less eccentric forms. Nor can one attribute it,
as Littré did, to a *crise de folie* and the influence of Clotilde de
Vaux. To concentrate on the earlier work is to realize that his
desertion of positivism is implied in the very terms of reference
he adopted for himself as Saint-Simon's young disciple: in the
discrepancy between his social and moral aims and the scientific
methods by which he was resolved to attain them. He illustrates
two recurrent nineteenth-century difficulties. How can one be a
positivist and yet provide an 'objective', authoritative ethical
system that will give direction and incentive for social man? If
we are confined to phenomena, ignorant of first causes and final
ends, how can we make the passage to such a system? And
secondly, can an ethic shorn of religious or metaphysical sanctions adequately replace the God-given morality of Christianity?
Nineteenth-century agnostics may attack the Christian religion
as vigorously as the *philosophes*, but they are less triumphant in
mood, often marked by regret and heart-searching. William
James's belief in the psychological value of religion and Durkheim's emphasis on its sociological utility are only two examples
of a widespread attitude throughout the century, as witness the
almost platitudinous respect for 'the religious sentiment' itself or
the many substitute-religions invented by social reformers and
metaphysicians alike. Comte is more confident and optimistic
than most but he shares these concerns. His ethical doctrine and

---

[70] M. Ginsberg, *The Idea of Progress—A Revaluation*, London, 1953, p. 35.
T. Whittaker remarks with equal justification: 'Comte has, indeed, an ethical
doctrine, but it is nowhere critically justified' (*Comte and Mill*, London, 1908,
pp. 52–53).

the Religion of Humanity are his answers to these two difficulties, and his later notions of a 'subjective method' and a 'subjective synthesis' and the primacy he gives to the emotions likewise stem from an awareness that the heart has demands as legitimate as those of the intellect. Delvolvé even urges that it is quite erroneous to see Comte as no more than 'le théoricien de la valeur suprême de la méthode scientifique et le père de la sociologie', whose later writings were mere aberrations. He considers Comte to be primarily a metaphysician and praises Ravaisson and Boutroux for perceiving 'le mouvement secret, qui entraîne la pensée comtienne par l'ascendant de la finalité vers la métaphysique'.[71] One need not agree with his evaluation of this metaphysics to accept his analysis. Comte is a reformer before he is a scientist, and it is small wonder that, sharing the preoccupations of his age, he should have ended as an archbishop.

[71] Delvolvé, op. cit., pp. v and iii. His references are to Ravaisson's *Rapport* and to E. Boutroux, *Science et religion dans la philosophie contemporaine*, 1908, and 'Auguste Comte et la métaphysique', *R.C.C.*, 1902, t. x, 1, pp. 769 ff., t. x, 2, pp. 206 ff., 547 ff., and 735 ff., and t. xi, pp. 57 ff. and 145 ff. A similar approach is found in Brunetière's *Sur les chemins de la croyance* and, from a more critical standpoint, in Caird, op. cit.

IV

LES VRAIS AMIS DU POSITIVISME (1)

ÉMILE LITTRÉ

1. *Littré and the Defence of Positivism*

THE reputation of Émile Littré (1801–81) rests chiefly on his philological studies—his translation of the works of Hippocrates (1839–61), his *Dictionnaire de médecine* (1855), his *Histoire de la langue française* (1862), and, supremely, the *Dictionnaire de la langue française* (1863–78). Yet these works are only a part of the immense achievement of this devoted, scrupulous savant. Translator of Strauss's *Life of Jesus*, Müller's manual of physiology, Schiller and Dante as well as Hippocrates; historian and philologist; student of literature; biologist, physiologist, and (the career for which he originally trained) medical scientist; member of the Académie des Inscriptions et Belles-Lettres, the Académie de Médecine, the Académie Française; frequent contributor to the *Revue des Deux Mondes*, the *Journal des savants*, the *Journal des débats*, and the *Revue germanique*; founder of the *Revue de philosophie positive* and, after 1870, first as *député*, then as *sénateur*, a political figure of considerable standing—it is little wonder that his contemporaries, Sainte-Beuve, Scherer, Caro, and many others, should emphasize the universality of his knowledge and the width of his intellectual range.[1]

He was also a philosopher, perhaps overshadowed in the perspectives of history by his master Comte but, nevertheless, during the second half of his life the very incarnation of the scientific attitude and the positivist philosophy. Dupanloup, in his polemic against Littré's candidature for the Académie Française in 1863 and in his own resignation when Littré was elected eight years later, was at least right in his assessment of his opponent's authority and influence. Martino points to the virulence of

[1] Cf. C. A. Sainte-Beuve, 'M. Littré', *Nouveaux Lundis*, t. v, 1866; E. Scherer, 'Émile Littré', *Études sur la littérature contemporaine*, t. vii, 1882; E. Caro, 'Émile Littré', *R.D.M.*, 1er avril 1882, pp. 516 ff. and 1er mai 1882, pp. 5 ff.; and E. Renan, 'Réponse au discours de réception de M. Pasteur', *Discours et conférences*, 9e éd., 1928.

contemporary attacks upon him as an indication of the prestige he attained and concludes by saying: 'il est évident qu'il a été pendant un demi-siècle une force morale considérable'.[2] It is this philosophical part of his work which concerns us here.

He was already thirty-nine years old before he read Comte's *Cours de philosophie positive*, the work which was to redirect his thinking and make him both a disciple of Comte and a leading champion of the positivist doctrine. He himself indicates the impact Comte's thought had upon him and contrasts his previous scepticism and his new-found conviction.

. . . Quand la philosophie positive m'apparut [he writes], je n'avais point de philosophie; j'avais renoncé depuis longtemps à toute théologie, et, depuis quelque temps, à toute métaphysique. Je me résignais, non sans un vif regret, à cet état négatif. L'ouvrage de M. Comte me transforma.

He was unable to mount by his own intellectual power to 'un point de vue universel qui me tînt lieu de métaphysique ou de théologie': Comte saved him from this negative position. 'Ce point de vue, M. Comte me l'a donné. Ma situation mentale en fut profondément modifiée; mon esprit devint tranquille, et la sérénité fut trouvée.'[3] His own practice as scholar and scientist received a unifying theoretical basis. His widely dispersed intellectual interests were related to each other and to a concerted movement of scientific advance. The pursuit of scientifically established knowledge which had always been his implicit aim now became the explicitly justified goal of his life's work. More than twenty years later he can still declare of Comte's philosophy: 'elle suffit à tout, ne me trompe jamais, et m'éclaire toujours'.[4]

The disciple amply repaid his debt. His *Analyse raisonnée du 'Cours', De la philosophie positive* (1845) was followed by *Application de la philosophie positive au gouvernement des sociétés et à la crise actuelle* (1849) and *Conservation, révolution et positivisme* (1852), both exploring the social consequences of the philosophy. His break with Comte occurred in 1852, but even this did not diminish his loyalty to the thought of the *Cours* and

---

[2] P. Martino, 'Le Second Empire', in *Littérature française*, edited by Bédier and Hazard, 1948–9, 2 vols., ii. 299.

[3] E. Littré, *Auguste Comte et la philosophie positive*, 2e éd., Hachette, 1864 [*A.C.*], pp. 662–3, 529.

[4] *A.C.*, p. ii.

in 1863 he published his most influential philosophical work, *Auguste Comte et la philosophie positive*—an exposition that shines with the lucidity Comte lacked and at the same time a penetrating assessment of Comte's limitations, for the task of a true disciple must include criticism, he affirms, 'cette critique de bon aloi qui n'écarte le faux que pour mettre en lumière le vrai'.[5] In the following year he published his famous 'Préface d'un disciple' to the second edition of the *Cours de philosophie positive* and in 1866 the article on 'Comte et Mill' in which he defends Comte against the charges made by Mill's *Auguste Comte and Positivism*. The foundation of the *Revue de philosophie positive* came in 1867, and he also collected some of his articles for it in *La Science au point de vue philosophique* (1873), which sought to illustrate Comte's classification of the sciences. Finally, three years before his death, he reissued *Conservation, révolution et positivisme*, adding *Remarques en 1878*, which amend and clarify his earlier views. Yet again he pays homage to Comte; his final complaint is not against Comte's method but against his own imperfect application of it. Even at the very end of his life, as he underwent great suffering, he still speaks of the positive philosophy as a faith that has given him serenity, purpose, and an ideal for his life.

La philosophie positive, qui m'a tant secouru depuis trente ans et qui, me donnant un idéal, la soif du meilleur, la vue de l'histoire et le souci de l'humanité, m'a préservé d'être un simple négateur, m'accompagne fidèlement en ces dernières épreuves.[6]

But this devotion to Comte could not undermine Littré's integrity or blind him to the defects of his teacher. His importance for any study of mid-nineteenth-century positivism lies above all in his refusal to accept the ideas—the errors, as he believed—of the *Système de politique positive* and the *Synthèse subjective*. By his separation from Comte he, more than any other individual, was responsible for dividing Comte's followers into the two groups of the orthodox and the dissident positivists. More firmly even than Mill he takes his stand upon the original teaching of the *Cours* and accuses Comte of forsaking his own method. Even against Comte himself he defends the pure positive

---

[5] *A.C.*, p. 664.
[6] Cited by Scherer, op. cit., p. 346.

doctrine and thereby preserves its intellectual virility against the disrepute into which his master's deviations might so easily have brought it. The disciple salvaged the essential elements of his master's thought and presented them with a force and persuasiveness that made them impossible to ignore. As one recent historian remarks, 'Littré a incarné le positivisme pur, philosophiquement et politiquement; il a noblement soutenu une cause que, sans lui, les fantaisies du maître auraient condamnée à une existence de petite chapelle.'[7]

Littré, one might say, is the Bossuet of nineteenth-century positivism, attacking every heresy, every improper modification, every misrepresentation, every unscientific theory that contradicted its strict philosophical doctrine. His criticisms were directed against both enemies and friends, against the Church and the eclectics and also against those *esprits mi-positifs et mi-métaphysiques*, to use his own phrase,[8] who sympathized with positivism, claimed to be its advocates, and benefited by its prestige, but who were in fact, in Littré's view, undermining its authority by their attempts to reinterpret its teaching. In turn, with greater or lesser kindliness, he therefore protects 'pure positivism' as he understood it against Comte himself, against Renan and all pantheists, against Berthelot and Spencer, against Mill and the English psychological school, and against the materialists. In the *Remarques en 1878*, one can add, he even upbraided himself and guarded the positivist position against his own errors.

To survey Littré's role as defender of orthodox philosophical positivism (as distinct, of course, from orthodox religious positivism) is to make clearer his own interpretation of that orthodoxy. It is also to prefigure to some extent our own analysis of Renan, Taine, and others, for Littré, too, was trying to estimate the real position of those mid-century thinkers who have been too simply classified as positivists. His criticisms of the positivist 'fellow travellers', as he considered them, are thus of special interest to us, and although some of them may seem invalidated by his own misconceptions concerning positivism, others remain as forceful as when first advanced.

[7] P. Martino, op. cit., ii. 300.
[8] E. Littré, 'Préface d'un disciple', in A. Comte, *Cours de philosophie positive*, 2ᵉ éd., Baillière, 1864, t. i [*Préf.*], p. xxxv.

2. *Littré and Comte*

It has been argued that Littré does not even accept the teachings of the *Cours de philosophie positive* in their entirety, and
that in his later years he whittles down the positive philosophy
to a single negation: nothing that is not observed can be known.[9]
It is difficult to support this view. Even the isolated admissions of
the *Remarques en 1878*, when read in their context, are closer
to stray self-questionings than to formal defections from Comte's
doctrine. As to his position before this, there can be little doubt
that he accepts whole-heartedly the major theses of the *Cours*. He
certainly shares the positivist theory of knowledge, its rejection
of metaphysics and *a priori* knowledge, its insistence on empirical
verification,[10] but he goes far beyond this. First, he stresses the
centrality of Comte's classification of the sciences. For Saint-
Simon, he argues, *la philosophie positive* was only a collective
term for all the sciences; Comte's greatest addition to this inadequate view lay in his ordering of them, and he adds in the 'Préface
d'un disciple' that this is one of the foundations of the positive
philosophy.[11] Littré also holds that the historical theories of the
Cours are '[une] portion essentielle de la philosophie positive'.
Kant and Turgot preceded Comte here, but Comte surpassed
them by relating history to sociology and making this final science
historically conscious.[12] Against Mill he contends that Comte
securely founded social science, and in 1873 he claims again:
'depuis lui, on a des idées précises sur la loi de l'histoire, la direction du progrès, la marche de la civilisation, le but de l'humanité'.[13]
Thirdly, Littré believes that the positive philosophy is a conception of the world and not merely, as Mill would have it, a conception of man or of the limits of the human mind. Here again
he sides with Comte: positivism is 'la conception du monde telle
qu'elle résulte de l'ensemble systématisé des sciences positives'.[14]
Although he dissents from the Religion of Humanity itself, he

---

[9] Caro, loc. cit., 1er mai 1882, pp. 17, 22–23; cf. G. Cantecor, *Comte*, nouv. éd.,
s.d., p. 167.

[10] *A.C.*, p. 45.

[11] *A.C.*, pp. 42, 44, 31 and *Préf.*, p. x; cf. E. Littré, *La Science au point de vue
philosophique*, Didier, 1873 [*La Science*], pp. ii–iii.

[12] *A.C.*, p. vii.

[13] E. Littré, 'La Philosophie positive; M. Auguste Comte et M. J. Stuart Mill',
R.D.M., 15 août 1866 [*C.M.*], pp. 840 ff., and *La Science*, p. vii.

[14] *C.M.*, pp. 829, 834.

even declares that, in so far as a religion is nothing more than a conception of the world, positivism can legitimately assume 'a role equivalent to the role of religions'.[15]

Littré also agrees with Comte's attempt to apply the positive philosophy in social action. The particular merit of this philosophy in the present age of social disorder is to have proposed 'un principe de doctrine et d'organisation . . . qui concentre en soi toute la vertu de la science positive'.[16] Again, despite reservations, he is sympathetic to the morality Comte erects. Positivism already possesses intellectual supremacy; it will soon gain moral ascendancy also. Love of humanity is its supreme moral principle, he says—a notion that transcends the Christian idea of charity by virtue of its interest in the past, present, and future progress of mankind. He even relates the advances of modern civilization to the spontaneous growth of this new love.[17]

Such are the principal respects in which Littré goes beyond simple epistemological positivism in his agreement with Comte. Despite this, however, Littré rejected the *Système de politique positive* and the *Synthèse subjective*—for reasons we must now examine.

His principal disagreements are expressed in the third part of *Auguste Comte et la philosophie positive*; basing himself on Comte's own dictum that 'the method is even more important than the doctrine', he attacks the non-positivist elements he discerns in the later works.

He objects, first, to the distinctively religious dogmas that Comte links with the moral creed of love for humanity. Whereas in the *Cours* 'le mot de religion n'est nulle part prononcé', after 1845 Comte's notion of a 'spiritual authority' is redefined in terms of a religion and humanity is erected as an object of worship. This contravenes the positive method, Littré submits.

La conception du monde étant posée comme il vient d'être dit, rien n'autorise à y choisir pour l'adorer, soit l'humanité, soit toute autre fraction du grand tout, soit le grand tout lui-même.[18]

Comte reverted to the theological state in fact, as becomes abundantly clear in the *Synthèse subjective*, where he even attributes

---

[15] *A.C.*, p. 524.
[17] *A.C.*, pp. 524–6; cf. *Préf.*, p. l.

[16] *Préf.*, p. xlvii; cf. *A.C.*, p. 672.
[18] *A.C.*, pp. 523–4.

faculties of feeling and action to such external objects as our planet and other habitable celestial bodies.[19]

Secondly, Littré attacks Comte's 'subjective method' and urges that it is radically opposed to the objective method of the *Cours*. It is metaphysical, based upon *a priori* notions, divorced from experience and experimental verification. Since this method ignores observed facts, 'rien ne l'arrête ni ne la borne': hence its attraction for Comte in the second part of his life. But its adoption was Comte's basic sin against his own earlier teaching, and Littré goes so far as to argue that he only accepted it as the result of a *crise de folie*.[20]

Connected with Comte's advocacy of the Religion of Humanity and of the subjective method is his subordination of the mind to the heart. This is the counterpart in the realm of *la morale* to the metaphysical theory of knowledge he has taken over: 'c'est, après avoir subordonné les déductions philosophiques à l'imagination logique, subordonner les déductions morales à l'imagination sentimentale'. Neither procedure has any place in the positive method. Nor is it justified by the facts to speak, as Comte does, of the intellect having usurped the rightful functions of the heart. To talk of 'l'insurrection moderne de l'esprit contre le cœur' is false both historically and psychologically, and it is also to condemn all the critical advances which have destroyed religious and metaphysical faith.[21] Comte was right to defend the Middle Ages against the superficial and prejudiced interpretations of the eighteenth century; but now, Littré severely concludes, he has allowed the Middle Ages to overwhelm him.

Finally, although he approves of Comte's postulation of love of humanity as the criterion of moral action, he rejects the assertion that *la morale* can become a seventh science. Here again Comte is committing 'une faute contre la méthode'.[22]

These are Littré's principal charges. Other less central criticisms concern Comte's *tableau cérébral*, adopted with modifications from Gall's phrenology, in which Comte accepts *a priori* views that cannot be verified; his identification of mathematics and logic; his restoration of fetishism; his re-establishment of the dogmatic notions and language of religion, all of them based upon

[19] *A.C.*, p. 571, referring to *Synthèse subjective*, t. i, 1856, p. 10.
[20] *A.C.*, pp. 534, 580 ff.   [21] *A.C.*, pp. 553-9.
[22] *A.C.*, p. 677.

arbitrary and unscientific considerations; and, worst of all, his belief (as expressed in the *Synthèse subjective*) that there are wills independent of man that intervene in the events of our world.[23] These latter views in particular mark a return to theological thinking on Comte's part—and perhaps no more damning chapter has been written about him than Littré's attack upon this *retour à l'état théologique*.[24]

Upon all these grounds he opposes Comte, in a tone of mingled regret, astonishment, and outraged sanity. It is false to think of Littré as a superficial or materialistic mind. He is aware of all the intellectual and emotional torment which the positivist questioning of religious belief can create, although he himself found an almost religious consolation in the positive philosophy. He, like Kant, could marvel at the starry heavens or, like Pascal, feel terror before their silence.[25] But the truth and the facts as he saw them held complete primacy over his emotional desires, and it was the truth and the facts that Comte was ignoring in his view. He even felt perhaps that his trust in Comte had been betrayed, and his reaction is identical to Mill's, both of them surprised and repelled by the later *comtisme*.

Aujourd'hui [he writes], tenant les derniers livres de M. Comte, j'en tourne les feuillets avec une douloureuse émotion; alors, tenant ses premiers ouvrages, je suivais avec un intérêt croissant les développements de cette pensée puissante qui devait me captiver.[26]

3. *Littré's Criticism of Materialism, Renan, Berthelot, and Spencer*

He also attacks other thinkers of his age who seemed to him to be falsely enlarging and adapting the positivist position to suit their own ends. This opposition is found in the 'Préface d'un disciple' above all.

In the first place he criticizes the materialists and firmly dissociates their philosophy from his own, for it is a gross error to imagine that materialism and positivism are synonymous. Materialism is a metaphysical doctrine which goes beyond the limits of observation by asserting that all phenomena derive from a material 'substance'. In common with Comte and Mill, Littré

---

[23] *A.C.*, '3ᵉ Partie', ch. iii and v.   [24] *A.C.*, '3ᵉ Partie', ch. v.
[25] Cf. Scherer, op. cit., pp. 343–5.   [26] *A.C.*, p. 569.

claims that positivism 'repousse comme vaines toutes les hypothèses, soit matérialistes, soit spiritualistes'. Both camps make
statements about a region that is strictly unknowable: this, he
adds, is the characteristic error of all metaphysics.[27]

Pantheism makes the same mistake, as he argues both here and
in his article on 'Comte et Mill',[28] and he accuses Renan and
Berthelot especially of a pantheistic deviation from positivism.
He bases his criticisms upon the exchange of views between the
two thinkers published in the *Revue des Deux Mondes* in 1863
under the title of 'Les Sciences de la nature et les sciences historiques'.[29] Unlike most metaphysicians, he points out, they claim
positivism's support for their systems—and it was this fact in
particular which aroused his opposition. Renan's theory of the
evolution of the world from its very origins up to the present is
largely conjectural, 'une hypothèse invérifiable', not 'un résultat
de l'observation': thereby it contravenes the positivist method.[30]
Secondly, Renan embraces the pantheistic view that God is immanent in the whole universe and in each creature within it,
gaining greater self-consciousness as the creature is the more
advanced upon the ladder of evolution. This is 'la pure doctrine
de l'hégélianisme', Littré remarks,[31] and in opposing it the positivist does not need to point to the inner improbabilities of the
system—God as both personal and impersonal, both in the Absolute and in the process of becoming. It is sufficient to stress that
here is a purely subjective notion for which there neither is nor
ever could be any scientific evidence whatever. As for the ethic
and the 'eschatology' Renan bases on this doctrine, they are even
more fragile than their fragile foundation.[32]

Berthelot is more congenial to Littré. His definition of positive
science is excellent. Unfortunately, he then goes on to advance
the notion of *une science idéale* whose aim is to seek first and final
causes, whose method is allegedly positivist but whose conclusions
are to be metaphysical. This is a mixture of mutually contradic-
tory elements, Littré declares. The only philosophy or *science
générale* compatible with positivism is 'la considération hiérar-
chique des sciences particulières, ou, en d'autres termes, de tout

[27] *Préf.*, pp. xxvi–xxviii. [28] *C.M.*, p. 837.
[29] 15 oct. 1863 and 15 nov. 1863. Both are reprinted in Renan's *Dialogues et fragments philosophiques*.
[30] *Préf.*, pp. xxix–xxx. [31] *Préf.*, p. xxxii.
[32] *Préf.*, pp. xxxii–xxxiii.

le savoir humain'. Berthelot's idea is 'une conception à base positive et à couronnement métaphysique', a typical product of 'l'esprit
mi-métaphysique et mi-positif, partagé entre des tendances con-
traires'. It will end by collapsing under the weight of its own
incompatibilities and its author will be led, either to construct an
Absolute, break with positivism, and make a complete return to
metaphysics, or else to renounce all thought of the Absolute and
ally himself whole-heartedly with positivism. Between the metaphysical and the positivist attitudes there can be no intermediate
stage.[33]

He next directs his critical fire upon Herbert Spencer's interpretation of the idea of the unknowable. He is writing in 1864,
and his knowledge of Spencer appears to derive largely from an
article by Laugel in the *Revue des Deux Mondes* (15 fév. 1864).
Once again he denies that anyone can be both a positivist and a
metaphysician, as Laugel claims Spencer to be. Spencer's argument, as resumed by his French interpreter, is that, given the
division between the knowable and the unknowable, science and
religion meet upon the shores of the unknowable. '*L'incognoscible*, c'est l'objet de toutes les religions; c'est en même temps
le dernier terme de toutes les sciences.' The antagonism between
science and religion is thus illusory: 'la religion et la science se
confondent en ce point [*l'incognoscible*]'. Such is the rather briefly
stated position which Littré then has little difficulty in destroying.
The notion of *l'incognoscible*, he says, is certainly due to Comte
and is an integral part of the positivist system. But Spencer is
guilty of a gross confusion between two *incognoscibles*. The unknowable for religion is its very object of attention, its central
preoccupation; the unknowable for science is a boundary at which
it is forced to halt. 'Être objet ou être limite sont deux notions
très-distinctes.' Moreover, theology pretends to have knowledge
of this unknowable and has based a social organization upon this
alleged knowledge; the *incognoscible* is *incognoscible* for Spencer
alone and not for the theologians. The unknowable recognized by
science, on the other hand, is really unknown; no scientist would
claim to know anything about it or to found any social policy or
any theory or law upon it. In fact, Spencer eventually deserts his
first definition and ends, like the theologians, by making an unverifiable assertion about this realm: he calls it 'the power of

[33] *Préf.*, pp. xxxv–xxxvii.

which the universe is a manifestation'. Nothing illustrates more clearly the impossibility of the reconciliation Spencer is trying to establish.[34]

4. *Littré and Mill*

Finally—and perhaps most interestingly for us—Littré takes Mill to task. His arguments are found in the article, 'Comte et Mill'. It has already been seen that Littré centres their main dispute on the question as to whether positivism is a way of thought about the world or a way of thought about man, and that he himself sides with Comte against Mill's limited epistemological conception. Littré recognizes that Mill philosophizes 'suivant le mode positif'. Why, then, is he antagonistic to certain aspects of the *Cours*? The answer is to be found in his excessive preoccupation with logic and the positivist theory of knowledge. Failing to recognize that positivism is first and foremost 'une conception du monde', he is led, incidentally, to underestimate Comte's originality by pointing out that the positivist approach had been adopted by numerous earlier scientists and thinkers. But above all, his restricted view prompts him to criticize Comte's treatment of sociology and negligent attitude to psychology.[35] In both spheres, Mill's misunderstandings derive from his misunderstanding of the positive philosophy itself. To take one crucial instance, when Mill accuses Comte of failing to provide an adequate criterion of scientific proof, he is giving a false primacy to logic. Littré's argument here brings us to the heart of his real position. Comte does provide a criterion of scientific truth, he asserts—that of sense-experience or verification. To this Mill could reply: How do you know that your observation, your verification are valid? This, as Littré seems to recognize, is the turning-point of the argument between them. His answer is worth quoting in full, for its confident urbanity conceals the most noteworthy divergence in his thought from the positivism of Hume and his successors—and from positivism as understood in this study.

Ici, tout au rebours de croire que l'expérience ait besoin de la

---

[34] *Préf.*, pp. xl–xliv.
[35] *C.M.*, pp. 856, 838, 848. In contrast to Mill, Littré sums up his attitude to psychology by saying: 'Si on définit la philosophie, comme je fais, une conception du monde, on se passe de la psychologie' (pp. 851–2).

logique, je crois que c'est la logique qui a besoin de l'expérience. Si les vérités scientifiques n'étaient vraies que logiquement, elles ne sortiraient pas du cercle des simples hypothèses; mais c'est quand l'expérience les a fournies que se fait la théorie logique de l'induction. Bien loin que la philosophie positive dépende de la logique, c'est la logique qui dépend de la philosophie positive. Ainsi . . . , comment connaît-on l'universalité de la loi de causation? Par l'expérience, non par la logique, car c'est une des excellentes opérations de la psychologie positive d'avoir démontré que la notion de cause n'est pas immanente à l'esprit humain.[36]

Such is Littré's position, and its influence permeates his interpretation of the scientific method and its results. Science gives not merely probabilities but certainties. It is not confined to the 'cercle des simples hypothèses', and he can thus speak of 'la certitude de la science positive'.[37] And in explaining the certainty given to us in 'direct' experience he argues that it is based upon intuition: 'la certitude scientifique est donc partout et toujours une certitude d'intuition'. His conclusion comes strangely from a positivist who has rejected the metaphysical notion of intuition. 'L'intuition [he declares], ne relevant que d'elle-même, constitue le criterium de la vérité objective, selon M. Comte et la philosophie positive.'[38] The tradition of Descartes's method of doubt, of Hume's scepticism and Kant's categories is here forgotten. And with Mill, significantly, Littré links Reid in England—and Kant on the Continent. He praises this 'psychological school' for its work in making psychology 'positive', but, like Mill, it has failed to construct a philosophy, and inevitably so, for 'l'étude de l'homme ne donnera pas la conception du monde'.[39] Scherer perceptively remarks, having equated positivism with 'agnosticism', that 'Littré, pas plus que Comte, ne paraît avoir connu la critique aussi décisive que subtile à laquelle Kant a soumis les anciennes données philosophiques'.[40]

There is even a tendency in Littré's thinking to slip into the very materialism he has condemned. In the 'Préface d'un disciple' he writes:

Le monde est constitué par la matière et par les forces de la matière:

[36] *C.M.*, p. 853.   [37] *Préf.*, p. xxxvii.
[38] *C.M.*, p. 854.   [39] *C.M.*, 857.
[40] Scherer, op. cit., pp. 342–3; Kant for him is 'le véritable père de l'agnosticisme'.

la matière dont l'origine et l'essence nous sont inaccessibles; les forces qui sont immanentes à la matière. Au delà de ces deux termes, matière et force, la science positive ne connaît rien.[41]

This is to endow abstractions, 'matter' and 'forces', with existence with a vengeance! And he makes a similar lapse in his book on Comte. 'Un phénomène naturel [he says] est celui qui dépend d'une matière et d'une force; et, comme je l'ai dit, nous ne connaissons pas d'autre espèce de phénomène.'[42] It is little wonder that materialism is one of the commonest charges made against him by his contemporaries. Caro, for instance, asserts that Littré is no more successful in remaining completely open-minded than any other positivist. Some, like Comte, have wandered into humanitarian 'mysticism'; others, like Spencer, into metaphysics; others, like Büchner and Moleschott, into straightforward materialism. Littré belongs to this last group, as is seen from his equation of man's 'soul' or 'mind' with the functioning of the nervous system.[43]

These differences between Littré and Mill—and especially the former's contention that positivism is more than a theory of knowledge—help to explain the variance in their judgement of the *Cours de philosophie positive*—as well as our own divergence from Littré's estimate of it. And if, although only on balance, one classes Littré as *un vrai ami du positivisme*, it is at this point that he least deserves such a title.

The second assertion that he makes in opposing Mill is related to his general position: it concerns the philosophical implications of the idea of the unknowable. We saw that he claims that this notion originates in positivism and resolutely opposes Spencer's attempt to utilize it in such a way as to reconcile science and religious faith. His attitude is made clear in his book on Comte. What cannot be known by scientific methods is absolutely inaccessible to the human mind. Yet inaccessible does not mean non-existent. The unknowable, he holds, 'apparaît sous son double caractère, la réalité et l'inaccessibilité'.[44] Thus far, Littré and Mill

---

[41] *Préf.*, p. ix. [42] *A.C.*, p. 43.

[43] Caro, loc. cit., 1er mai 1882, pp. 27–32. Renouvier discerns in Littré's thought 'une métaphysique matérialiste' ('De la philosophie du dix-neuvième siècle en France', *L'Année philosophique — Première Année (1867)*, 1868, pp. 36 ff.). Cf. the notorious definition in the *Dictionnaire de médecine*: 'HOMME. Animal mammifère de l'ordre des primates, famille des bimanes. . . .'

[44] *A.C.*, p. 519.

are in agreement; beyond this point they diverge. Littré takes issue above all with Mill's assertion that positivism does not necessarily exclude belief in a supernatural. Mill believes that the positivist may form his own opinion upon religious questions, in accordance with the weight he attaches to the alleged evidences of design and to the other arguments for the existence of God, provided always that he acknowledges that these questions only allow of conjecture and never of knowledge. Littré, in his reply, links this view with Spencer's concept of the *incognoscible*. Even to allow the possibility of a Divine Designer is to reject the positivist principles whereby any notions of first or final causes or of the intervention of wills independent of the natural order are banished from philosophy. Positivism does not leave one free to think whatever one will about first or final causes.

Non, il ne laisse là-dessus aucune liberté; sa détermination est précise, catégorique, et le sépare radicalement des philosophies théologique et métaphysique: il déclare les causes premières inconnues. Les déclarer inconnues, ce n'est ni les affirmer ni les nier, et c'est, quoi qu'en dise M. Mill, laisser la question ouverte dans la seule mesure qu'elle comporte.[45]

One of the inadequacies of Mill's definition of positivism is precisely that it leaves open the question of the existence of a supernatural. The purely psychological doctrine of the relativity of our knowledge 'ne ferme pas la voie aux causes premières'. It merely proves that we only know phenomena: 'elle ne prouve pas que cela même, qui n'est aperçu de nous que phénoménalement, n'est pas au fond partie et manifestation d'un absolu, s'il est un absolu'.[46] Comte's doctrine, on the other hand, in which positivism is 'une conception du monde', effectively precludes any metaphysical speculation.

Three comments may be made with regard to Littré's attitude here. First, his belief that one can prove (in the way that Comte allegedly has and Mill has failed to do) that phenomena are not manifestations of an Absolute is itself an infringement of his principle that what lies behind phenomena, whether it be an Absolute or not, is utterly unknowable. Elsewhere in the same article, in fact, Littré excludes the possibility of any such proof; 'la rigueur de la preuve et l'objectivité veulent ici que l'on ne nie

[45] *C.M.*, p. 863.   [46] *C.M.*, p. 857.

pas, que l'on n'affirme pas . . .'.[47] That he should sometimes suggest that some such denial or affirmation can be made is a strange inconsistency in his system, deriving firstly from his suspicion of any view which seemed to reopen the door for metaphysics and as well from his occasional lapse into the view that 'reality' is wholly to be equated with what can be observed.

Secondly, it is not certain that he altogether understood Mill's standpoint. How else can one explain the misconception contained in his argument? He writes against Mill:

Faire résoudre la question des causes premières dans un mode de philosopher qui partout en a constaté expérimentalement l'insolution, introduire l'absolu dans un mode de philosopher qui ne comporte que le relatif, concevoir une connaissance là où ce mode de philosopher met rigoureusement l'inconnu, c'est non pas concilier, mais juxtaposer les incompatibilités.[48]

The obvious reply is that Mill does not claim that it is possible to 'resolve' the question of first causes or have 'knowledge' about the unknowable: he merely points out that, granted we cannot resolve or know anything about it, we can still form our personal conjectures if we wish to do so.

Thirdly, despite the errors into which Littré falls at this point, his attitude looks forward to an assertion commonly made by twentieth-century positivists. His underlying thesis is that it is as meaningless to speak about conjectures concerning the unknowable as to speak about knowledge of it. Even individual opinions are philosophically nonsensical when they refer to a realm which is inaccessible to observation. He believes that we can contemplate this vast, impenetrable sea of the unknowable and the sight of it may move or inspire us. 'Je n'interdis point à l'esprit de se perdre, avec l'indéfinissable frémissement que cause l'abîme, dans l'espace et dans le temps sans borne. . . .'[49] 'C'est un océan qui vient battre notre rive, et pour lequel nous n'avons ni barque ni voile, mais dont la claire vision est aussi salutaire que formidable.' Later he adds, in a mood of growing elevation: 'Rien n'élève plus l'âme que cette contemplation: par un concours qui ne s'était pas encore

[47] C.M., p. 863. Cf. La Science, p. 562: 'La science positive professe de n'y [in the domain of the unknowable] rien nier, de n'y rien affirmer; en un mot, elle ne connaît pas l'inconnaissable, mais elle en constate l'existence. Là est la philosophie suprême. . . .'
[48] C.M., p. 864.   [49] Préf., pp. xxx–xxxi.

produit, elle excite dans l'esprit le besoin de comprendre et de se soumettre, de se résigner et d'agir.'[50] But contemplation and scrutiny do not lead to insight; the sea remains as mysterious and mist-shrouded as before. We experience only 'la satisfaction indi-viduelle de la contemplation, qui donne essor à des élans de senti-ment et de poésie; et l'on confond deux domaines, quand on reporte en la science ce que la contemplation poursuit en ses loin-tains voyages'.[51]

As he thus firmly bars all entry to the unknowable, Littré's attitude is not a superficial scepticism or the product of cynicism but a cool and half-regretful recognition of human limitations. The triumphs of the scientific method may inspire a legitimate pride, but pride must always be tempered by the vision of the minuteness of man's knowledge compared with the immensity of his ignorance. Introducing a collection of his own scientific articles, he characteristically concludes by saying of man in his search for knowledge:

... quelque vaste espace qu'il parcoure ..., quelque immensité qu'il traverse, d'autres immensités s'ouvrent à perte de vue; et il revient résigné à ignorer, mais assez fortifié par ce qu'il sait pour aspirer indéfiniment à savoir davantage.[52]

5. *Littré and Ethical Standards*

Whilst Littré is certainly the foremost spokesman of the posi-tivist philosophy during the Second Empire, his understanding of it owes too much to Comte, one may feel, not to involve those lapses from strict fidelity that have just been noted. A similar mingling of orthodoxy and occasional heresy is also seen in his treatment of ethics.

His ethical views are difficult to clarify, for only infrequent passages relate to them; his stature as a moral philosopher is undeniably slight, as he would have admitted. If he avoids for the most part the fallacies of Comte and Renan, that is at the cost of almost complete silence. Yet the question cannot be entirely ignored as to how far he tries to base an ethical code upon the unpromising foundation of the positivist theory of knowledge. In the conclusion of his book on Comte he points out three

[50] *A.C.*, pp. 519, 525.   [51] *Préf.*, p. xxxi.
[52] *La Science*, pp. vii–viii.

principal lacunas in positivism as Comte has established it—first, 'l'économie politique', secondly, 'la théorie cérébrale', and thirdly, '[une] théorie subjective de l'humanité', under which heading he includes *la morale, l'esthétique*, and *la psychologie*. He believes that Comte was wrong to regard political economy as a false science; he deplores his respect for Gall's cerebral theory and hopes for a better treatment of this most complicated and difficult part of biology.[53] By 'théorie subjective de l'humanité' Littré means above all a study of 'les conditions formelles sous lesquelles la connaissance s'exerce'.[54] But beyond this psychological study it must also comprise an examination of the ways in which men arrive at their ethical and aesthetic judgements. That, at least, would appear to be his view, for his *dicta* here are far from clear. On the one hand, he condemns Comte for making *la morale* the seventh science in the hierarchy of the sciences, and yet on the same page he can speak of the need for 'une science de la morale' and 'une [science] de l'esthétique et de la psychologie'.[55] In the 'Préface d'un disciple', too, he praises Berthelot for placing 'l'ordre moral' 'sous la catégorie de la science positive'. His exposition of Berthelot's approach does something, however, to clarify his own opinions. The scientific knowledge of human nature, with which he here links this 'moral science', is to be based upon 'l'observation des phénomènes du monde moral, révélés soit par la psychologie, soit par l'histoire et l'économie politique'.[56]

Littré himself attempts a study of the origins of our moral concepts, from both the psychological and the historical points of view. In an article in the *Revue de philosophie positive* he argues that morality derives psychologically from the two conflicting impulses of egoism and altruism.[57] He sums up his rather insubstantial theory by saying:

toute la morale est une dérivation de deux impulsions, l'égoïsme et l'altruisme, qui eux-mêmes proviennent: l'un de la nécessité de nutrition qui est imposée à la substance organisée pour qu'elle subsiste comme individu, et l'autre, de la nécessité d'aimer qui lui est imposée fondamentalement par l'union des sexes pour qu'elle subsiste comme espèce.[58]

[53] *A.C.*, pp. 674-5.   [54] *A.C.*, p. 676.
[55] *A.C.*, p. 677.   [56] *Préf.*, p. xxxiv.
[57] 'Des origines organiques de la morale', t. vi, 1870, pp. 5-23.
[58] *La Science*, pp. 346-7.

Unfortunately, this analysis, even if valid, could not justify us in attributing a higher value to altruism than to egoism and in so far as Littré looks forward to the growth of the former at the expense of the latter, he is expressing a purely subjective preference. In another article written at the same time, 'Origine de l'idée de justice', he attempts an historical examination of the same general question.[59] He rejects, naturally enough for a positivist, the idea of an innate moral sense. 'Plus j'examine la justice, plus il me semble que, loin d'être primordiale, innée, élémentaire, elle est secondaire, acquise et complexe.'[60] Seeking its primitive origin, he finds that 'l'idée primordiale de justice est compensation, dédommagement, indemnité'. Given this, he adds:

il n'est pas difficile de discerner l'élément psychique qui lui a donné naissance. C'est celui qui fait que nous reconnaissons intuitivement la ressemblance ou la différence de deux objets. A égale B, ou A diffère de B est le dernier terme auquel tous nos raisonnements aboutissent comme futur point de départ.[61]

Here again it is hard to believe that this rather inadequately clarified view provides a sufficient explanation. One can note to his credit that he criticizes utilitarianism for confusing 'l'utile' and 'le juste', and his discussion of free will also is interesting if slight. The question of justice involves that of free will, he agrees, but one's answer to this latter problem does not affect society's right to punish what it considers to be crimes. Whether one is a determinist or accepts what Littré somewhat tendentiously calls 'la liberté métaphysique' makes no difference. 'La société a droit sur le malfaiteur'—by virtue of two principles, 'celui de dédommagement ou de justice, celui de vengeance ou de talion'. At the same time, society has a duty to increase the inner psychological freedom of its citizens. He remarks pertinently in this connexion:

La liberté de l'homme ne consiste pas en ce qu'un motif plus faible l'emporte sur un plus fort; cela est impossible; elle consiste à augmenter le nombre des motifs dans l'esprit de l'individu, afin que leur conflit l'éclaire et le soustraie à la toute-puissance d'un motif unique.

This can best be done by education, he thinks.[62]

[59] *Revue de philosophie positive*, t. vi, 1870, pp. 161–74.
[60] *La Science*, p. 332.   [61] *La Science*, pp. 339–40.
[62] *La Science*, pp. 341–6.

Yet Littré seems to dispose too easily of the difficulties of arriving at moral judgements. He makes ethical choice so like an elementary arithmetical calculation that his portrayal of it perhaps fails to correspond to our own experience. Moreover, although he has dismissed the moral intuition theory as metaphysical, he himself ends with an intuition theory hardly distinguishable from it. 'L'idée de justice [he says he has tried to show] n'est pas autre chose que la dérivation d'un fait purement intellectuel, extrêmement simple, véritablement intuitif, celui qui constate l'identité de deux objets.' This might just pass in isolation, but he also alleges more strikingly:

Quand nous obéissons à la justice, nous obéissons à des convictions très semblables à celles que nous impose la vue d'une vérité. Des deux côtés, l'assentiment est commandé: ici il s'appelle démonstration; là il s'appelle devoir.[63]

In reality Littré makes the same ethical assumptions as Comte, Renan, and their generation of agnostic humanists, and the criteria he adopts are no more philosophically justified or proof against the attacks of a thorough-going ethical relativism than theirs. For him, as for them, the progress of humanity is the source of moral conviction. Positivism, he says, has given him a thermometer by which he can judge; it offers

cette double échelle qui montre, dans l'histoire de l'humanité, la décroissance du surnaturel et la croissance du naturel, la décroissance des notions subjectives et la croissance des notions objectives, la décroissance du droit divin et la croissance du droit populaire, la décroissance de la guerre et la croissance de l'industrie. . . . Là est la source de convictions profondes, obligatoires pour la conscience; et, en attendant que ce thermomètre, accomplissant sa marche, fixe le destin des opinions, poursuivons loyalement et vaillamment ce que, dans la sincérité de notre cœur, nous considérons comme le digne objet d'une vie mortelle.[64]

Here Littré goes beyond what is deducible from the positivist doctrine, and in particular his views illustrate the anti-clerical and socialistic motives often linked with it in the later nineteenth century.

[63] *La Science*, pp. 346, 341.
[64] *Préf.*, pp. xlvii–xlviii. Cf. his *Préface* to his translation of D. F. Strauss's *Life of Jesus*, 2ᵉ éd., 1853.

Such as it is, this personal ethic is Littré's not ignoble standard of value. It allows him to assert, for example, that the growth of scientific knowledge proves that there has been 'un mouvement vraiment ascensionnel dans la civilisation et une évolution'.[65] Again, it leads him to attribute to society a further duty, 'essentiel aussi', beyond the duty to increase by education the inner liberty of its members. Deserting philosophy for the field of political action, he declares this duty to be 'celui de diminuer la force et le nombre des mauvais motifs en réglant mieux la répartition de l'avoir commun, en établissant la plus stricte justice entre les classes, en donnant la prérogative au travail, et en la retirant au parasitisme'.[66] The same standard permits him to affirm also: 'Plus l'homme vit au dehors de son égoïsme, plus il se sent amélioré et heureux.' And it likewise dictates his vision of man's progress through the centuries and his picture of

cet idéal réel qu'il faut connaître (science et éducation), aimer (religion), embellir (beaux-arts), enrichir (industrie), et qui de la sorte tient toute notre existence, individuelle, domestique et sociale sous sa direction suprême.[67]

Although Littré attributes his perception of this ideal to his contact with the positive philosophy, he is following here his own aspirations rather than the facts of experience. Caro, in his study of Littré, remarks that the most dramatic and serious question posed by nineteenth-century thought is whether science can provide men with ideals, and he is clearly justified when he goes on to say that Littré has failed to show that it can.[68] But at least it is not certain, especially in view of the vagueness with which his ideas are expressed, that he believed that science or the scientific method had given him his moral creed. At times he seems rather to suggest that our ethical beliefs must—for the time being at least—be personal and that we can only follow the ideals which, 'dans la sincérité de notre cœur, nous considérons comme le digne objet d'une vie mortelle'.[69] We cannot be sure that he would have insisted, as Comte did, that his ethical creed rested upon a scienti-

[65] *A.C.*, p. 671.
[66] *La Science*, p. 346.
[67] E. Littré, *Conservation, révolution et positivisme*, 2ᵉ éd., Bureau de la philosophie positive, 1879, p. 395.
[68] Caro, loc. cit., 1ᵉʳ mai 1882, pp. 35, 37 ff.
[69] *Préf.*, p. xlviii.

fic basis or that it embodied more than his personal moral recommendations. And we cannot therefore conclude that in advancing it he is deserting the positivist position.

Our general conclusion must be similar. To the last—or at least until his death-bed conversion to Catholicism, if such it was[70]—he remains one of the few broadly faithful positivists of his age. Though he does at times abandon the rigorous orthodoxy to which he aspired, so that one may wonder whether even he is divided between his allegiance to Comte and his allegiance to the positivist method, he is nevertheless the most persuasive defender of that orthodoxy during these years.

[70] Cf. P. H. Loyson, 'La Vérité sur la mort de Littré', *La Grande Revue*, t. 62, 1910, pp. 469–83, and 'Mémoires inédits de mon père sur la mort de Littré', *La Grande Revue*, t. 101, 1920, pp. 353–62. Cf. also the account of his death (although Littré is not named) given in F. von Hügel, *Essays and Addresses on the Philosophy of Religion*, London, 1931–3, 2 vols., i. 3–4.

V

LES VRAIS AMIS DU POSITIVISME (2)

CLAUDE BERNARD'S *INTRODUCTION À L'ÉTUDE DE LA MÉDECINE EXPÉRIMENTALE*

1. *Bernard's Positivism*

Positivism claims that the scientific methods alone can give us knowledge. But what are their aims and conditions and what is their nature? Comte and Littré both attempt to answer these questions, and so also do Renan and Taine. Yet the most famous and comprehensive study of scientific methodology during the Second Empire comes from Claude Bernard in his now classic *Introduction à l'étude de la médecine expérimentale*, published in 1865. This work demands consideration here, however briefly, because, as will be submitted, it expresses even more closely than the works of Littré the standpoint of true philosophical positivism.

Claude Bernard (1813–78) was a scientist rather than a philosopher, preoccupied throughout his career by the experimental study of medicine: the *Introduction* itself is the fruit of more than twenty-five years spent in laboratory research. Yet behind the scientific work that won the respect of Pasteur and many others there lies, unavoidably, a theory of knowledge, and in the last thirty years there has been a marked revival of interest in Bernard's philosophy. Lamy, Sertillanges, Cotard, and Faure, for example, have all written books treating Bernard as a thinker in his own right.[1] In the same period have been published several philosophical *inédits* from his pen, most notably *Philosophie*, *Pensées*, and Delhoume's edition of the *Principes de la médecine expérimentale*, the first draft of the uncompleted major work for

---

[1] P. Lamy, *Claude Bernard et le matérialisme*, 1939; A. D. Sertillanges, *La Philosophie de Claude Bernard*, 1944; H. Cotard, *La Pensée de Claude Bernard*, Grenoble, 1945; J. L. Faure, *Claude Bernard*, 1926. Cf. also E. Dhuront, *Claude Bernard, sa vie, son œuvre*, 1937, and P. Mauriac, *Claude Bernard*, 1941, the latter unfavourable to Bernard as a philosopher.

which the *Introduction* itself was to serve as *discours préliminaire*. Nor is this degree of attention historically disproportionate: he was one of the most influential thinkers in the intellectual circles of his age, chiefly by reason of the *Introduction*, though also through his scientific books and articles and his lectures at the Sorbonne. He, even more than fellow scientists like Marcelin Berthelot or Pasteur, popularized the notion of experimental science, and, as Bergson and others have remarked, the *Introduction* was the *Discours de la méthode* of the nineteenth century.[2] For his contemporaries he was an incarnation of 'the man of science', and his work on diabetics, the role of the nervous system in digestion and secretion, and other biochemical problems richly illustrated the fruitfulness of its methods. Even in this way he encouraged the spread of the positivist philosophy, whether he wished it or not, for his admirers were almost inevitably led to feel that science and knowledge were synonymous; Zola's *Le Roman expérimental* is only the most notorious illustration of the scientist's profound *philosophical* impact.

Bernard's aim is practical and not philosophical, however. 'Conserver la santé et guérir les malades'—these are the opening words of the *Introduction* and they indicate its overriding concern: to make medical knowledge more effective and reliable by making it more scientific.[3] He wants first and foremost to turn medicine into an experimental science, and this prompts his painstaking exposition of the experimental method. And to this end he wishes to exclude all extraneous considerations and to preserve unity in the laboratory by avoiding the dissensions of philosophy. '. . . Le meilleur système philosophique consiste à ne pas en avoir', he remarks; we must sharply distinguish the theories of an experimental scientist—which are hypotheses verified by experiment—and doctrines held, whether by theologians, metaphysicians, or even scientists themselves, without a 'critical and experimental verification'. There are no philosophical strings to the scientific method. Experimental medicine, like the other natural sciences, has no need to adopt any metaphysical creed:

[2] H. Bergson, 'La Philosophie de Claude Bernard', *La Pensée et le mouvant*, 1934, p. 257.
[3] C. Bernard, *Introduction à l'étude de la médecine expérimentale*, Baillière, 1865 [*Introd.*], p. 5.

elle ne sera ni vitaliste, ni animiste, ni organiciste, ni solidiste, ni humorale, elle sera simplement la science qui cherche à remonter aux causes prochaines des phénomènes de la vie à l'état sain et à l'état morbide.[4]

Bernard is thus certainly not trying to convert his readers to the positivist philosophy as such. Indeed, he explicitly condemns it: 'le positivisme qui, au nom de la science, repousse les systèmes philosophiques, a comme eux le tort d'être un système'.[5] Yet his assertion of neutrality is deceptive: his arguments reveal over and over again his adherence to the positivist theory of knowledge.

His conception of philosophy is particularly instructive. He thinks it 'une excellente gymnastique de l'esprit' even though it contains 'des tendances systématiques et scolastiques'. The philosophical spirit of inquiry can serve as a stimulus to the scientist; philosophers communicate to scientific thought 'un mouvement qui la vivifie et l'ennoblit', for they keep alive 'l'aspiration éternelle de la raison humaine vers la connaissance de l'inconnu'.[6] But this is double-edged praise indeed, for it consecrates his view that philosophy deals with the unknown, not with the known. Science may neglect what is still covered in mystery; philosophy can remedy this 'en agitant sans cesse la masse inépuisable des questions non résolues'. The 'union' of science and philosophy is useful to both: 'elle élève l'une et contient l'autre'.[7] Philosophy has no higher value, however. It may point science 'vers la cause ou vers la source des choses'; but earlier he has emphasized that we can never have any knowledge of first or final causes.[8]

It is true that we can attain 'subjective truths', as opposed to the 'objective truths' revealed by the experimental method. These truths, he explains, recalling Descartes, 'sont celles qui découlent de principes dont l'esprit a conscience et qui apportent en lui le sentiment d'une évidence absolue et nécessaire'.[9] This notion might seem at first sight to open the way for religious and metaphysical knowledge.[10] But Bernard at once comments that mathematical truths are the prototype of what he has in mind. In this field we are rewarded by truths which are 'absolute'—'c'est-à-dire

---

[4] *Introd.*, pp. 384–7.   [5] *Introd.*, p. 387.
[6] *Introd.*, pp. 89, 387.   [7] *Introd.*, pp. 390, 392.
[8] *Introd.*, p. 88; cf. p. 51.
[9] *Introd.*, p. 51.
[10] Sertillanges does interpret it in this way (op. cit., p. 30).

indépendantes de la réalité', he quietly but quite conclusively adds. The mathematician begins with a certainty—'*Ce point de départ étant donné*'—and therefore ends with a deduction that is equally certain—'tel cas particulier en résulte nécessairement'. The scientist, in contrast, is confined to the conditional and relative and can only say: '*Si ce point de départ était juste, tel cas particulier en résulterait comme conséquence.*'[11]

Theologians and metaphysicians also claim 'absolute knowledge', Bernard believes, and it follows from his treatment of mathematics that they would be justified *if* they allowed that, like mathematical truths, their conclusions were 'indépendantes de la réalité'. As it is, they pretend to describe reality, and he therefore condemns them and asserts the 'sterility' of their discussions. Their theories are the 'ideal creations' of man's mind: it is foolish to believe that they tell us anything about the actual world.[12] Where the scientist is marked by modesty, never daring to claim that he holds 'absolute truth', aware at every moment of 'son ignorance relative et absolue', the theologian and metaphysician are distinguished by excessive pride. They ignore the limits of human knowledge, and contrasting 'le raisonnement expérimental' and '[le] raisonnement scolastique' he tartly comments:

La scolastique veut toujours un point de départ fixe et indubitable, et ne pouvant le trouver ni dans les choses extérieures, ni dans la raison [as the mathematician does], elle l'emprunte à une source irrationnelle quelconque: telle une révélation, une tradition ou une autorité conventionnelle ou arbitraire.[13]

These words leave little doubt as to his real position. He is not, whatever he claims, confining himself to the scientific method whilst leaving strictly open the question as to whether there are other methods of knowledge. He is affirming, both implicitly and explicitly, that the scientific method is our only means of knowing reality. One must not be misled by the disarming protestations of philosophical impartiality with which he concludes his book. In reality he is Mr. Hyde the positivist as well as the scientist Dr. Jekyll.

[11] *Introd.*, pp. 52, 82.
[12] *Introd.*, p. 48. Cf. C. Bernard, *Philosophie, manuscrit inédit*, edited by Chevalier, Boivin, 1938, pp. 36–37: 'Un homme qui trouve le fait le plus simple fait plus pour la recherche de la vérité que le plus grand philosophe du monde.'
[13] *Introd.*, pp. 49, 69, 86–87.

It is therefore not surprising that his account of the experimental method should reiterate the principles of the positivist
theory of knowledge. His primary emphasis is on observation and
experiment. In terms anticipatory of the 'verification principle'
he declares that the essential condition of a scientific hypothesis
is to be experimentally verifiable:

En effet, si l'on faisait une hypothèse que l'expérience ne pût pas
vérifier, on sortirait par cela même de la méthode expérimentale pour
tomber dans les défauts des scolastiques et des systématiques.[14]

Secondly, he rejects all alleged *a priori* knowledge. He points out
that the preliminary 'scientific idea', 'fondée sur une intuition ou
un sentiment vague des choses', begins as an *a priori* postulation.
But this is not to claim *a priori* knowledge; only when the 'idea'
has been justified experimentally can it be said to be known. The
aim of the scientific method is precisely to transform such *a priori*
conjectures into 'une interprétation *a posteriori* établie sur l'étude
expérimentale des phénomènes'.[15] Thirdly, the method seeks the
laws of phenomena. Bernard emphasizes as strongly as Comte
that observation alone is sterile. 'L'accumulation indéfinie d'observations ne conduirait à rien', and one of his complaints about
the medicine of his day is that it is still lingering 'dans les ténèbres
de l'empirisme'. Observation only becomes fruitful when it seeks
to formulate and to verify scientific hypotheses, and he asserts, in
words that have a wider application than to scientists alone: 'Un
fait n'est rien par lui-même, il ne vaut que par l'idée qui s'y
rattache ou par la preuve qu'il fournit.' True science does not
merely list phenomena; it seeks to know 'leurs rapports mutuels
et complexes de causalité'. And thus he says in concluding the
first part of the work: 'Toute la philosophie naturelle se résume en
cela: *Connaître la loi des phénomènes.*'[16] Only thus can man
become master of the natural world.

Such is the method whose workings Bernard goes on to illustrate in the later parts of the *Introduction*. One need not follow
here his persuasive elaboration of his subject,[17] but two of his

[14] *Introd.*, p. 59.   [15] *Introd.*, p. 48.
[16] *Introd.*, pp. 46, 76, 93, 55, 100.
[17] See, for example, his discussion of the importance of intuition in the formation of the 'experimental idea' (pp. 57 ff.) and of the place of deduction and
induction in the scientific methods (pp. 78 ff.).

more important claims call for comment. First, as has already become evident, he insists that the knowledge which the method establishes will always be relative and provisional. Unlike a mathematical truth, a scientific truth 'n'est jamais que relative au nombre d'expériences et d'observations qui ont été faites'. Although no fact may so far have been observed which contradicts a particular scientific conclusion, this does not exclude the possibility that such a fact may be discovered in the future. Scientific theories are thus inevitably 'des vérités partielles et provisoires'; they represent only 'l'état actuel de nos connaissances'.[18] Consequently, Bernard establishes doubt as a basis of the method, formulating it by saying: 'La conclusion de notre raisonnement doit toujours rester dubitative quand le point de départ ou le principe n'est pas une vérité absolue.' In the natural sciences, he adds, 'la règle unique et fondamentale de l'investigation scientifique se réduit au doute'.[19]

It is this insistence upon the provisional nature of scientific knowledge that was welcomed by Bergson in particular.

Bien avant que les philosophes eussent insisté sur ce qu'il peut y avoir de conventionnel et de symbolique dans la science humaine, [Bernard] a aperçu, il a mesuré l'écart entre la logique de l'homme et celle de la nature.[20]

This way of stating Bernard's view is to turn what was a confession of ignorance into an affirmation, but in so far as he was a forerunner of the pragmatists it is noteworthy that his position is still that of positivism. Bernard's reticence compares sharply with the more audacious claims which Renan and Taine made for science, but it is Bernard and not Renan or Taine who is the consistent positivist. And it is because he is faithful to it that one of his recent admirers can write, contrasting his ideas with the absurdities of Le Roman expérimental:

La science, au vrai sens du mot, n'avait rien promis que ce qu'elle pouvait donner, et qu'elle donna; l'œuvre de Claude Bernard, entre autres, est là pour en témoigner.[21]

18 Introd., pp. 53, 63; cf. pp. 56, 81.
19 Introd., p. 86.
20 Bergson, op. cit., p. 264.
21 P. Martino, 'Le Second Empire', in Littérature française, edited by Bédier and Hazard, 1948–9, 2 vols., ii. 304.

2. Bernard's Notion of 'Determinism'

Doubt is a basis of the scientist's method, but one thing he cannot doubt if he is to be a scientist is the principle of 'determinism'. Where the sceptic doubts even this, the true scientist doubts only his own interpretations, for 'le déterminisme des phénomènes', as Bernard insists time and again, is 'le principe absolu de la science'.[22] His development of this idea is perhaps his most original contribution to the discussion of scientific method.

What is meant by 'le déterminisme'? Bernard firmly separates its scientific usage—which he says he first established—from its philosophical sense. 'Determinism' must not be confused with 'fatalism', a doctrine exactly opposite to his own, he maintains.[23] 'Le déterminisme' in his sense means '*la cause prochaine ou déterminante* des phénomènes'—and elsewhere he prefers the term 'condition' to 'cause', for, he says, the 'determinism' of a phenomenon is the sum of the conditions which must be set up in order infallibly to reproduce it. He also differentiates between the 'determinism' of a phenomenon and its 'essence' (a notion he never develops) and urges that we can only know and act upon the former and never upon the latter.[24] Bernard's principle of determinism thus amounts to no more than a belief in the regularity of the phenomenal world the scientist is concerned with, a belief that, given exactly the same 'conditions', the same phenomenon will always be observed. It is a working assumption that is necessary for science if it is to formulate laws and make predictions; it is 'useful' in the pragmatist sense. But it is only 'un axiome expérimental' and not a metaphysical dogma; it is 'absolute' only in the mathematical sense noted earlier—'this axiom granted, such and such consequences follow'.[25] It is true that all our scientific observations to date have confirmed this assumption, but Bernard's normal position is not that 'undetermined' phenomena do not and cannot present themselves; it is that, if they did, they would fall outside the scope of the scientific method. Speaking in his

---

[22] *Introd.*, p. 69; cf. pp. 94, 383.

[23] C. Bernard, *Pensées, Notes détachées*, Baillière, 1937, p. 61, and *Introd.*, p. 383. Cf. also 'Du progrès dans les sciences physiologiques', *R.D.M.*, 1er août 1865, p. 647: 'Le mot *déterminisme* a une signification tout à fait différente de celle du mot *fatalisme*. . . . Le fatalisme est . . . anti-scientifique à l'égal de l'indéterminisme.'

[24] *Introd.*, pp. 383, 116.   [25] *Introd.*, pp. 79, 115.

Discours de réception à l'Académie Française (1869) about the
idea of contingency and the problem of free will he remarks:

> Nous ne voulons pas nier l'importance de ces grands problèmes qui
> tourmentent l'esprit humain; mais nous voulons les séparer de la
> physiologie, les distinguer, pour que leur étude relève de méthodes
> absolument différentes.[26]

Bergson reminds us that even Bernard's master, Magendie, believed in the operation of a capricious indeterminacy in the realm
of human physiology,[27] and the insistence upon the principle of
determinism has to be understood against that background. That
apart, however, he wishes to avoid contentious questions and
to remain philosophically impartial in the practical interests of
experimental medicine.

He has thus no intention of denying the reality of human free
will or of abetting the doctrine of fatalism, and one can note that
his definition of determinism is acceptable to libertarians like
Paul Janet, Chauffard, and Sertillanges.[28] If certain ambiguities
remain, they do not really jeopardize his position. It is true that
on occasion he seems to assert that scientific laws are *known* to be
more than convenient summaries of the observed facts. 'Le rapport d'un phénomène à une cause déterminée est nécessaire et
indépendant de l'expérience', he argues. Again, he speaks of 'laws'
and 'forces' as 'governing' or 'directing' phenomena even though
we do not observe the laws and forces themselves.[29] This is not
conclusive evidence of a jump into metaphysics perhaps, but
nevertheless he does not always treat determinism as just a working assumption. He sometimes suggests that we have *a priori*
knowledge of it, referring, for example, to 'le *déterminisme absolu*
des phénomènes dont nous avons conscience *a priori*'. At first
sight it seems merely a matter of definition to say that if an undetermined fact were observed, it would be an unscientific fact,
but behind the principle that 'la science repousse l'*indéterminé*'
there sometimes lurks a doctrine about the 'essence' of the natural

---

[26] Cf. Sertillanges, op. cit., p. 147.

[27] Bergson, op. cit., p. 261.

[28] P. Janet, 'La Méthode expérimentale et la physiologie à propos des travaux
récents de M. Claude Bernard', *R.D.M.*, 15 avril 1866, pp. 908–36; and E.
Chauffard, 'Claude Bernard — Sa Vie et ses œuvres', *R.D.M.*, 15 nov. 1878, pp.
272–310. Janet remains wistfully puzzled, nevertheless, as to the possibility of
reconciling the notion of human free will with Bernard's 'determinism' (loc. cit.,
p. 933).   [29] *Introd.*, pp. 94, 84.

world. 'L'expérimentateur ne crée rien [he remarks]; il ne fait qu'obéir aux lois de la nature.' Or again he alleges:

Dans les corps vivants comme dans les corps bruts les lois sont immuables, et les phénomènes que ces lois régissent sont liés à leurs conditions d'existence par un déterminisme nécessaire et absolu.[30]

This may only be a restatement of the 'experimental axiom', but one would like to be reassured that he is not forgetting his own dictum that 'absolute truths' are 'independent of reality'.

Yet even this would in no way commit him to fatalism. It is still open to him to agree that human free will may operate to change 'physiological conditions'; he is only maintaining that *if* in different instances those conditions are identical, the concurrent phenomena will be identical. And thus, when he writes in the *Introduction*: 'L'organisme créé est une machine qui fonctionne nécessairement en vertu des propriétés physico-chimiques de ses éléments constituants', this does not exclude human freedom. This may still operate in the 'creation', the continuous formation, of an organism—of the physico-chemical state of the brain, for example.[31] Bernard is placing outside the scope of science all questions concerning '*causes* of conditions'—which we cannot observe—and limiting it to the study of the 'conditions'. He himself represents the 'causes' of the phenomena of living organisms by such terms as 'l'idée directrice' or 'la force vitale', but these are merely speculative postulations, and he condemns both vitalism and materialism, for they go beyond this tentative suggestion by asserting that 'the vital force' does—or does not—exist. He uses these terms to *indicate* causes; the vitalists and materialists pretend to *describe* them. The distinction he has in mind is perhaps most clearly expressed in the *Principes de médecine expérimentale*:

[30] *Introd.*, pp. 95–96, 148, 118. The 'experimental axiom' is defined as follows: '*chez les êtres vivants aussi bien que dans les corps bruts les conditions d'existence de tout phénomène sont déterminées d'une manière absolue*' (p. 116).

[31] *Introd.*, p. 147. I am indebted here to Sertillanges's argument (op. cit., pp. 176–200). P. Mauriac, in contrast, sees him as 'un piètre philosophe' because of 'la contradiction qui est au centre même de sa doctrine'; 'obligé d'admettre la force vitale, Claude Bernard ne veut connaître que le déterminisme, qui en est la négation' ('La Figure tourmentée de C. Bernard', *Mercure de France*, 15 oct. 1938, pp. 282–3). Mauriac, in my view, fails to distinguish between Bernard's suggestions about the unobserved realm of 'causes' and his verifiable assertions about the observed realm of 'conditions'.

On peut dire certainement qu'il y a dans les êtres vivants la force vitale qui donne à l'être son évolution, sa forme. Cette forme est indépendante de la matière [here he himself makes a statement about the unknowable]; c'est le *pouvoir législatif* qui est au-dessus de la matière et qui la dispose; mais le *pouvoir exécutif* de cet arrangement est tout à fait matériel et physico-chimique. De même un peintre réalise son idée par les propriétés physico-chimiques des couleurs. . . .

And in a note on the idea of determinism he adds: 'J'ai employé ce mot pour dire tout simplement que tout phénomène de la nature avait ses *conditions déterminantes*', and asks whether he ought to have used a barbarism like 'conditionnalisme' in place of 'déterminisme'.[32]

3. *Bernard's Attitude to Scientism and Metaphysics*

Opposed to any confusion between the working determinism of the scientist and a fatalist philosophy, Bernard is no less on his guard against any attempt to pass from positivism to scientism: here again he is a true disciple of the positivist philosophy. He rejects the claim of scientism that science alone can offer a new ethic of life and reorder civilization. He roundly condemns Comte's notion of the positive society, alleging, somewhat unfairly, that it would be 'le règne du rationalisme pur, le règne de la tête et la mort du cœur'; he even adds: 'Des hommes ainsi faits par la science sont des monstres moraux.' Human nature cannot be changed by science but only 'by charity, by Christianity', and whilst science may influence the development of a civilization, it cannot modify its 'principles', nor can it give moral guidance.[33] Understandably in view of the scientism of acknowledged 'positivists' of his day, like Comte, Renan, and Taine, though unfairly ignoring the religious and metaphysical elements in their thought, he even condemns the positivist philosophy:

Les positivistes sont dans l'erreur la plus profonde possible en pensant que l'humanité marche avec la science. Ils croient effacer les religions, c'est-à-dire le sentiment qui y correspond. Jamais cela

[32] C. Bernard, *Principes de médecine expérimentale*, Presses Universitaires de France, 1947, pp. 243, 265.
[33] *Philosophie*, pp. 27, 39.

n'arrivera. . . . Jamais la métaphysique non plus ne disparaîtra: c'est encore une erreur de la philosophie positiviste.[34]

As this assertion confirms, he believes it is a mistake to proscribe metaphysical questionings and religious aspiration. 'L'homme [he says] aura toujours besoin de croire, de raisonner, de prouver et conclure.'[35] He attacks Comte's view that the three 'states' are mutually exclusive and tries to preserve a place for metaphysical and religious belief alongside the acquisition of scientific knowledge. Both are an essential part of man's nature; we need to believe just as we need to eat, and thus he can conclude: 'Il ne faut donc pas chercher à éteindre la métaphysique ou le sentiment religieux de l'homme, mais l'éclairer et le faire monter plus haut.'[36] Like Pasteur, he submits, though he himself lacked faith, that religious belief and scientific honesty are compatible, and he is said to have declared on his death-bed: 'Ce n'a jamais été mon intention de porter à la religion la moindre atteinte.'[37]

Does this mean that he abandons positivism? Some critics have thought so and find 'un spiritualisme nouveau' in his work; one even believes that on certain essential points his thought is completely in accord with orthodox Catholic philosophy.[38] This is to overlook, however, his insistence that religious and metaphysical knowledge is impossible, that we cannot advance beyond belief in these realms. He is careful always to distinguish the three processes of belief, reasoning, and experimental proof.[39] He remains to the end a metaphysical agnostic. 'Si notre sentiment pose toujours la question du *pourquoi* [he argues in the *Introduction*], notre raison nous montre que la question du *comment* est seule à notre portée. . . .'[40] And at the conclusion of his final *Leçons sur*

---

[34] *Pensées*, p. 64.

[35] *Introd.*, p. 47. He adds that the scientist utilizes all three modes of thought (p. 50).   [36] *Philosophie*, pp. 28, 38, and *Pensées*, p. 64.

[37] Cited by Sertillanges, op. cit., p. 35. His death-bed statements are a matter of dispute, however.

[38] Ibid., pp. 8, 10. Cf. F. Ravaisson, *Rapport sur la philosophie en France au dix-neuvième siècle*, 1904, pp. 134–6; and E. Caro, 'La Métaphysique et les sciences positives — I: L'École expérimentale', *R.D.M.*, 15 nov. 1866, pp. 430–41. Faure, on the other hand, regards him as a materialist. Far better than either view is Cotard's conclusion: 'Claude Bernard, s'il est parfois métaphysicien par le langage, ne l'est jamais dans le sentiment et l'étude des réalités' (op. cit., p. 61).

[39] Cf. *Introd.*, pp. 47–50.

[40] *Introd.*, p. 142. It is true that on occasions he seems to desert the view that

les phénomènes de la vie he remarks that we are forced by the limits of human knowledge to 'mortify' our minds, as religious ascetics mortify their bodies by material privations, 'mortifier [l'esprit] par la privation de certaines questions et par l'aveu de notre impuissance'. Even though we may think—or rather feel, Bernard says—that there is something lying beyond our 'scientific prudence', we can have no knowledge of it.

Si après cela [after our scientific explorations] nous laissons notre esprit se bercer au vent de l'inconnu et dans les sublimités de l'ignorance, nous aurons au moins fait la part de ce qui est la science et de ce qui ne l'est pas.[41]

He does not deny the 'importance of those great problems which torment the human mind', but in our musings upon them, in his view, we can do no more than explore 'les sublimités de l'ignorance'.

This moderation is typical of Bernard, and his significance in the history of positivist thought during these years springs from it. He is content to stand by the pure positivist position, to claim knowledge only where he has verification. He withstands the temptation to offer his readers a new ethic, metaphysics or religion in the name of science, just as he also avoids the metaphysical doctrine of fatalism. And whilst he readily admits that religious and metaphysical speculation is rooted in man's very nature, as a consistent positivist he suggests no method for its pursuit: each man must choose his own beliefs.

Only five years later, as the Second Empire ends, almost precisely the same position will be adopted by Théodule Ribot (1839–1916). Founder of the *Revue philosophique* and author of works on *L'Hérédité* (1873), *Les Maladies de la mémoire* (1881), *Les Maladies de la volonté* (1883), and other subjects, including Schopenhauer's philosophy, Ribot leads the way in establishing a new

science can never know first causes and to postulate the theoretical possibility of working back from knowledge of efficient causes to knowledge of a first cause —for example, in *Philosophie*, p. 15. But he adds here, rather mysteriously: 'Mais alors ce sera la fin du monde.' Cf. *Introd.*, p. 223: 'Certainement nous n'arriverons jamais au déterminisme absolu de toutes choses; l'homme ne pourrait plus exister.' Cf. also the testimony of his friend Paul Bert: 'Il n'est ni matérialiste... ni spiritualiste' (*L'Œuvre de Claude Bernard*, Introduction de Duval, Notices par E. Renan, P. Bert et A. Moreau, Baillière, 1881, p. 84).

[41] Cited by Chauffard, loc. cit., p. 301.

approach to psychology in France—the experimental approach, exactly parallel to Bernard's new method for medical science. He invokes as his predecessors British psychologists like Mill, Spencer, Bain, and Lewes, and his first book, *La Psychologie anglaise contemporaine* (1870), is as much a manifesto as Bernard's *Introduction*, seeking to wean psychology from its former *a priori* and introspective ways. In his Introduction he discusses the relation of science and philosophy—and arrives at the same conclusions as Bernard.

Originally, he points out, philosophy included within its scope every aspect of life, but gradually the sciences have won their independence, and now psychology in its turn must break free and adopt exclusively the scientific methods, banishing all consideration of first and final causes and of the nature of the 'soul'. Meanwhile, the range of philosophy has become ever more restricted, and ultimately, Ribot predicts, it will be confined to 'les spéculations générales de l'esprit humain sur les principes premiers et les raisons dernières de toutes choses'.

Elle sera la métaphysique, rien de plus. Ce qui occupera alors les philosophes et ce qui constituera leur domaine propre, ce sera cet inconnu sur lequel chaque science s'établit et qu'elle abandonne à leurs disputes.[42]

Ribot is far from despising these metaphysical studies: they can point the sciences towards new problems and they can discuss the status of the laws and ever-wider generalizations put forward by the sciences. Hence he goes on to criticize the 'positivists' of his day for trying to proscribe metaphysics altogether. They are right to say it cannot be a science, for it cannot verify or prove the truth of its assertions. They are right to purge the experimental sciences of all remaining metaphysical elements—as Ribot himself is attempting to do for psychology.

Mais condamner toutes les recherches sur les raisons dernières comme une illusion dangereuse et vaine, considérer comme perdu le temps qu'on y consacre, vouloir en guérir l'esprit humain comme d'une infirmité chronique, c'est en réalité l'amoindrir. . . . Chercher sans espoir n'est ni insensé, ni vulgaire; on peut entrevoir, sinon trouver.[43]

[42] T. Ribot, *La Psychologie anglaise contemporaine*, 3ᵉ éd., Alcan, 1896, p. 16.
[43] Ibid., p. 21.

To seek is as 'noble' as to find, and unproven 'ideas' may be as valuable to man as verified 'facts'. Philosophy should thus remain as 'une tentative éternelle sur l'inconnu', and we may well be glad that it can never resolve all the questions posed by human ignorance. Metaphysicians are (in Vacherot's phrase) 'poets who have missed their vocation', 'des poètes qui ont pour but de reconstituer la synthèse du monde', but for whose 'grands poèmes' we can be grateful. Of philosophy he says in conclusion:

Ne dût-elle rendre à l'intelligence d'autre service que de la tenir toujours en éveil, que de l'élever au-dessus d'un dogmatisme étroit, en lui montrant ce mystérieux *au delà* qui dans toute science l'entoure et la presse, elle l'aurait servie assez.[44]

Ribot, like Bernard, thus stands by the strict positivist position, eschewing both scientism and the over-assertive negations of the atheist. His mature career falls outside our scope, but the ideas he expresses in 1870 serve to indicate that Bernard's philosophy, a salutary and much-needed corrective for Second Empire thought, was not to lack support in the century's final decades.

[44] Ibid., pp. 20, 22.

VI

FROM POSITIVISM TO SCIENTISM (2)

ERNEST RENAN

1. *Introduction*

'No one knew better than Renan how to gild positivism with religiosity and throw around the operations of the scientific intellect a vague aroma of the infinite.' Thus judges an American critic, whilst a French contemporary remarked: 'Il donne aux hommes de sa génération ce qu'ils désirent, des bonbons qui sentent l'infini.'[1] But this common view projects the dilettantism of Renan's final years on to his whole career and underestimates both his intense concern with religion and the gravity of his divided intellectual allegiance throughout most of his life.

Born in 1823 at Tréguier in Brittany, of a race whose characteristic, he says, is its religious idealism,[2] he was brought up to revere the traditional pieties of the Church, his native bent for the mystical was confirmed by his environment and his teachers, and in 1838 he entered the seminary of Saint-Nicolas-du-Chardonnet, directed by Dupanloup, to train for holy orders. Ironically, the next seven years, here and at Issy and Saint-Sulpice, develop above all his intellectual, critical powers; he was taught, he tells us, 'l'amour de la vérité, le respect de la raison, le sérieux de la vie',[3] and he finally concluded that these were incompatible with Christian belief. On 10 October 1845 he left Saint-Sulpice and, after a period of academic study and private teaching during which he was befriended by Berthelot, he turned to the philological researches that were to make him famous. Yet he brought from Saint-Sulpice a longing for religious faith as well as a critical, scientific attitude, a longing that was to be one pole of his thought.

---

[1] I. Babbitt, *The Masters of Modern French Criticism*, Boston and New York, 1912, p. 271; and X. Doudan, *Mélanges et lettres*, 1876–77, 4 vols., iv. 143.
[2] E. Renan, *Souvenirs d'enfance et de jeunesse*, éd. Collection nouvelle, Calmann-Lévy, s.d. [*Souv.*], pp. 65, 68.
[3] *Souv.*, p. 118.

As he acknowledges in the closing paragraph of *L'Avenir de la
science,* that youthful testament of faith written in 1848 and 1849:

j'ai été formé par l'Église, je lui dois ce que je suis, et ne l'oublierai
jamais. . . . Celui que Dieu a touché sera toujours un être à part. . . .
Ô Dieu de ma jeunesse, j'ai longtemps espéré revenir à toi enseignes
déployées et avec la fierté de la raison. . . .[4]

There is romanticism here and a certain self-pity, but there is
also sincere regret, and all his life he tries to convince himself
that although he has left the Church he has never left or betrayed
Christ. To seek truth is to follow Christ, and he even imagines
Christ speaking to him in somewhat Gidean terms: 'Abandonne-
moi pour être mon disciple.' Sometimes he talks more bitterly of
his loss of faith and accuses others of being responsible for it. It
may be his Catholic teachers. It may be the religious state of
France, which allows no Protestant compromise between Catholic
dogma and agnostic free-thought. It may even be God Himself.
'Dieu m'a trahi, monsieur', he tells his *directeur* in 1845, and he
concludes *L'Avenir de la science* with the words: 'Adieu donc,
ô Dieu de ma jeunesse! . . . quoique tu m'aies trompé, je t'aime
encore!'[5]

The same religious emphasis affects his work as a *philologue,*
excepting only his early linguistic studies—from the articles
collected in *Études d'histoire religieuse* (1857) to his two major
achievements, the *Histoire des origines du christianisme* (1863–83)
and the *Histoire du peuple d'Israël* (1887–93)—and his attitude to
Christianity is always respectful even whilst he embalms its
realities in the pages of *La Vie de Jésus.* It is only in the final
years before his death in 1892, under the corrosive effect of re-
newed scepticism and popular esteem, that he deserves the charge
of playing lightly with sacred things.

Renan is essentially *un être de dialogue,* who can best express
the fluctuations of his thought in the form of the *dialogue philosophique* or the *drame philosophique.* Certainly, too, there is in
him an unwillingness to conclude which helps to explain both
his praise of irony and the obscurities and contradictions which
have irritated many of his readers. He distrusts the *esprit de
système* and he praises the dialogue form, significantly, 'parce

---

[4] E. Renan, *L'Avenir de la science—Pensées de 1848,* 23ᵉ éd., Calmann-Lévy,
1929 [*A.S.*], p. 492.   [5] *Souv.,* pp. 274–5, 266, 278, and *A.S.,* p. 492.

qu'elle n'a rien de dogmatique et qu'elle permet de présenter successivement les diverses faces du problème, sans que l'on soit obligé de conclure'.[6] He values his state of mental alternation, claiming that most of humanity shares it, and he is fond of stressing the disparities in his heredity—the clash of the Breton and the Gascon—and his early life—the contrast between Tréguier and the sophistication of Paris. 'Je suis double', he writes, and again, with more than a little satisfaction:

j'étais prédestiné à être ce que je suis, un romantique protestant contre le romantisme, un utopiste prêchant en politique le terre-à-terre, un idéaliste se donnant inutilement beaucoup de mal pour paraître bourgeois, un tissu de contradictions ...[7]

Yet it would be mistaken to dismiss him on account of this innate and also cultivated vacillation of mind. A narrower, more concentrated thinker might have erected a more logically consistent system; he could never have awakened response and understanding in such a diversity of readers. The breadth of Renan's reading and sympathies, the ambiguities of his thinking, his astonishing eclecticism, so baffling to more logical minds—these symptoms of his *état de dialogue* help to account for the extent of his influence in the later nineteenth century. Nor do they justify the accusation of dilettantism, for they also conceal one of the clearest examples in the whole century of the conflict between an inherited religion and a triumphant science. Renan's works epitomize all the heart-searching, the regrets, the earnest determination to be intellectually honest, that mark the debate between science and religion. Unlike Matthew Arnold he cannot reconcile the two and remain within an established Church, and such is his honesty that despite his wistful glances towards Protestantism he deplores the Liberal Catholic theology of his day, 'ce fade compromis, bon pour les laïques, qui a produit de nos jours tant de malentendus'.[8] Yet unlike those who withdrew into pessimism he fervently believes that what is indispensable in

[6] E. Renan, *Dialogues et fragments philosophiques*, 12ᵉ éd., Calmann-Lévy, 1925 [*D.F.P.*], pp. v-vi. (The following abbreviations are also used to indicate quotations from the *Fragments*:

MA = 'La Métaphysique et son avenir' (janvier 1860);
LB = 'Les Sciences de la nature et les sciences historiques—Lettre à M. Berthelot' (août 1863).
The titles of other *Fragments* quoted are given in full.)
[7] *Souv.*, pp. vii, 127, 63.   [8] *Souv.*, p. 265.

religion can be retained, although outside the Christian faith, and can be integrated with the science of his age.

Hence his cult of science is linked with a desire to find a new religion in which the traditional concepts of Christianity, excepting the supernatural, will be reinterpreted and made scientifically respectable. Speaking of the impact on him of German scholarship and philosophy, he declares: 'C'était bien là ce que je cherchais, la conciliation d'un esprit hautement religieux avec l'esprit critique.' He wishes to abandon as little of Christianity as is compatible with rejecting the idea of the supernatural.[9] Faguet remarks that Renan has two faiths—one of the feelings and the soul, the other of reflexion and the reason.[10] His hope was to escape from this ambivalence and for a good part of his life he seems to have believed that he had done so. As we trace his progress from *L'Avenir de la science* through the *Études d'histoire religieuse* (1857), the *Essais de morale et de critique* (1859), 'La Métaphysique et son avenir' (1860) and the 'Lettre à Berthelot' (1863) to the *Dialogues philosophiques* (written in 1871), we shall find not only a deeply religious nature, a man given to contemplation and introspection and disposed towards the infinite and the ideal,[11] but also a new religious creed for a scientific age. He claims to offer something far more genuine and inward than 'des bonbons qui sentent l'infini', and his attempt should command greater respect than it has sometimes received. Certainly he realized the difficulty of his task:

'Ce que vous cherchez n'est pas trouvable', disent les positivistes pratiques (les seuls dangereux), les politiques railleurs, les athées. Certes, on ne connaîtra jamais la formule de l'infini vivant . . . mais on ne réussira pas davantage à persuader à l'homme qu'il soit vain de désirer connaître l'ensemble dont il fait partie et qui l'entraîne malgré lui.[12]

If he finally failed, this is hardly surprising, for he sought to fuse positivism with a religion that would have to be far more than an *élargissement* of that philosophy if it was to satisfy his aspirations

---

[9] *Souv.*, pp. 256, 302.
[10] E. Faguet, *Politiques et moralistes du dix-neuvième siècle*, 1903, 3 vols., iii. 375.
[11] Cf. Faguet's analysis of his 'priestly' characteristics (ibid., iii. 374-5). Renan himself claims to have remained the pupil of his Catholic teachers even in his moral behaviour (*Souv.*, pp. 306 ff.).
[12] *D.F.P.*, p. xiii.

—that was, in fact, often a contradiction of the presuppositions from which he started.

2. *Renan's Theory of Knowledge*
(a) His rejection of metaphysics and the supernatural

The conflict between his positivist starting-point and his religious aspirations is best seen in his conception of a 'religion of science', but first his views on the problem of knowledge must be sketched. He begins from the assertion that all knowledge must be based on observation, preferably linked with experimentation. The method of the natural sciences has become 'le *criterium* de certitude pratique des modernes'.[13] The immediate and most important consequence is that he rejects the Christian faith on the ground that the supernatural and the miraculous have never been scientifically verified and that we thus have no reason to postulate their existence. Many occurrences once regarded as miraculous can now be explained in terms of scientific laws, and we may believe that science will soon account likewise for any other similar events. Thus Renan embraces and often reiterates Malebranche's dictum: 'Dieu n'agit pas par des volontés particulières.'[14] 'Ce n'est pas d'un raisonnement, mais de tout l'ensemble des sciences modernes que sort cet immense résultat: Il n'y a pas de surnaturel.' Belief in a divine revelation disappears simultaneously, and the rejection of the supernatural and hence of the possibility of revealed knowledge is for him the central tenet of positivism, one of the few matters on which he feels certainty.[15] And it is this—and not, he affirms, metaphysical, political, or moral reasons—that leads him to disavow Christianity, although we must add to it the doubts provoked by his studies in biblical criticism.[16]

He was also brought to reject metaphysics as traditionally conceived. His views are best seen in his reply to Vacherot's *La Métaphysique et la science* (1858), entitled 'La Métaphysique et son avenir' (1860). Although Vacherot shares a certain positivism of outlook with Renan, he holds that metaphysics, though not

[13] *A.S.*, p. 442, and *D.F.P.*, p. 284, MA.

[14] *D.F.P.*, p. 3, p. 249, 'Lettre à Adolphe Guéroult', and p. 319, MA.

[15] *A.S.*, pp. 47, 412, and *D.F.P.*, p. 10; cf. *La Vie de Jésus*, 24ᵉ éd., Calmann-Lévy, 1895, p. ix.

[16] *Souv.*, p. 262. Cf. P. Lasserre, *La Jeunesse d'Ernest Renan*, 1928, 2 vols., and especially ii. 219.

yet a science, can quickly become one, just as the natural sciences have before it. Renan begins his review by noting the lack of metaphysical speculation at the present time. Hegel is dead; Schelling sterilely repeats a philosophy that ignores science; Cousin's metaphysics will deceive only those who are ignorant of the fact that it was undermined in advance by the *critique* of Kant and his followers; the Scottish school has ceased to concern itself with the problems of metaphysics and devotes itself to linguistic analysis. Only the positivist school remains, 'debout, active, pleine d'espérance, s'attribuant l'avenir', but its first principle is precisely the rejection of all metaphysical thinking.[17] The few examples of current metaphysics which Renan commends are Séguin's *Introduction à l'esthétique,* Renouvier's first two *Essais de critique générale,* and Véra's work on Hegel. But their isolation and the general ignorance about them only serve to confirm 'l'incapacité philosophique de l'heure présente' and to suggest that metaphysical philosophy has no foreseeable future. Hegel, Hamilton and Cousin 'ont posé tous trois à leur façon . . . la fatale borne après laquelle la spéculation métaphysique n'a plus qu'à se reposer'.[18] These facts are not the result of a chance development; they reflect a new situation in philosophy, a situation of disintegration in which theology and the positive sciences are dividing between themselves its former province. Furthermore, those who might have devoted themselves to philosophy are now working in the more rewarding field of the natural sciences: 'les vrais philosophes se sont faits philologues, chimistes, physiologistes'. Renan's attitude follows logically from his epistemology. If metaphysics claims to reach its conclusions by an abstract intellection working from axioms which are unverified or unverifiable by experience, then it is not a branch of knowledge at all. What element of genuine knowledge there may be in past metaphysical systems will be found to derive from the observation of facts and never from *a priori* reasoning. This was the principle which Aristotle, one of the founders of metaphysics, always respected: '[il] ne cherche à construire la science que par l'étude des faits et l'observation des détails'. To admit metaphysics 'comme une science distincte', 'c'est contredire la tendance générale des études de notre temps'.[19]

[17] *D.F.P.*, pp. 274, 260, MA.   [18] *D.F.P.*, p. 263, MA.
[19] *D.F.P.*, pp. 284–6, MA.

This does not mean that metaphysical philosophy must necessarily be abandoned. It should be regarded not as a science but as
an art—comparable to poetry or painting. Thus conceived, it will
be the sum of man's speculations, hypotheses, and 'dreams' about
the universe and human life, although these should always begin
from the facts revealed by observation and the positive sciences.
As such and provided no higher claim is made for it, it is a
legitimate object of human thought. 'Le rêve est bon et utile',
says Euthyphron in the first *Dialogue philosophique*, 'pourvu
qu'on le tienne pour ce qu'il est. Souvenez-vous du grand principe
de Hegel: "Il faut comprendre l'inintelligible comme tel."'[20] To
this extent he would agree with Vacherot that metaphysics has
a future, a future that will endure as long as reasoning human
beings.

Si l'on entend par métaphysique le droit et le pouvoir qu'a l'homme
de s'élever au-dessus des faits, d'en voir les lois, la raison, l'harmonie,
la poésie, la beauté (toutes choses essentiellement métaphysiques en
un sens); si l'on veut dire que nulle limite ne peut être tracée à l'esprit
humain, qu'il ira toujours montant l'échelle infinie de la spéculation . . .; si la science qu'on oppose à la métaphysique est ce vulgaire
empirisme satisfait de sa médiocrité, qui est la négation de toute
philosophie, oui, je l'avoue, il y a une métaphysique.[21]

Renan therefore declares that he is not denying the possibility of
metaphysics. One could perhaps wish that he had defined its
epistemological status rather more closely. His dislike of 'ce vulgaire empirisme satisfait de sa médiocrité' perhaps suggests a
certain turning away from the scientific attitude. Yet at no point
does he claim for metaphysics thus understood that it achieves
any new knowledge, and if he went no further than this, he would
not transgress the bounds of positivism.

(b) 'Science' and 'Philosophy'

Renan rejects Vacherot's claim that metaphysics can become
scientific, but he then goes on to develop his own conception of

[20] *D.F.P.*, p. 9.
[21] *D.F.P.*, pp. 282–3, MA. At one point in the 'Lettre à Berthelot' he seems to
suggest a rather different future for metaphysics: 'Mathématiques pures, logique,
métaphysique, autant de sciences de l'éternel, de l'immuable, nullement historiques, nullement expérimentales, n'ayant aucun rapport avec l'existence et
les faits. . . . Ne nions pas qu'il n'y ait des sciences de l'éternel; mais mettons-les
bien nettement hors de toute réalité' (*D.F.P.*, p. 175).

'philosophy'. His distinction between 'metaphysics' and 'philosophy' is not always clear, but broadly he thinks of the former as
pretending to be 'une science première' which deduces philosophical conclusions from *a priori* abstractions, whereas the latter
is to be 'une science universelle' which builds up its conclusions
from scientific facts. The one starts from *a priori*, the other from
a posteriori foundations. This notion of 'philosophy' is of the
greatest importance to Renan, and whilst his maturer formulation
of it is found in his review of Vacherot, it is also one of the central
ideas of *L'Avenir de la science*. Here we have an almost dithy-
rambic statement of a theory that by 1860 has become more
guarded—and more equivocal.

In the letter prefaced to *L'Avenir de la science* he tells us that
the equation of science and philosophy was the dream which inspired him as he listened to the lectures of the great orientalist
Burnouf at the Collège de France in 1848:

> En écoutant vos leçons sur la plus belle des langues et des littéra-
> tures du monde primitif, j'ai rencontré la réalisation de ce qu'au-
> paravant je n'avais fait que rêver: *la science devenant la philosophie*,
> et les plus hauts résultats sortant de la plus scrupuleuse analyse des
> détails.[22]

At times Renan speaks as if the sciences are indeed only of real
value in so far as they 'become' philosophy. 'Que reste-t-il, en effet,
si vous enlevez à la science son but philosophique?' he asks. 'De
menus détails . . . fort indifférents pour celui qui voit dans la vie
une chose sérieuse, et se préoccupe avant tout des besoins religieux
et moraux de l'homme.' In his confidence in the future of this new
'scientific' philosophy, he can affirm:

> ce n'est donc pas une exagération de dire que la science renferme
> l'avenir de l'humanité, qu'elle seule peut lui dire le mot de sa destinée
> et lui enseigner la manière d'atteindre sa fin.

Science alone can provide man with 'les vérités vitales'; the
separation of science and philosophy is no longer necessary—they
become one and the same thing. At the height of his youthful
enthusiasm, he asserts:

> Ce n'est pas sans quelque dessein que j'appelle du nom de *science*
> ce que d'ordinaire on appelle *philosophie*. . . . Oui, il viendra un jour

[22] *A.S.*, p. 4 (my italics).

où l'humanité ne croira plus, mais où elle saura; un jour où elle saura
le monde métaphysique et moral, comme elle sait déjà le monde
physique. . . .[23]

Thus we may escape from the 'shipwreck of scepticism' on moral
and metaphysical questions to which positivism might have
seemed to condemn us. We have a criterion of practical certainty
in the method of the physical sciences, and we can attain a similar
certainty, though with greater difficulty, in the field of what will
henceforth be 'the moral sciences'.[24]

What is the nature of this 'science' which will yield a new
philosophy? Renan's answer is far from clear, and in particular
he uses the term la science in differing senses. The French language itself presented an initial source of confusion between
la science as knowledge or learning, une science as a branch of
knowledge, and la science in the sense of natural science. Renan
adds other ambiguities. Thus he equates la science with '[l']exer-
cice régulier de l'esprit humain', or again he cites Aristotle as
its supreme practitioner. A little later he associates it with '[les]
délices de l'idéal', with '[la] vérité, [la] sincérité de la vie', with
'[la] sainte poésie des choses'.[25] And he is continually transposing
these different senses and persuading himself that the characteristics of la science in one sense are also those of la science in
another sense. There is a distinct element of verbal self-deception
in his work, as the usage of l'existence to be noted shortly further
illustrates; part of his system at least amounts to an exercise in
linguistic magic.

The idea of a new scientific philosophy—or philosophical
science—reappears in the Essais de morale et de critique, where
he pictures each branch of human knowledge bringing its results
'en tribut à la science universelle',[26] but it is more fully explored
in 'La Métaphysique et son avenir'. Having banished the notion
of an a priori metaphysical science, he again advances his conception of philosophy as 'une science du tout', built up out of the
knowledge given by the separate sciences. This is not to lower the
function of philosophy, he stresses, but to propose a far nobler
mission for it. It is to be 'le résultat général de toutes les sciences,
le son, la lumière, la vibration qui sort de l'éther divin que tout

[23] A.S., pp. 39, 36, 38, 91.   [24] A.S., p. 443.
[25] A.S., pp. 92, 114, 123.
[26] E. Renan, Essais de morale et de critique, 10ᵉ éd., Calmann-Lévy, 1928, p. 81.

porte en soi'. Indeed, the great ages of philosophy have always treated it in this way, as a study based on the scientific discoveries of their time and not as an *a priori* construction. 'Tous les grands philosophes ont été de grands savants'—Aristotle, Roger Bacon, Descartes, Leibniz, Kant.[27] Only in periods of philosophical decline is philosophy elevated to the rank of an independent branch of knowledge—in such thinkers as the scholastic philosophers of the late Middle Ages, Malebranche in the immediate post-Cartesian period, and Schelling and Hegel in the nineteenth century. Thus Renan can say: 'La philosophie semble ainsi aspirer à redevenir ce qu'elle était *à l'origine*, la science universelle.'[28]

What kind of status does Renan now attribute to this 'science du tout'? At times he may appear more cautious than in *L'Avenir de la science*; at other moments he is hardly less audacious. He sometimes presents it as purely conjectural, beginning from knowledge of the sciences but not itself attaining any further scientific insights. Here his idea is very close to the future he held out to metaphysics—as comparable with art and poetry. 'Chaque être vivant a eu son rêve qui l'a charmé, élevé, consolé: grandiose ou mesquin, plat ou sublime, ce rêve a été sa philosophie.' Moreover, we can never hope for an absolute knowledge or any certainty in this 'science': 'elle est toujours relative, toujours incomplète, toujours perfectible'; 'la gloire de la philosophie n'est pas de résoudre le problème, mais de le poser'.[29] This is a modest and unobjectionable proposal. Under cover of it, however, his suggestions are more far-reaching. Renan never gives a direct answer to the question as to whether this 'science' offers us knowledge which we did not previously possess. At times—under pressure, as it were—he will speak of philosophy as the individual's 'dream'; but the synonyms he coins for philosophy all imply a higher status for it than this and again (as in *L'Avenir de la science*) he lays particular emphasis upon the term 'science'. Thus it is described as 'la science universelle', as 'la science du tout', as 'le *résultat* général de toutes les sciences', as 'la vraie philosophie des *réalités*', as 'la science du monde et de l'humanité', as (in a more guarded moment) 'moins une science qu'un côté de toutes les sciences'.[30] Quietly, but very effectively, he surrounds philosophy

[27] *D.F.P.*, pp. 283, 266, 290, 291, MA.   [28] *D.F.P.*, p. 265, MA (my italics).
[29] *D.F.P.*, pp. 287, 280, 332, MA.
[30] *D.F.P.*, pp. 265–6, 304, 312, 286, MA (my italics).

with what might not unfairly be called a verbal cocoon of 'scientific' authenticity. One even sometimes feels that he was a master
of the principle of 'innocence by verbal association'. Were he
pressed, he would remind us of his subjectivism; were his use of
la science questioned, he would admit that he was using it in a
wider sense than a thinker like Comte or the adherents of 'ce
vulgaire empirisme satisfait de sa médiocrité' or than those
érudits 'qui trop souvent ne voient dans leurs travaux que l'ali-
ment d'une curiosité assez frivole',[31] and he would regret that we
had mistaken his meaning. It would be presumptuous and almost
certainly false to imply that he had any intention of deceiving. It
seems rather as if he quite sincerely deceives himself at these
moments. With two different sides of his mind, he is perfectly
able to conceive of philosophy as a man's 'dreams' and to imply
that it is a purely speculative addition to the sciences, that it poses
questions rather than resolving them; and then to make this
philosophy the straightforward equivalent of 'l'étude de la nature
et de l'humanité' and to allege: 'En résumé, philosopher, c'est
connaître l'univers.'[32] He is equally sincere when, having previously spoken of philosophy as an equivalent of poetry or art, he
goes on to link the aims of science with the aims of philosophy
and claims: 'La science n'a réellement qu'un seul objet digne
d'elle: c'est de résoudre l'énigme des choses, c'est de dire à
l'homme le mot de l'univers et de sa propre destinée'; or when
he links philosophy with 'la science du monde et de l'humanité,
la science de l'universel *devenir*, aboutissant comme culte à la
poésie et à l'art, et par-dessus tout à la morale'.[33]

In this exposition of the nature of 'philosophy', nevertheless,
Renan does not explicitly claim that it will discover any truths
not already present in the sciences from which it begins, and one
cannot therefore say that he openly forsakes the positivist standpoint here. He often implies that it will do so, but he would, if
need be, disown these implications.

(c) His conception of philologie

The individual science which he believes will be a particularly
rewarding starting-point for philosophy is his own special field
of study, *philologie*, 'la science de l'humanité'. In the past philo-

[31] *D.F.P.*, p. 295, MA.   [32] *D.F.P.*, p. 292, MA (my italics).
[33] *D.F.P.*, pp. 296, 312, MA.

sophy began from the study of Nature, but in the future it is more likely, he thinks, to begin from the study of man and his intellectual history.[34] In *L'Avenir de la science* he even identifies 'philosophy' with *philologie*; it is this science above all which 'becomes' philosophy and for which he therefore predicts so important a future. And it is in studying his description of *philologie*, as Parodi quoting Le Dantec remarks, 'que l'on peut voir son "scientisme" . . . s'élargir singulièrement, et parfois se rapprocher presque de son contraire'.[35] Renan himself claims that in its method it does not differ at all from the physical and mathematical sciences.[36] But it is hard to feel that he substantiates this view.

His conception of *philologie* and its methods is already clearly seen in *L'Avenir de la science*. This study of man, he says, will be based on the experimental and descriptive method of all the sciences.[37] Like Comte he urges science to proceed to its greatest conquest.

One can note at once that Renan nowhere makes evident in what way his new science will be experimental. Though he defines it as 'l'expérimentation universelle de la vie humaine',[38] he fails to suggest any possible lines for experiment. In fact he leaps from this idea to the idea of a descriptive study of human history without showing any awareness that they are by no means identical. At best Renan can reply that *philologie* is based on empirical evidence and is therefore compatible with the positivist theory of knowledge.

Philologie, he urges, is essentially concerned with the history of the development of man's mind. It must be an historical study, first, because 'la science d'un être qui est dans un perpétuel *devenir* ne peut être que son histoire'. Change and advance are everywhere apparent in the world; the whole of Nature is ceaselessly evolving, and Renan even equates this *éternel devenir* with the reality of the universe. It follows that all the sciences must consist of the history of their selected aspects of the world.[39] Here Renan reaffirms the great principle of Heraclitus and looks

---

[34] *D.F.P.*, p. 292, MA.

[35] D. Parodi, *Du positivisme à l'idéalisme — Philosophies d'hier*, 1930, p. 202.

[36] *D.F.P.*, p. 243, Introduction to 'Lettre à A. Guéroult', citing his brochure, *La Chaire d'hébreu au Collège de France*, 1862.

[37] *A.S.*, p. 265.   [38] Ibid.

[39] *A.S.*, p. 132, and *D.F.P.*, pp. 155–6, LB.

forward, too, to Boutroux and Bergson's emphasis on the all-importance of *la durée*—in Nature and in man, for humanity also is progressing: it is 'l'armée immense qui s'avance à la conquête du parfait'.[40]

Secondly, *philologie* must be the history of man's *mind*: 'c'est la *science des produits de l'esprit humain*'.[41] By studying the civilizations of the past and their languages and documents the *philologue* will be able to trace the whole evolution of the human spirit. And Renan adds that the farther back into the past one can penetrate, the more rewarding will be one's investigations, for in the primitive stage man's creation was spontaneous and unreflective. Under the influence of the German *Völkerpsychologie* and scholars of primitive poetry like Wolf, he comes to believe that the myths and legends achieved collectively and anonymously in humanity's youth are far richer sources of knowledge about the human spirit than the highly pondered, individualistic works of the succeeding ages of reflection and analysis.[42] Consequently, he is able to rescue the religions of the past from the ignominy to which Comte and the *philosophes* had consigned them. Religions become relevant to science—and beyond science, to philosophy—so that Renan can draw up his own *loi des trois états* and urge that whereas in the first stage of human history men were religious but not scientific and in the second stage scientific but not religious, in the third and final stage they will be both scientific and religious.

Les mythologies ne sont plus pour nous des séries de fables absurdes et parfois ridicules, mais de grands poèmes divins où les nations primitives ont déposé leurs rêves sur le monde suprasensible.[43]

Renan is here following such German scholars as Heyne, Niebuhr, Müller, Bauer, and Strauss, but what he fails to make clear is why a positivist should be interested in '[des] rêves sur le monde suprasensible'. Such a position is symptomatic, though, of the movement away from positivism implicit in his conception of *philologie* and its tasks.

He now passes beyond this standpoint, however, and argues that this study of the development of the human mind will reveal that the goal towards which evolution in general and human

[40] *A.S.*, p. 195.
[42] *D.F.P.*, p. 301, MA.
[41] *A.S.*, p. 138.
[43] *A.S.*, pp. 308, 266.

evolution especially are moving is 'la conscience', ever greater self-awareness and mental self-control. And having adopted this belief, he then goes even further and founds the ethic of his new 'science of humanity' upon the movement towards consciousness. Since this is the direction in which man is going, we may equate the moral good with it. The search for knowledge becomes a primary virtue, and the aim of true religion 'la culture intellec-tuelle'.[44]

There are two major weaknesses in Renan's case here. The first is the fallacious leap from 'this is' to 'this is good'; we shall return to this in discussing his ethical views. The second, which is especially pertinent to his notion of *philologie*, is that he believes consciousness is the goal of human evolution precisely because he begins by concentrating on the history of man's mind. A different approach might have led him to the conclusion, for instance, that consciousness is a mere accident in the evolutionary story and that the processes of evolution tend to work against rather than for its survival. In the 'Lettre à Berthelot' he gives a conjectured history of the universe. The first period is the atomic; the second the molecular; the third the solar period; the fourth is the planetary period when our own Earth started its existence; the fifth is the period in which each planet went through the stages of evolution revealed to us by geology, botany, zoology, and physiology; the sixth period is the age of 'l'humanité incon-sciente'; the final epoch is the period of historic times covering the last 6,000 years or so. From this survey Renan concludes that two elements explain the universe, 'le temps et la tendance au progrès'.[45] We may certainly accept as important the elements of time and development and, for argument's sake, progress, but what is completely unjustified is to conclude that 'le progrès vers la conscience est la loi la plus générale du monde'. Consciousness is wholly absent in the first five periods of universal history, although Renan assures us that the first period already held 'the germ of all that was to follow'.[46] It can hardly be said to exist even in the period of 'l'humanité inconsciente'. It is empirically verified only for the last, relatively short period out of the aeons of time comprising the previous six periods. It is not the compulsion of the facts that guides Renan here but the conclusion

[44] *A.S.*, p. 326. [45] *D.F.P.*, pp. 175–7, LB.
[46] *D.F.P.*, pp. 181, 175, LB.

he wishes to reach, and his conclusion itself is presupposed in his very equation of the 'science of man' with the history of man's mind. This unjustified equation in itself, quite apart from any other fallacies or confusions, is sufficient to invalidate Renan's 'ethic of the intellect'. Above all, it offers a salient example of his desertion of the positivist principle that deduction must always be from a comprehensive survey of verified facts.

At the same time one can state more precisely one's objection to his conception of 'philosophy'. 'La Métaphysique et son avenir' may not openly claim that 'la science du tout' can yield new knowledge, but Renan does claim scientific respectability for its conclusions.[47] This imposes an obligation to pursue it in a scientifically reputable way. Renan does not live up to this obligation— as Berthelot implicitly argues in his reply to Renan's letter on 'Les sciences de la nature et les sciences historiques'. In 'la science idéale' (which is Renan's 'philosophy'), he says,

il n'y a de probabilité qu'à la condition de s'appuyer sur les mêmes méthodes qui font la force et la certitude de la science positive.[48]

Renan does not fulfil this condition, and, as we must now see, his account of the methods of *philologie* gives no grounds for expecting that he would.

(d) *The methods of* philologie

Renan rejects the supernatural and the Christian religion in the name of scientific honesty, but in discussing the methods of *philologie* he abandons his strict positivist position. His attitude to Comte and Proudhon is significant. Comte, he urges, approaches human nature as a physicist or a chemist might; his method is too mechanical and limited to capture 'l'infinie variété de ce fond fuyant, capricieux, multiple, insaisissable, qui est la nature humaine'. He seeks to reduce the varied, complex manifestations of human activity to a totally inappropriate simplicity. Even

---

[47] It has been persuasively argued (Colin Smith, 'The Fictionalist Element in Renan's Thought', *French Studies*, Oxford, ix, 1955, pp. 30–41) that his philosophy is most fruitfully studied as a system of 'as if' 'fictions' and that he himself sometimes thinks of it as such. One can certainly accept this view if it is agreed that on other occasions Renan forgets that his 'fictions' are no more than this and claims that they form a 'science' and are built upon scientifically established facts and that 'to philosophize is to know the universe'.

[48] *D.F.P.*, p. 195, 'La Science idéale et la science positive—Réponse de M. Berthelot'.

worse perhaps in Renan's eyes, he discounts literature as relevant evidence for the study of a society; for Comte, he declares, 'la morale, la poésie, les religions, les mythologies, tout cela n'a aucune place, tout cela est pure fantaisie sans valeur'. He also restricts himself to studying the recent past of western Europe. Comte is dominated by *l'esprit de système*; thus he is unable to follow 'les lignes infiniment flexueuses de la marche des sociétés humaines'.[49] Proudhon, likewise, is too abstract and logical in his method: 'sa science n'est ni poétique ni religieuse'. He has failed to understand that in the human sciences 'l'argumentation *n'est rien*, et que la finesse d'esprit est tout'.[50] In a word, they are not philologists and are therefore incapacitated for the study of man.

The positivist approach, it now appears, is inadequate as it stands for the task of establishing the science of humanity. Refer-ring to the methods of the physical sciences, he says: 'l'effort doit tendre à élargir ce cercle'. In philological science, 'les faits aperçus finement sont . . . le seul *criterium* de vérité'[51]—and Renan's use of the word 'finement' represents a considerable abandonment of orthodox positivism. As he says:

notre rationalisme n'est donc pas cette morgue analytique, sèche, négative, incapable de comprendre les choses du cœur et de l'imagina-tion, qu'inaugura le XVIIIᵉ siècle; ce n'est pas l'emploi exclusif de ce que l'on a appelé 'l'acide du raisonnement'; ce n'est pas la *philo-sophie positive* de M. Auguste Comte, ni la critique irréligieuse de M. Proudhon.

The 'rationalism' postulated by Renan is 'l'usage simultané et harmonique de *toutes les facultés*'.[52] Imagination and intuition are quite as valid means in the search for knowledge as observa-tion and logical reasoning. The strict analytical method would be appropriate only if applied to what is dead and thus static: 'on lie facilement les épis quand ils sont coupés ou abattus par l'orage, mais non tant qu'ils vivent'. To seize the living in its state of temporal flow, he maintains,

les lois étant . . . d'une nature très délicate, et ne se présentant point de face comme dans les sciences physiques, la faculté essentielle est celle du critique littéraire, la délicatesse du tour, la ténuité des aperçus, le contraire en un mot de l'esprit géométrique.[53]

---

[49] *A.S.*, pp. 149–50; cf. p. 513, note 117.
[50] *A.S.*, pp. 151–2 (my italics).   [51] *A.S.*, pp. 442, 153.
[52] *A.S.*, pp. 65–66 (my italics).   [53] *A.S.*, pp. 307, 150–1.

Renan is already closer to Bergson than Comte or Littré, and this is still clearer in his adumbration of a *loi des trois états*. The first stage of man's intellectual evolution, illustrated by primitive peoples, is that of syncretism, of spontaneity as opposed to reflection, 'où les facultés, dans leur fécondité créatrice, sans se regarder elles-mêmes, par leur tension intime, atteignaient un objet qu'elles n'avaient pas visé'. In this manner man developed his languages and religions; they grew as plants grow, without conscious thought, products of 'cette force créatrice de la raison spontanée'. Renan is in fact very close to the view of many of his fellow *philologues* that primitive man was given 'une première révélation', lost by reflective, modern man, which can only be regained by the study of early mythologies. The second stage is that of analysis, when the human mind becomes conscious of itself, an age of abstractions and fierce intellectual controversy. He even refers to this stage as 'l'abîme de l'analyse', a period in which true reflection was abused, for analysis has no power to create. He comes to the brink of regretting that men ceased to be instinctive and became rational and argues that in some ways analysis is inferior to syncretism: 'celui-ci saisissait la vie complète, et l'analyse ne la saisit pas'.[54] Yet it does represent an advance on balance in that the earlier stage was inexact and could give no more than a first general view of life and the universe. Renan consequently looks forward to a third 'state', synthesis, 'la réflexion complète'. Superficially synthesis and syncretism are alike: the former will make available to us once more the latter's rich insights of instinct, discounted and obscured during the age of analysis, and at one point he equates 'la critique' with '[une] *intuition* vraie de l'humanité'.[55] But synthesis also presupposes analysis; it fuses both approaches to truth to attain 'une unité supérieure'.[56]

This conception of synthesis, distantly echoing the Hegelian dialectic, certainly differs from Bergson's idea of 'intellectual intuition' in that the latter is less dependent upon prior ways of knowing. Yet the description of philological method that Renan now develops within this wider context does suggest a certain similarity. This method must above all be appropriate to its subject-matter, and since *philologie* deals with the 'spontaneous

[54] *A.S.*, pp. 259, 261, 309, 89, 308.   [55] *A.S.*, p. 259 (my italics).
[56] *A.S.*, pp. 308, 312.

activity' of primitive, pre-analytical man, the distinctions of a rigid logic will be quite out of place. In this field of study, 'les résultats de la critique ne se *prouvent* pas, ils s'aperçoivent; ils exigent pour être compris un long exercice et toute une culture de finesse'.[57] It is the *esprit de finesse*, perceptive of 'considérations délicates' and 'nuances', that is required. The *philologue* must submit himself to the subject of his study, seek to penetrate it by a process of *sympathie*, to relive within himself the psychological states of primitive man and grasp them in their entirety. Thus he will need '[la] pénétration la plus intime des secrets de la psychologie spontanée' and '[une] nature enfantine et sérieuse, capable de s'enthousiasmer du spontané et de le reproduire en soi au sein même du réfléchi'.[58] Erudition is a prerequisite but must be supplemented by an act of imaginative sympathy.

One may well think this an apt method for studying the history of the human spirit, but it is noteworthy that Renan has moved emphatically away from an approach based upon observation and analysis. He is here far closer to Bergson than to any nineteenth-century positivist—in his emphasis upon universal flux and upon the primacy of spontaneous activity in human history; in his diagnosis of the limitations of the analytic intelligence when it tries to understand temporal reality and humanity's development; and in his stress on the necessity for a kind of intuition, in which the scholar grasps his subject-matter in its entirety. Yet a further resemblance is found in Renan's view of truth. Elsewhere he claims that philology will yield general laws as evident and sure as the laws of natural science. At other times, and perhaps more frequently, he admits that the reality of human life is too complex and many-sided to be reducible to neat systems and laws. It would be absurd, he believes, that any one system should hold 'le dernier mot de la réalité'. A system is 'une épopée sur les choses', and he likens scientists to poets, each producing different variations upon the same theme. There can be too great a precision in the sciences: only geometry can be formulated in clear axioms and theorems. 'Ailleurs le vague est le vrai.' Truth is to be sought in 'les nuances', and its discovery requires a sensitive, undogmatic mind prepared to abstain, where necessary, from reaching a conclusion, ready to realize that science always abstracts from reality and never

57 *A.S.*, p. 298.
58 *A.S.*, p. 162.

encompasses it entirely.[59] Even in 1848, in *L'Origine du langage*, he applies this principle to physics and asserts that recent work in physics has shown that its chief laws 'ne sont vraies qu'en un certain état moyen'; they cease to be verified 'dans les cas extrêmes'.[60] Here Renan perhaps anticipates not only Bergson but also Henri Poincaré's conception of scientific laws as 'useful hypotheses'.

3. *The Religion of Science. (i) Renan's attitude to religion*

The 'science of man' will also lead us to a new religion—'la religion de la science'. What does he want of it?

We saw that Renan regards Comtian positivism as too abstract and intellectual, too lacking in the flexibility of outlook that can combine science with poetry, religion, and the insights of the heart in a higher synthesis. Comte excludes all but the mechanical from his consideration, Renan thinks; the arts, religion, and the works of the imagination are all outside the scope of his interest—he is 'un esprit borné'. He is here unjust to Comte and his Religion of Humanity. Yet it is perhaps true that the needs which Comte was aware of intellectually, first and foremost, perhaps through his contact with Saint-Simon in particular, and only came to recognize emotionally under the influence of Clotilde de Vaux, Renan always felt as a thirsting of his own soul. To listen to Comte legislating for the new poetry, for example, of his religion is to suspect that he was unresponsive to the very nature of true poetry. Renan is far more sensitive and aesthetically alive, and when he speaks of human longing for beauty or for an ideal, the first-hand experience out of which he talks is unmistakable. Very few nineteenth-century writers were more innocent than Renan of the rationalist dichotomy between the realm of thought and the realm of feeling and imagination.[61] Basically, his distrust of Comte and of *l'esprit de système* derives from his belief that thought, feeling, and imagination are intimately related in human nature and that a system which satisfies the intellect but ignores the feelings is an impoverishment and distortion of human life. His own method of synthesis seeks to overcome the distinction

[59] *A.S.*, pp. 57–58.
[60] E. Renan, *L'Origine du langage*, 2ᵉ éd., Calmann-Lévy, 1858, p. 243.
[61] Cf. the 'Existentialist' interpretation of Renan presented in J. Chaix-Ruy, *Ernest Renan*, 1956.

between the intellect as the vehicle of thought and the soul as the vehicle of sensibility, to make thought imaginative and sensitive and to discipline feeling by the control of facts and erudition. His approach to the poetry of primitive peoples is typical. He never falls into what he regards as the error of those who try to confine poetry to an 'aesthetic' sphere. He interprets the texts of the ancients as revelations of their authors' vision of life, even though his emphasis upon the delicacy of response required shows his awareness of the dangers of translating the emotive and imaginative statements of poetry into the logical statements of philosophy. His distrust of the 'age of analysis' stems from the same rebuttal of a dissociation of intellect and sensibility. For him poetry and religious feeling are as much an expression of thought as the logic of the analytical philosopher. Thus he can even affirm that the true history of philosophy is the history of man's religions.

L'homme accompli serait celui qui pourrait être à la fois poëte, philosophe, savant, homme vertueux, et cela non pas par intervalles, mais par une intime pénétration à tous les moments de sa vie, qui serait poëte alors qu'il est philosophe, philosophe alors qu'il est savant....[62]

There is a further difference between the two thinkers. Comte conceives of his Religion of Humanity primarily as a social stimulus, as an incentive to the self-sacrifice and moral betterment that the 'positive' society requires. In part, no doubt, Comtian religion expresses Comte's own feeling for religion, but it is still doubtful whether he ever whole-heartedly valued religion as more than a concession to a weak human nature still needing the objects of devotion appropriate to the theological stage.

Renan's attitude reflects his own inwardness, his own spirituality, formed in his childhood amongst pious Bretons and in his youth at his Catholic seminaries. Where one might say that Comte's approach is for most of his life cynical, in a sense, Renan's is fundamentally sincere. Comte utilizes religion as a means: Renan ardently desires it as an end. He seems far more aware of the strength of man's religious need. 'Ce qui est de l'humanité, ce qui par conséquent sera éternel comme elle, c'est le besoin religieux, la faculté religieuse.' And in a preface to La Vie de Jésus he declares:

[62] A.S., p. 278, and D.F.P., p. 309, MA; cf. A.S., p. 11.

Fausses quand elles essayent de prouver l'infini, de le déterminer, de l'incarner, si j'ose le dire, les religions sont vraies quand elles l'affirment. . . . Le dernier des simples, pourvu qu'il pratique le culte du cœur, est plus éclairé sur la réalité des choses que le matérialiste qui croit tout expliquer par le hasard et le fini.

Life, to be meaningful, must be lived in a religious spirit. The atheist is not merely an unbeliever; his approach to life is frivolous and superficial. Only a religious faith can imprint upon man the high seriousness without which existence becomes mean and self-centred.[63]

The tension in Renan's thinking between his positivism and the 'religion' he erects in place of Christianity is therefore far more marked than in Comte's system; and Renan's *scientisme*, his attempt to derive a religion from science, is more far-reaching than in perhaps any other thinker of his time. Whereas for Comte the important aspect of religion is, broadly speaking, organizational—so that his Religion of Humanity could legitimately be dubbed 'Catholicism minus Christianity'—for Renan quite the contrary is true. Comte wishes to preserve the outward signs and rituals of religion—hence his careful hierarchical scheme of 'priests', complete with the amount of their stipends, and his provision of feast-days and ceremonies. Renan wishes to salvage the *beliefs* of his former faith and the individual experiences of prayer, worship, and the submission of the humble believer. Their respective attitudes to religious freedom are significant. Comte would ban dissension and religious toleration. Renan, for whom religion is above all a private experience, considers personal freedom essential. Religion is a matter over which the State should have no power whatever.[64] This view also determines his attitude to the Catholic Church. As is well known, he lamented that Protestantism, with its belief in tolerance, was not a practical alternative for a Frenchman, that he had to choose between the opposite poles of Catholic orthodoxy and *la libre pensée*. His belief was that dogmas—the petrifications of organizational religion—pass, whereas personal piety is eternal in the human heart. The best guide in the religious life is neither an organized, dogmatic Church nor a Bible that is regarded as infallible, but

---

[63] *A.S.*, pp. 483, 78, and *La Vie de Jésus*, p. xxxi, 'Préface de la 13e édition'.

[64] Cf. in particular his *Nouvelles études d'histoire religieuse*, Calmann-Lévy, 1884, *Préface*.

the moral inspiration of the heart.[65] Where Comte is the Catholic of positivist religion, Renan is its Nonconformist.

Renan's desire for a religion is nowhere more explicit than in his views on the ultimate aims of science. Science is of value only in so far as it is capable of replacing the religion of the past. It alone can give man a new creed and a moral law.

La science est donc une religion; la science seule fera désormais les symboles; la science seule peut résoudre à l'homme les éternels problèmes dont sa nature exige impérieusement la solution.

The aim of science is to teach man his final end, to make him grasp the true meaning of life, to join with art, poetry, and virtue to formulate 'le divin idéal qui seul donne du prix à l'existence humaine'. Thereby science can become 'religious and poetical'.[66]

Renan's insistence on this poetical value of science in its religious function is characteristic. He always felt that the 'natural religion' of earlier positivists, particularly of the *philosophes*, was only an intellectual husk, 'sorte de théologie mesquine, sans poésie, sans action sur l'humanité'.[67] He despises that pale theism in which God is postulated as the prime mover, as the great clock-maker. He rejects a creed with no place for love of God or for the wonderment, humility, and growth in sanctification of the believer. Religion, for him, cannot be purely intellectual. 'L'art, la poésie et la religion sont, en théodicée, supérieurs à la philosophie'; 'Dieu est le produit de la conscience, non de la science et de la métaphysique.'[68] Renan's attitude to religion expresses itself, therefore, in an attempt to unite the scientific and the emotional, the data of research and the insights of the heart.

4. *The Religion of Science. (ii) Renan's conception of God*

What is the content of this 'religion of science'? In what way can an historical study of the development of the human mind yield a religious faith? How can a transition be made from the natural to a notion of 'God'?

Renan's bold reply depends above all on the idea of progress, an idea which, as Javary remarks in his *Idée de progrès* (1851), was the seminal concept of the age. Almost every element in Renan's

[65] D.F.P., p. 329, MA, and A.S., p. 355.
[66] A.S., pp. 23, 31, 108, 91, 301.   [67] A.S., p. 473.
[68] D.F.P., p. 323, MA.

'religion' was in fact a commonplace in European thought of the mid-nineteenth century. What lends him his interest for the historian of ideas is the fusion of different philosophies of progress that he achieves, and this also highlights his movement away from positivism. We must therefore digress briefly to indicate these philosophies.

(a) Previous theories of progress and Renan's relation to them

Two main treatments can be discerned in the history of the idea of progress in the fifty years prior to L'Avenir de la science.[69] One may be termed the Hegelian treatment, the other the Comtian, although each individual thinker introduces minor variations upon one or other of the two dominant themes. Broadly speaking, both views have in common the belief in progress itself, secondly, a belief that determinism reigns in human history, and thirdly, a belief that the direction of progress is most intimately linked with the advance of the human mind. Thus progress in the systems of Fichte and Hegel is seen as a necessary consequence of the nature of reason, and for Cousin the evolution of humanity is related to a necessary evolution of thought. Similarly, in Comte's system progress mirrors the movement from the theological and metaphysical states to the positive state, and man's history is pre-eminently the history of his ideas. For Saint-Simon, likewise, it is dominated by the alternation of intellectual construction and criticism. In England, Buckle maintains the same thesis—progress is determined by the intellect and not by man's emotional and moral faculties, which are stationary. Even Jouffroy, in his 'Réflexions sur la philosophie de l'histoire' (1825), although not a determinist, interprets it in terms of 'the fatality of intellectual development'.

Beyond those similarities, however, the two treatments diverge. Hegel's interest in progress derives from his belief that through an understanding of its movement he can penetrate to ultimate reality, the Absolute. Since the Absolute realizes itself through historical evolution, to seize its nature we need only to discern the direction of that evolution. Comte and Saint-Simon, in contrast, interpret the past in order to make predictions and influence the society of the future, and a similar social preoccupation is

[69] Particularly helpful studies are J. B. Bury, The Idea of Progress, London, 1920, and M. Ginsberg, The Idea of Progress—A Revaluation, London, 1953.

found in Fourier and in the *Introduction à la science de l'histoire* of Buchez (1833), where history is defined as a science whose end is to foresee the social future of the human species. Progress is in fact invoked by most of the social reformers of this period—by Proudhon, for whom it is 'the railway of liberty'; by Leroux, who sees it in terms of the breaking down of social classes; by Michelet and Quinet; by Louis Blanc, whose journal was entitled *Revue du progrès*.[70] Hegel, in comparison, refuses to apply his study of man's development to political and social ends. For him, moreover, the aim of progress has now been achieved—in his own system, in which the Absolute has finally become fully conscious of itself—whilst on the political level the Prussian monarchical state is its final and highest external expression. Hegel's is a closed system which has nothing to say or to predict concerning the future. Comte's, on the other hand, looks forward—even though it also is a closed system in that it does not postulate any further evolution beyond the positive stage. The opposing orientations of the two systems are well seen in their attitudes to philosophy. For Comte and Saint-Simon, philosophy, interpreted as the scientific study of man and society, enables them to legislate for a utopian future. Hegel concludes the preface to his *Philosophy of Right* by saying:

> One word more about giving instruction as to what the world ought to be. Philosophy in any case always comes on the scene too late to give it. As the thought of the world, it appears only when actuality is already there cut and dried after its process of formation has been completed. . . . The owl of Minerva spreads its wings only with the falling of the dusk.[71]

A second major difference concerns the method by which the law of progress is discovered. Hegel and Fichte adopt an *a priori* method. Since progress is a necessary result of the nature of reason, its direction can be deduced without any reference to actual experience. Comte's approach is to be empirical, based upon an

---

[70] On the views of Proudhon and other French social thinkers of the period, cf. M. Leroy, *Histoire des idées sociales en France*, t. ii, *De Babeuf à Tocqueville*, 1950, and t. iii, *De Comte à Proudhon*, 1954. This brief sketch omits the theory of progress inspired by occultism found in Ballanche, for example, in which progress and primitive harmony are closely linked.

[71] G. W. F. Hegel, *The Philosophy of Right*, translated Knox, Oxford, 1942, pp. 12–13.

analysis of the actual events of history. Logically, since he believes progress is determined by the direction in which the human mind develops, Comte might have adopted an *a priori* method, and in fact he remarks that the principal aspects of society in the monotheistic period could have been deduced in this way. In fact, however, his philosophy purports to be scientific and not metaphysical.[72]

The last main difference lies in the respective views of the two systems on the final aim of the whole process of evolution. For the most part, the French thinkers discern a movement towards greater happiness in one form or another. This is true above all of the social reformers—of Proudhon, Michelet, and Quinet, for whom progress means the triumph of liberty; of Leroux and his disciples, who link it with greater equality; of Saint-Simon, for whom the goal is social happiness achieved through socialism; and of Fourier, whose law of passional attraction is used to fight the decline of happiness produced by recent 'civilization'. Although they may identify the aim of progress with the particular political principle they themselves support, they view the establishment of liberty or equality or fraternity chiefly as a means to greater human well-being. Comte himself is the greatest exception to this generalization.[73] Progress for him is expressed in the better organization of human society and a fuller adaptation of man to his environment, and although happiness may well be their by-product, it is not their justification or ultimate aim. None the less, both Comte and the French social reformers of the period are agreed that progress is manifested above all in the development of society, that is, in a primarily external fashion.

The German idealists, by comparison, locate progress in the realm of the internal—in the mind of humanity or of the Absolute. The final aim for Hegel, we saw, is the Absolute's consciousness of itself. For Fichte the goal is related to humanity rather than an Absolute, but for him, too, self-consciousness is the end to which men are moving—what he terms the full realization of 'freedom', by which he means not a political liberty but a state of complete consciousness opposed to the state of wholly instinctive

[72] Cf. Bury, op. cit., p. 253, and J. Baillie, *The Belief in Progress*, Oxford, 1950, pp. 118 ff.

[73] Other exceptions are Jouffroy, Guizot (for whom the aim is both social betterment and the development of individual life), and Cousin (whose views derive from Hegelianism).

behaviour. Likewise, Kant in his hesitant treatment of progress—which for him is not inevitable—places its criterion outside the increase of happiness or scientific and material achievements. It is to be judged by reference to moral amelioration, morality lying in conscious obedience to an external moral law. A perfect society would imply a reign of reason in which all men obeyed the categorical imperative and treated their fellows as ends in themselves. Herder, too, in his *Ideen*, although concerned with happiness and with the transformation of society by intelligent action, particularly stresses the development of man's highest faculties.

This division is inevitably imperfect. Fichte, for example, differs from Hegel: his is not a closed system, he looks forward to a re-organized society in the future and emphasizes the role of the savant in planning that society in very much the same manner as do Saint-Simon and Comte. Again, moral improvement is irrelevant to Hegel, whereas to Kant it is the very criterion of progress. Or again, Schelling resembles his fellow idealists in interpreting history as a progressive revelation of divine reason, but he rejects the determinism of Hegel. Yet in general outline the distinction is a valid one. The German idealists' approach is *a priori* in method and metaphysical in intention, aiming to reveal the nature of the Absolute, and progress for them means the attainment of greater self-consciousness. Their opponents are interested above all in applying their discoveries to a future society, they oppose the metaphysical pretensions of the idealists and allege that their own method is empirical, and they believe that progress is moving towards greater social cohesion involving, for most of them, an increase in human happiness.

Whatever its imperfections, this distinction does serve to indicate that Renan fuses elements from both systems into a new synthesis. He has the Comtian interest in the future and in the organization of society, and he claims to base his system upon the same empirical method. At the same time he takes over the Hegelian beliefs that the process of evolution is to be equated with the progressive realization of the Absolute, which he baptizes as 'God', and secondly, that progress is towards completer self-consciousness. To this amalgam he adds a moral emphasis that is absent in Hegel and Fichte and that exists in Comte only as a means to a social end—an emphasis which makes him reminiscent of Kant at times.[74]

The result is a reinterpretation of the idea of progress in terms of a religious system. Where Hegel is concerned with a metaphysical conception of the Absolute, Renan puts forward his religious conception of God. Where Comte thinks of a specific society, Renan thinks of humanity in general. Yet since it is to be founded on the scientific method, he can justifiably, on his assumptions, claim his new creed as a religion of science—a religion, not a mere metaphysics, and a scientific religion, not a religion of the traditional *a priori* and supernatural kind.

(b) Evolution and God

The second certainty expressed by Philalèthe in the *Dialogues philosophiques* as he surveys the universe from which he has just banished the supernatural is that a progression is revealed in its workings, a ceaseless *devenir*, activated by an impulse not unlike Bergson's *élan vital*, 'un ressort secret qui pousse le possible à exister'. The mechanical materialism of the *philosophes* appears to him 'une des plus grandes erreurs qu'on puisse professer'. Moreover, the mistake of believing in final causes lying behind the universe is not the belief in final causes itself but the belief that they existed prior to the universe: in fact, they should be located 'dans la catégorie du *fieri*, de la lente évolution'.[75]

A similar progression is visible in the human realm. Man's history is not an aimless succession of isolated events but 'une tendance spontanée vers un but idéal'. This was Hegel's greatest discovery, in his opinion, and it is from him that Renan takes over the *a priori* and strikingly unpositivist assertion that the development of the universe and of humanity is synonymous with the progressive creation of a final cause that the one terms the Absolute and the other God. With the achievement of that complete consciousness to which Renan looks forward 'God' will be 'realized': thus 'the divine work of progress' is to create God. And whilst man's search for knowledge constitutes 'le grand agent de

---

[74] Cf. his assertion as early as 1845: 'Oui, cette Allemagne me ravit, moins dans sa partie scientifique que dans son esprit moral. La morale de Kant est bien supérieure à toute sa logique ou philosophie intellectuelle, et nos Français n'en ont pas dit un mot' (*Souv.*, p. 339).

[75] *D.F.P.*, pp. 22–25.

la conscience divine', the whole universe is moving in the same direction.[76]

Thus far Renan's 'God' is little more than an honorific title bestowed upon the goal of universal evolution. But he rapidly adds to this basic concept and ends with a deity possessing marked affinities with even the God of Christianity.

Renan believes that everything, including progress, must have a cause. He has already banished the notion of a first cause existing *prior* to the process of progress, but he believes that a first cause can and does coexist with—or, rather, within—this process. Surveying human life in the *Dialogue* on *Certitudes*, Euthyphron says he admits that 'une volonté supérieure se sert de nous, et fait quelque chose par l'humanité'.[77] Théophraste develops the same view: 'L'idéal apparaît . . . comme le principe de l'évolution déifique, comme le créateur par excellence, le but et le premier moteur de l'univers.'[78] What had been postulated as the aim of progress is now also regarded as its cause: 'l'idéal' or 'God' is both the cause and the effect of the evolutionary movement. He appears to have had the analogy of plant germination and growth in mind and he often uses it to express his idea on the point. In his 'Lettre à Berthelot', for example, he refers to 'le germe fécond de progrès' and asserts: 'Il faut admettre dans l'univers ce qui se remarque dans la plante et l'animal, une force intime qui porte le germe à remplir un cadre tracé d'avance.'[79] But he appears to be misled by his analogy, for his attempt to transfer it to the notion of an 'Ideal' that is both cause and effect ends in a further example of verbal confusion. The problem is well posed by Euthyphron: 'Vous pensez alors, comme Hegel, que Dieu n'est pas, mais qu'il sera?' To this Théophraste replies: 'Pas précisément. L'idéal existe; il est éternel; mais il n'est pas encore matériellement réalisé; il le sera un jour.' It is upon this theme that Renan

[76] *A.S.*, p. 222, and *D.F.P.*, p. 58. It has been argued (e.g. by E. Caro, *L'Idée de Dieu et ses nouveaux critiques*, 1864) that in his earlier works God is no more in his view than the 'catégorie de l'Idéal' in the human mind. Whilst he does advance this view, he also embraces an Hegelian notion of 'God' even in *L'Avenir de la science* and claims: 'quand l'humanité ne sera plus, Dieu sera, et l'humanité aura contribué à le faire . . .' (p. 222).

[77] *D.F.P.*, p. 49. He seems to overlook his assertion earlier in the same dialogue that there is in the observable universe 'aucune trace de l'action d'êtres déterminés, supérieurs à l'homme et procédant par des volontés particulières' (p. 10).

[78] *D.F.P.*, p. 54.

[79] *D.F.P.*, pp. 177–8, LB.

elaborates—in a passage that is central for his whole theology and must be quoted in its entirety to reveal the verbal sleight of hand in regard to the idea of 'existence' that it involves. Théophraste is the speaker, and referring to 'l'idée', by which is meant 'God' or 'l'idéal' in Renan's usage of them, he says:

> L'idée est une virtualité qui veut être; la matière lui donne la concrétion, la fait passer à l'être, à la réalité. Les deux pôles de l'univers sont ainsi l'idéal et la matière. Rien n'est sans la matière; mais la matière est la condition de l'être, non la cause de l'être. La cause, l'efficient appartiennent tout entiers à l'idée. *Mens agitat molem.* C'est l'idée qui est réellement, qui seule est et aspire sans cesse à une pleine existence en suscitant les combinaisons matérielles aptes à sa production.
>
> Nous arrivons ainsi à n'attribuer la parfaite existence qu'à l'idée, ou plutôt à l'idée consciente d'elle-même, à l'âme.[80]

Thus Renan again belies his positivism by embracing a notion of existence which no positivist could accept. And on this linguistically dubious basis he develops his ideas about the nature of God. 'Dieu sera et Dieu est. En tant que réalité, il sera; en tant qu'idéal, il est.'[81] First, God is in the making and His complete existence will be the fulfilment of the entire evolution of the universe. Secondly, God is at the same time the cause of that evolution. Thirdly, since the evolution of all things is the 'creation of God', Renan at times accepts an explicit pantheism:

> Dieu n'est pas seulement au ciel, il est près de chacun de nous; il est dans la fleur que vous foulez sous vos pieds, dans le souffle qui vous embaume, dans cette petite vie qui bourdonne et murmure de toutes parts, dans votre cœur surtout.[82]

Beyond this, fourthly, God also exists *outside* the whole process of evolution—despite Renan's assertions to the contrary. In the 'Lettre à Berthelot' he reaffirms his view that God is 'en voie de se faire'. But to go no farther would leave one with 'une théologie fort incomplète'.

> Dieu est plus que la totale existence; il est en même temps l'absolu. Il est l'ordre où les mathématiques, la métaphysique, la logique sont vraies; il est le lieu de l'idéal, le principe vivant du bien, du beau et du

vrai. Envisagé de la sorte, Dieu est pleinement et sans réserve; il est éternel et immuable, sans progrès ni *devenir*.[83]

This passage shows how far from positivism and how close to the orthodox Christian conception of God he has wandered. It might sometimes have seemed earlier that Renan's God existed only in man's mind—as when he writes in 1848 that God is 'le résumé transcendant de ses [humanity's] besoins suprasensibles, *la caté-gorie de l'idéal*'.[84] But later this position is inverted: God is not the creation of man's moral conscience; man's conscience is the creation of God, and Renan is affirming: 'La vertu de l'homme est en somme la grande preuve de Dieu.'[85]

Such discrepancies are perhaps the outcome of the incompatible aims Renan had before him. Claiming to reject any method not based on observation, he yet wishes to arrive at a religion that includes a doctrine of God—that is, of the unobservable. His method confines him to men's ideas about God and can logically never furnish a bridge to knowledge of the reality or non-reality with which those ideas correspond. Positivism conflicts with his desire for a transcendental faith, and it is not surprising that he should eventually be led by the latter to a denial of one of the basic tenets of the former:

La nature n'est qu'une apparence; l'homme n'est qu'un phénomène. Il y a le fond éternel, il y a l'infini, la substance, l'absolu, l'idéal; ... il y a, selon l'expression juive ... *celui qui est*.[86]

Where positivism claims that our knowledge is confined wholly to the realm of phenomena, Renan here claims a knowledge that would be attainable only if that phenomenal world were trans-cended by the human mind. This is perhaps the best known of Renan's self-contradictions, and it is difficult to feel that Séailles succeeds in diminishing it.[87]

5. *The Religion of Science. (iii) Renan's ethical ideas*

Renan also adds to his system a moral imperative which is entirely absent from Hegel and is introduced by Comte largely

[83] *D.F.P.*, pp. 184–5, LB.
[84] *A.S.*, p. 476. Cf. E. Renan, *Études d'histoire religieuse*, 3e éd., Calmann-Lévy, 1863, p. 419.   [85] *D.F.P.*, p. 30.
[86] *D.F.P.*, p. 252, 'Lettre à A. Guéroult'.
[87] G. Séailles, *Ernest Renan*, 1895, pp. 193–4.

as a social expedient. But since he has abandoned the supernatural sanction of the Christian ethic as unscientific, he now has
to seek a more scientifically based moral code.

He finds a sanction in 'Nature', not unlike his positivistic predecessors, Diderot, D'Holbach, and Helvétius, but their injunction
to 'follow Nature' is reinterpreted to read: 'follow the direction of
evolution'. He also differs from them as to the message given by
the voice of Nature. For the *philosophes*, it urged man to pursue
happiness as the supreme end in life. To Renan it speaks in sterner,
less eudaemonistic terms. The goal is the increase of consciousness,
the cultivation of an awareness that is intellectual first and foremost—so that he can refer to his religion as 'le progrès de la raison,
c'est-à-dire de la science', as 'la religion de l'esprit'[88]—but is also
moral and aesthetic. The perfect man, we saw, must combine a love
of virtue and beauty with a cult of learning and philosophy.[89] Nor
is it only the hedonism of the *philosophes* that is surpassed. By
1871, if not earlier, even their humanism is abandoned. Surveying
the evolution of life from a mid-nineteenth-century vantage-point,
Renan now emphasizes that man is only one species in a long line
of living forms; it has itself replaced earlier species and will in
turn be supplanted by higher types of life. A certain anthropo-
centricity remains: 'l'absolu de la raison', Théophraste claims,
though not to be attained by man, will be achieved by 'quelque
chose d'analogue à l'humanité'.[90] None the less the goal of evolution lies beyond man, whose reward and 'immortality' will be in
'le souvenir de Dieu', and man will be sacrificed—and rightly so—
to the attainment of this goal.

Here is a turning-point in the history of the idea of progress.
Almost all his predecessors, idealists and positivists alike, with
the outstanding exception of Hegel, had associated its goal with
humanity. Even Hegel held that the Absolute had achieved self-
consciousness in his own system, that is, in and through a human
mind. In startling contrast, Renan places the end outside man:
God alone exists, whilst man is 'only a phenomenon', used and
deceived by Nature for its own ends.[91] This had not been his view
in *L'Avenir de la science*: there the progress of humanity is justified for its own sake, and he can assert:

[88] *A.S.*, pp. vii, 473.   [89] *D.F.P.*, p. 309, MA, and *A.S.*, p. 11.
[90] *D.F.P.*, p. 67.
[91] *D.F.P.*, p. 252, 'Lettre à A. Guéroult', and pp. 40–42, 45.

Ma conviction intime est que la religion de l'avenir sera le pur *humanisme*, c'est-à-dire le culte de tout ce qui est de l'homme. . . .[92]

It is perhaps the supreme irony of that 'religion', when it is fully worked out, that it should prove to be a super-humanism to which man must be subordinated and whose political counterpart is seen in Renan's *aristocratisme*. And one may also wonder if it is not characteristic of the manner in which the absolute idealism deriving from Hegel so often ends by sacrificing the reality of man to the reality of the Absolute.

This change is in part explained by the wider perspectives opened out by nineteenth-century theories of the evolution of the species. But perhaps an even more fundamental reason lies in the impulse that led Renan to seek not merely a new ethic but a new religion. The very heart of a religion is to be turned towards a being utterly surpassing the human believer, and it is perhaps the need to worship, to abase himself, that drives him to set his God beyond the grasp of man.

But how are we to pass from a description of the direction of progress to the injunction that we ought to assist this movement —even though it may ultimately replace us by a superior species? In answering this question he is betrayed into further difficulties which it is hard to believe that he ever resolved.

Four possible doctrines were open to him. First, one may main-tain that progress is determined and inevitable and that man, like the rest of the natural world, will be swept along by it whether he wishes it or not. In such a situation it is only wisdom to accept this inevitability with resignation; man's only possible freedom lies in his recognition of necessity. Alternatively, one may hold that man has free will, that he may co-operate with the movement of progress or refuse to do so, and one may further assert that this movement is good or that it is evil—in a more generalized form, that Nature is good or evil. Finally, one may argue that man has free will but that historical development is morally neutral, that the whole concept of an ethic is foreign to it and that it is idle and fallacious to seek a sanction for any ethical system in it.

Renan's distinction is to affirm all four of these incompatible views, although his support of the view that Nature is evil is only momentary. It is a noteworthy achievement even for so catholic

[92] *A.S.*, p. 101; cf. p. 381.

and subtle a mind as his. Philalèthe begins his exposition of the two certainties that compose his theology by denying the intervention of a supernatural in the natural order: Nature operates according to general laws which are never suspended, even to aid a virtuous man or a just cause. 'La nature est d'une *insensibilité* absolue, d'une *immoralité* transcendante, si j'ose le dire.'[93] At this point, Renan's standpoint is a mingling of the two ideas that Nature is morally neutral and that it is evil—a view adopted in order to evict the supernatural. But when he is developing his conviction that Nature is evolving towards a goal, he embraces a different notion: 'le mal, c'est de se révolter contre la nature. . . . Son but est bon; veuillons ce qu'elle veut.' Eudoxe even speaks of 'le joyeux alléluia de la nature'.[94] The contradiction is transparent: the immorality of Nature which he had previously postulated yields to what is an almost religious confidence in its goodness. Yet Renan does not leave the contradiction in its simple state. He agrees that Nature employs deceits and frauds in order to further its ends.

L'homme est lié par certaines ruses de la nature, telles que la religion, l'amour, le goût du bien et du vrai, tous instincts qui, si l'on s'en tient à la considération de l'intérêt égoïste, le trompent et le mènent à des fins voulues hors de lui.[95]

We are in a sense the victims of Nature, like gladiators killing each other for a cause which is not their own. What he does not explain is the further dichotomy within the natural order which he has introduced—between, on the one hand, the morally good end he attributes to it and, on the other hand, the egotism and self-interest that are natural in both men and animals. This is particularly evident in his treatment of man's virtuous, self-sacrificing action which, in his view, constitutes 'la grande preuve de Dieu'. Renan admits that in most cases man has 'un intérêt actuel à ne pas être vertueux'; Nature, through all man's instincts, would seem to counsel non-virtuous action. Yet it is the virtuous action which in fact represents true obedience to Nature. 'Obéir à la nature est pour nous collaborer à l'œuvre divine.'[96]

The point of interest is not the contradiction, however, but the reason behind it. It is the positivist in Renan who observes the

[93] *D.F.P.*, p. 13 (my italics).   [94] *D.F.P.*, pp. 46, 44.
[95] *D.F.P.*, p. 43.   [96] *D.F.P.*, pp. 30, 38.

insensibility of Nature and the natural egotism of man. It is the Renan in search of an ethic who postulates that Nature's goal is none the less good and ought to be pursued by man.[97]

Notwithstanding, Renan provides a moral imperative for his system, and he supports it by two arguments in particular. The first is based on the claim that the goal of Nature's progress is good, from which Renan draws the conclusion that man has a moral duty to further it. The second argument is that man is compelled to do so whether he wishes it or not. Nature will always triumph over him: 'la moralité se réduit ainsi à la soumission'.[98] The juxtaposition of these two assertions is especially clear in the passage in which he considers Schopenhauer. This confrontation with the German pessimist is a crucial moment for Renan. For Schopenhauer illustrates a crisis in the history of ethical thought based on the concept of Nature. Whereas the *philosophes*, Herder, and many German Romantics believe in general that Nature is good, Schopenhauer asserts that it is evil: the natural life is the sphere of tormenting will. Romantic optimism is replaced by Romantic cynicism and revolt. The wise man will oppose Nature and attempt to stifle desire and will within himself, seeking in art a temporary respite from suffering and in self-abnegation release from an unhappy universe. This is the moment at which the optimistic conception of Nature is seen to derive from just that religious, indeed Christian view of the universe which many of its adherents had rejected.

Renan is clearly aware of the importance of Schopenhauer's standpoint, and it is therefore all the more interesting to see him trying to meet it.[99] He correctly interprets it as 'la révolte, la haine contre le tyran'. But the German thinker was guilty of a contradiction. He admits that Nature has a goal and he perceives the deceitful tactics by which Nature moves towards it; but he fails to acknowledge that this is sufficient to establish an objective moral law and that virtue lies henceforth in willing acceptance of life as it is—'obéir à la nature . . . est déjà une loi'. Against Schopenhauer Renan asserts: 'Si la nature a un but, il faut s'y prêter.' One might have suspected him at this point of having

[97] Renan is here following a path well trodden by the *philosophes*. Cf. in particular B. Willey's study of Helvétius and D'Holbach in *The Eighteenth-Century Background*, London, 1940.

[98] D.F.P., p. 43.

[99] D.F.P., pp. 40–45.

failed to see that the significance of *The World as Will and Idea*
lies in its rejection of what its author regarded (in common with
Renan) as an objective law. But he goes on to interpret Schopenhauer in precisely this sense, as 'un homme non résigné à la
nature, qui prétend aller contre ce qu'elle veut'. He now adduces
two arguments against this attitude of revolt:

> En premier lieu, cela est coupable; en second lieu, cela est inutile;
> car la nature triomphera toujours; elle a trop bien arrangé les
> choses . . . ; elle atteindra, quoi que nous fassions, son but, qui est de
> nous tromper à son profit.

So Renan proceeds to enunciate the equivalent in his new religion
of the Christian 'sin against the Holy Spirit': 'Cette révolte de
l'homme est le crime par excellence, le seul crime à vrai dire qu'il
y ait.' Against Schopenhauer he affirms: 'Le grand homme doit
collaborer à la fraude qui est la base de l'univers.'

These somewhat strident tones cannot hide the inadequacy of
Renan's reply. If we must obey, the injunction that we ought to
obey can have no meaning. In reality, Renan has transferred
allegiance from his youthful faith in the goodness of God to
a faith that is equally unscientific in the goodness of Nature.
Positivism has entered to destroy the former; it has itself been
cast out to permit acceptance of the latter.

6. *The Religion of Science. (iv) Its 'creed' and 'religious practices'*

When Renan has reached his notions of 'God' and of the goal
of morality, the way is open for him to reintroduce in a newly
interpreted form the concepts and practices of the Christian
Church which he had renounced. It is not merely the idea of God
that finds a place within his new creed. He is able to give a sense
to many other facets of his former Catholicism.[1] Immortality may
have lost something of its supernatural connotations, but it still
has a meaning. We live eternally by virtue of the small contribution we have made to universal progress; 'c'est dans le souvenir
de Dieu que les hommes sont immortels'. No action, even the
action of the primitive savage, is ever wholly lost. Even an insect

---

[1] On this aspect of his thought, cf. J. Pommier, *La Pensée religieuse de Renan*, 1925.

eating a leaf, Renan maintains, accomplished something that contributed to the eternal march of evolution. The belief in immortality is now linked with 'cette invincible confiance de l'humanité dans l'avenir'.[2] Even Paradise is not a wholly illusory concept. Science has destroyed the idea of a supernatural paradise, but paradise may be brought down to earth and will finally be established 'quand tous auront part à la lumière, à la perfection, à la beauté, et *par là* au bonheur'.[3] Nor is the element of the mysterious and the transcendental banished from religion. 'Ce mystère infini que nous entrevoyons dans un nuage' will always remain an enigma, '[sur laquelle] il sera toujours aussi impossible à l'homme de se satisfaire que d'abdiquer la recherche'. We can never possess more than 'des lambeaux de vérité'; God has willed that men should only see through a glass darkly. Addressing himself to the 'Père céleste', he cries: 'Tu n'as pas voulu que ces doutes reçussent une claire réponse, afin que la foi au bien ne restât pas sans mérite, et que la vertu ne fût pas un calcul'.[4] Even in 1890, in the preface he wrote for *L'Avenir de la science*, he sees his scientific religion as

la doctrine transcendante selon laquelle le but de l'humanité est la constitution d'une conscience supérieure, ou, comme on disait autrefois, 'la plus grande gloire de Dieu'.

The Eternal remains, as immovable as in the creed of the Church: 'La nature n'est qu'une apparence; l'homme n'est qu'un phénomène. Il y a le *fond éternel*, il y a l'infini. . . .' The religion of science, he goes on, like the religion of the Christian theologians, has as its aim to embrace the Infinite; the experimental method has revealed 'cet infini réel, que jamais [l'homme] n'atteint dans les plus hardies excursions de sa fantaisie'.[5] Objective virtue also remains, and with it a doctrine of evil. In 1848 he equates this evil with lack of intellectual culture, in 1871 with revolt against Nature and its purposes. Likewise, the moral conscience and '[les] instincts divins du cœur de l'homme' are as foremost in his religion as in Christianity. Even sanctification still has a sense, for the new religion is 'une façon de prendre la vie entière en voyant sous toute chose le sens idéal et divin, et sanctifiant toute la vie

[2] *D.F.P.*, pp. 52, 139, and *A.S.*, p. 223.
[3] *A.S.*, p. 330.
[4] *D.F.P.*, pp. 332–3, MA.   [5] *A.S.*, pp. xvi, 96.

par la pureté de l'âme et l'élévation du cœur'.[6] Worship, furthermore, is directed now to its true object, for 'la vraie façon d'adorer
Dieu, c'est de connaître et d'aimer ce qui est'.[7] Prayer remains
'comme hymne mystique' and as a means of self-examination,
having been purged of its superstitious and self-centred elements.[8]
Again, the Christian believer's love for God is re-expressed but
not discarded. 'Aimer Dieu, connaître Dieu, c'est aimer ce qui
est beau et bon, connaître ce qui est vrai.' To be religious is to
know and love the truth of things, and in his reverence the
Renanian believer will experience all the humility and submissiveness of the Christian.[9] He will even feel an equivalent of the
Christian's sense of communion with his fellow adherents. 'Voilà
la grande, la suprême, l'*internelle* consolation', remarks Eudoxe
in the first *Dialogue philosophique*, 'songer qu'on fait partie d'un
ensemble qui va sûrement à ses fins....'[10] The joys of the Christian
believer, Renan assures us, are nothing in comparison with the
joys that he has experienced 'dans la pure contemplation du beau
et la recherche passionnée du vrai'; the religion of science is 'une
religion tout aussi suave, tout aussi riche en délices, que les cultes
les plus vénérables'.[11] Even the hope of resurrection is preserved.
Renan asks at the close of his 'Lettre à Berthelot': 'Pourquoi le
règne de l'esprit, fin de l'univers, ne serait-il pas ainsi la résurrection de toutes les consciences?'—for 'en Dieu vivent . . . toutes les
âmes qui ont vécu'. And he goes on to affirm that 'la résurrection
finale se fera par la science, soit de l'homme, soit de tout autre
être intelligent'.[12] The new religion will also have a priesthood,
composed of philosophers, scholars, artists, and poets. They will
revive 'le sacerdoce poétique des premiers civilisateurs' and be
guardians of 'la vraie *théologie*'—'la science du monde et de
l'humanité'—whilst the churches of the religion, finally, will be
the reformed schools, the *scholae*, of the future.[13]

    In these ways Renan is able to give a new meaning to the doc-
trines, practices, and personal experiences which he had known
as a Catholic. God, immortality, religious hope, paradise, mystery
and the transcendental, the Eternal, an objective moral law, a

---

[6] *A.S.*, pp. 475, 473.   [7] *A.S.*, p. 126.
[8] *D.F.P.*, p. 14.
[9] *D.F.P.*, p. 326, MA, and *A.S.*, p. 474.
[10] *D.F.P.*, p. 44.   [11] *A.S.*, p. 318.
[12] *D.F.P.*, pp. 189–90, LB.
[13] *D.F.P.*, p. 312, MA (my italics), and *A.S.*, p. 165.

doctrine of evil and trust in the inner light of conscience, sanctification, worship, prayer, the love of God by the believer, the experiences of humility, submissiveness and wonderment, the communion of all believers, the joys of religion, resurrection, a theology, a priesthood, and new churches—the list is comprehensive and strong evidence of his search to formulate a creed that had inevitably, if it were to satisfy the innermost needs of Renan himself, to outsoar the limitations of the positivist method.

7. Renan's Final Scepticism

This chapter has been concerned with Renan's constructive philosophy in the years between 1848 and 1871. In studying his relationship to the positivist philosophy one need not follow him into the political discussions of *La Réforme intellectuelle et morale* or into his reinterpretation of the early history of the Christian Church and the history of Israel (upon which his reputation as a scholar must be judged). But one must stay to notice the final transformation of Renan's philosophy into the ironic scepticism of his last years. For a second time the religion in which he believed crumbled away. These last years of popular acclaim and of excessive literary facility are indeed years of philosophical disintegration. It is painful, for anyone who has come to respect his ardour and high-mindedness, to survey the breakdown of his former faith, of his sincerity and even of his integrity. Already in the preface to the *Dialogues philosophiques*, written five years after the *Dialogues* themselves, his attitude is becoming more ironic—and more trivial. We need not take any philosophy too seriously: 'la bonne humeur est . . . le correctif de toute philosophie'.[14] Increasingly he falls back upon his positivist starting-point and, for the rest, accepts a subjective ethic of pleasure. Truth is confined to positive, ascertained facts, and beyond that we can only form our own illusory dreams. Renan still speaks in the same tones of priestly elevation, and the search for truth remains a kind of 'religion' for him. The religion which he and Berthelot have had in common, he says, 'cette religion, c'était le culte de la vérité'.[15] Even our philosophical dreamings are given a quasi-religious importance: 'Être assez puissant pour se créer

---

[14] *D.F.P.*, p. xviii.
[15] E. Renan, *Discours et conférences*, 9e éd., Calmann-Lévy, 1928, p. 232.

un rêve où l'on vive à l'abri des turpitudes ambiantes, tel est, en définitive, je crois, le but de tout effort humain.'[16] He may now be suspected of playing lightly with sacred matters, and it is to this period of his life that Séailles's hard but just words apply:

Renan ajoute quelque chose à Voltaire, il invente une forme nouvelle du blasphème, le blasphème sacerdotal, qui n'est que la familiarité avec les choses sacrées, poussée jusqu'à l'impertinence, une manière de se mettre à l'aise avec Dieu et les saints. . . .[17]

Behind this new attitude lies his realization that his efforts to construct a new religion have been vain. 'Nous ne savons pas, voilà tout ce qu'on peut dire de clair sur ce qui est au delà du *fini*.' Philosophy is an idle game. To the young people of his day he says: 'c'est inutile de se donner tant de mal à la tête, pour n'arriver qu'à changer d'erreur. Amusez-vous, puisque vous avez vingt ans, travaillez aussi.' He himself ends with an unrefined hedonism, with a Gidean sensualism without the early Gidean innocence. 'La chose du monde la plus philosophique et la plus saine' is now to teach 'toutes les nations à rire en français'. Still, we may notice, he dresses his advice in the language of the metaphysical priest: 'On entre par la gaieté dans les vues les plus profondes de la Providence.'[18] He says again, in what is an unwitting confession of philosophical bankruptcy:

Le moyen de salut n'est pas le même pour tous. Pour l'un, c'est la vertu; pour l'autre, l'ardeur du vrai; pour un autre, l'amour de l'art; pour d'autres, la curiosité, l'ambition, les voyages, le luxe, les femmes, la richesse; au plus bas degré, la morphine et l'alcool; la plus dangereuse erreur, en fait de morale sociale, est la suppression systématique du plaisir.[19]

We may agree with his conclusion; but the remainder of his assertion witnesses to the failure of his life-long search for an objective code of values. Now he even describes the historical and philological sciences on which his system had been founded as 'petites sciences conjecturales qui se défont sans cesse après s'être faites, et qu'on négligera dans cent ans'.[20] The conclusion of all his aspirations is scepticism, summarized when he writes in

[16] Letter to Séailles, cited by Séailles, op. cit., p. 362.
[17] Ibid., p. 303.
[18] E. Renan, *Feuilles détachées*, 17e éd., Calmann-Lévy, 1922, pp. 17, 263.
[19] Ibid., p. 382 (my italics).   [20] *Souv.*, p. 230.

a letter to Séailles: 'Ah! dire la vérité, vivre selon la vérité! mais n'est-il pas fou d'y penser, dans le monde où nous vivons?'[21] At best he suggests on occasion, as in the 'Examen de conscience philosophique' published in the *Revue des Deux Mondes* in 1889, that we can act and choose *as if* God and the soul existed; but even this only consecrates his view that man must be resigned to permanent ignorance.

8. *Conclusion*

John Stuart Mill referred to Comte as a morality-intoxicated man. Renan, by Comte's side, is a religion-intoxicated man. 'J'étais né prêtre *a priori*', he states; 'je ne fus pas prêtre de profession, je le fus d'esprit.' He declares himself 'un prêtre manqué'.[22] Throughout this chapter we have stressed his inner need of a religion to replace the supernatural faith he had rejected and the tension that is thereby created between his 'religion of science' and his positivist presuppositions. It was the building of a creed that should be more than the emasculated theism of the eighteenth century, that should be religious in the way that Catholicism is religious, that led Renan, again and again, to betray the tenets from which he began. The full extent of his deviation from positivism may be measured by recalling Comte's definition of the metaphysical state.

Dans l'état métaphysique, qui n'est au fond qu'une simple modification générale du premier [l'état théologique], les agents surnaturels sont remplacés par des forces abstraites, véritables entités (abstractions personnifiées) inhérentes aux divers êtres du monde, et conçues comme capables d'engendrer par elles-mêmes tous les phénomènes observés....[23]

This is a surprisingly exact description of Renan's system, even to the observation that it represents little more than a modification of the theological state.

The failure of his religious search—for failure it is, as his final scepticism only serves to confirm—cannot wholly detract from its grandeur or its significance. As a philosopher, judged by the normal standards of academic philosophy, Renan is marked by

---

[21] Séailles, op. cit., p. 361.
[22] *Souv.*, pp. 134, 129, 136.
[23] A. Comte, *Cours de philosophie positive*, 2ᵉ éd., 1864, 6 vols., i, 9.

too many contradictions and ambiguities. Yet no French writer of his period epitomizes so well one of the characteristic intellectual developments of the century. From Catholic Christianity he passes to positivism; from positivism he moves to a religion of humanity and science; from that emerges a religion of the ideal, a creed surpassing humanity itself; and the final disintegration of his faith issues into a scepticism in which, outside the few certainties of a strict positivism, all values and all criteria of judgement are equalized.

VII

FROM POSITIVISM TO SCIENTISM (3)

HIPPOLYTE TAINE

1. *Introduction*

(a) Unity and duality in Taine's work

ONE's first impression of Taine (1828–93) is of the astonishing diversity of his interests and achievements. By the age of thirty-five his studies of La Fontaine (1853) and Livy (1856) and the *Histoire de la littérature anglaise* (1864) had established him as an historian of literature and thought and *Les Philosophes français du dix-neuvième siècle* (1857) as a philosophical polemicist. By the age of forty, having been appointed Professor at the École des Beaux-Arts in 1864, he had won a reputation as an art historian and critic with works on Italian, Flemish, and Greek art, later collected as *La Philosophie de l'art* (1882). By forty-five or earlier, following *De l'intelligence* (1870), he was acknowledged as a founder of scientific psychology, whilst before he was fifty he had published the first volume of *Les Origines de la France contemporaine* (1875–93), the great work that was to bring him controversial fame as an historian. And to these we also have to add his volumes of *Essais de critique et d'histoire* (1858, 1882, and 1894), books on his travels in the Pyrenees, Italy, and England, the four volumes of his *Correspondance*, and a novel.

Yet his work does possess its underlying unities—a unity of aim and a unity of method. His lifelong goal was to explore human psychology, to contribute to '[cette] grande enquête sur l'homme' which he regarded as the very purpose of contemporary thought, and all his individual books are essays in psychology. Studying works of literature and art, he tries to penetrate to the minds of their creators, to 'explain' their artistic products by their mental state as formed by the interacting influences of *race*, *moment*, and *milieu*, and (Bourget points out[1]) the books he

[1] P. Bourget, *Essais de psychologie contemporaine*, 1926, 2 vols., i. 235.

especially admires—by Michelet, Balzac, Saint-Simon, Shakespeare, Swift, and Carlyle—are for him examples of 'living
psychology'. As Faguet neatly suggests, 'l'étude de l'homme par
l'histoire, l'histoire par l'histoire littéraire, l'histoire littéraire par
l'étude des grands écrivains—telle pourrait être l'épigraphe de
tous ses livres de critique'.[2] And when he turns to history and
sociology—to Robespierre or Napoleon, for example—he attempts
to analyse the workings of the human spirit in the concrete affairs
of life. From this point of view *De l'intelligence* is the culmination
of his career. He planned a companion volume, *De la volonté*, but
his historical work—motivated by that moral and political *examen
de conscience* which preoccupied French intellectuals after 1870—
prevented him from writing it. Had it appeared, as the last of his
works, it would have made even more evident the central aim of
all his research.

His work derives no less marked a coherence from the method
he employed. The principal texts of his discourse on method comprise the preface to the *Essai sur Tite-Live*, the prefaces and final
chapters of *Les Philosophes français*, the celebrated *Introduction*
to the history of English literature, the discussion of Mill in the
Histoire itself, and parts of *De l'intelligence*, and it is this method
which he applied in turn in the fields of literature, art, history,
and psychology and propounded in his studies of other philosophers. His entire work sought to justify a single, universal method
by showing its fruitfulness in these various subjects.

Taine was not only a scholar and scientist, however; he was also
a philosopher. Behind the method lies a theory of knowledge, and
behind all the individual sciences lies the greatest and most universal science, metaphysics. Philosophy even more than psychology inspired him throughout his life. As a young man he writes
to Prévost-Paradol 'Je veux être philosophe'; he thinks of himself
not as 'un critique qui voudrait peindre' but as 'un critique qui
essaye de philosopher'.[3] Later, having completed the *Histoire de
la littérature anglaise*, he complains of the time it has cost him:
philosophy is worth more than history, he adds. And towards
the end of his life, in 1891, he can declare yet again: '. . . j'ai

    [2] E. Faguet, *Politiques et moralistes du dix-neuvième siècle*, 1903, 3 vols.,
iii. 261.
    [3] *Hippolyte Taine, sa vie et sa correspondance*, Hachette, 1902–7, 4 vols.
[*Corr.*], i. 56; and H. Taine, *Essais de critique et d'histoire*, 14ᵉ éd., Hachette,
1923 [*Essais*], p. v.

toujours aimé, sinon la métaphysique proprement dite, du moins la philosophie, c'est-à-dire les vues sur l'ensemble et sur le fond des choses'.[4]

It is here, in the philosophical substratum of his work, that the unities of his various monographs are replaced by division and ambiguity. The duality we shall discern is perhaps paralleled in his whole character. Zola believed that in Taine a poet and a rationalist were in conflict, whilst Jules Lemaître saw in him *un poète-logicien*.[5] He combines 'a Germanic imagination' and 'a Latin reason',[6] and many of his most striking generalizations are not the scientific discoveries he alleged but brilliant imaginative intuitions.[7] Yet this personal dualism can be over-stressed. Taine is primarily an intellectual, far removed from Renan's spiritual reveries. Where the one seeks a religion, the other seeks a metaphysics. *La raison raisonnante* is Taine's dominant faculty and intellectual truth his chief goal. As early as 1849 he is writing to Prévost-Paradol:

Considère que je n'ai jamais rien fait que par la volonté et l'intelligence, parce que la nature en moi était mauvaise et rebelle, que je n'ai compris les arts que par la pensée, et le beau que par la philosophie et l'analyse.[8]

Thus he sharply distinguishes the intellectual spheres of science and philosophy from religion, ethics, and poetry; and dissenting from Bourget's view that he is a pessimist, he says with asperity: 'Être pessimiste ou optimiste, cela est permis aux poètes et aux artistes, non aux hommes qui ont l'esprit scientifique.'[9]

This was how he thought of himself and how his contemporaries thought of him. For Boutroux, despite their philosophical differences, he offers 'l'exemple d'une grande intelligence et d'une grande âme vouée toute à la recherche sincère de la vérité',[10] whilst the young Paul Bourget and his fellow students could feel

<hr/>

[4] *Corr.*, ii. 268 and iv. 332.
[5] E. Zola, *Mes Haines: Causeries littéraires et artistiques*, 1880, p. 205, and J. Lemaître, *Les Contemporains*, s.d. (Boivin), 8 vols., vi. 311.
[6] E. Boutmy, *Taine, Scherer, Laboulaye*, 1901, p. 35; cf. Bourget, op. cit., i. 211.
[7] Cf. the interesting discussions of occasional resemblances between Taine and Bergson in G. Barzellotti, *La Philosophie de H. Taine*, 1900, pp. 165–7, and A. Chevrillon, *Taine—Formation de sa pensée*, 1932, pp. 135–47.
[8] *Corr.*, i. 79.
[9] *Essais*, p. 48, and *Corr.*, iv. 333.
[10] Cited by V. Giraud, *Essai sur Taine*, 6e éd., s.d. (Hachette), p. 175.

of him: 'Celui-là du moins n'a jamais menti.'[11] Honesty and devotion to truth are no insurance against error or ambiguity, however, and a salient feature of Taine criticism is the widely divergent interpretations that have been advanced about his philosophical position. Many have seen him as the supreme positivist of his time: this is the view of contemporaries like Scherer, Caro, and Paul Janet and of later historians like Faguet, Weber, Benrubi, Lalande, and Meyerson.[12] Others, like Lenoir and Kahn, have maintained that he is an idealist, a disciple of Hegel and Spinoza, whilst one of Taine's best expositors, Rosca, cogently argues that it is wholly erroneous to link him with positivism.[13] Yet others, including Boutmy, Giraud, and René Berthelot, agree he is not a positivist but, unlike Rosca, do not assign him to the idealists.[14] Finally, Fouillée and Höffding suggest that he began in positivism but ended in idealism, whilst Mill and Barzellotti believe he holds an intermediate position between the two.[15]

These divergences are arresting and are not wholly explicable (as Rosca sometimes implies) by misconceptions and faulty scholarship on the part of Taine's commentators. In part it may be true that whereas in the heat of controversy Taine appeared to be a positivist, a longer perspective shows him to have been an idealist. Certainly since his death and the publication of such thorough studies as those of Giraud and Barzellotti his thought has appeared more complex and less easily categorized than many of his contemporaries might have acknowledged. Certainly, too,

---

[11] Bourget, *Essais de psychologie contemporaine*, i. 201.

[12] E. Scherer, *Mélanges de critique religieuse*, 1860; E. Caro, *L'Idée de Dieu et ses nouveaux critiques*, 1864; P. Janet, 'La Crise philosophique et les idées spiritualistes en France—I', *R.D.M.*, 15 juillet 1864, pp. 459–90; Faguet, op. cit., iii. 254; A. Weber, *Histoire de la philosophie européenne*, 1914, pp. 536–7; I. Benrubi, *Philosophische Strömungen der Gegenwart in Frankreich*, Leipzig, 1928, pp. 17–23; A. Lalande, *Vocabulaire technique et critique de la philosophie*, 1951, p. 793; E. Meyerson, *Identité et réalité*, 1912, pp. 2, 44.

[13] R. Lenoir, 'L'Idéalisme de Taine', *R.M.M.* xxiii, 1916, pp. 859–78; S. J. Kahn, *Science and Aesthetic Judgment—A Study of Taine's Critical Method*, London, 1953; D. D. Rosca, *L'Influence de Hegel sur Taine théoricien de la connaissance et de l'art*, 1928, p. 245.

[14] Boutmy, op. cit., p. 21; Giraud, op. cit., p. 44; R. Berthelot in Lalande, op. cit., p. 793.

[15] A. Fouillée, *Le Mouvement idéaliste et la réaction contre la science positive*, 1896, p. xvi; H. Höffding, *Philosophes contemporains*, 1907, pp. 67–68; J. S. Mill, *Dissertations and Discussions*, London, 1867–75, 4 vols., iv. 111–18; Barzellotti, op. cit., *passim*.

his reputation as a positivist derives to some extent less from what he wrote than from the impassioned atmosphere in which he wrote it: his belief in determinism, his devotion to the sciences, the anger aroused by his historical works combined to make him an obvious target for those who used the label of 'positivist' to discredit their opponents. Yet even in his lifetime Ravaisson, like Fouillée a little later, can allege signs of a latent idealism in Taine's philosophy.[16] Even when allowances are made for error and prejudice in the critics themselves, the disagreements about his place in nineteenth-century thought remain challenging: they can only be fully explained, it will be submitted, by reference to a conflict of loyalties in Taine himself.

(b) The search for certainty and completeness

If Taine is first and foremost an intellectual, we must look at the cast of his mind rather than his entire personality in order to find the sources of his philosophical ambiguity.

Two requirements dominate his thinking: he seeks a knowledge distinguished by both certainty and completeness. He was not made for that 'negative capability' of which Keats writes, when a mind is content to be in doubts, mysteries, and uncertainties. Doubt and scepticism or anything less than a synthesis of human knowledge are for him only the transitory stages of intellectual advance, for he possesses an unbounded confidence in the powers of man's mind. 'Je vois les limites de mon esprit, je ne vois pas celles de l'esprit humain', he asserts,[17] and since this attitude is basic to any explanation of his metaphysical hopes, it will be valuable to consider it in more detail.

An intellectual emphasis is unmistakable even in his youth. In the *Introduction* to a projected work on *La Destinée humaine*, written when he was only nineteen, he tells of the crisis he underwent at the age of fifteen.[18] Until then he had unquestioningly accepted the Christian teachings, but suddenly reason, 'comme une lumière', had forced him to question his faith. 'Ce qui tomba d'abord devant cet esprit d'examen, ce fut ma foi religieuse.' He rejects all authority except that of his own mind, and scrutinizing the doctrines of God, immortality, and moral duty he

[16] F. Ravaisson, *Rapport sur la philosophie en France au dix-neuvième siècle*, 1904, p. 105. [17] Cited by Barzellotti, op. cit., p. 129.
[18] *Corr.*, i. 21–25.

finds mere probabilities. He becomes a sceptic and, reminding us of Descartes's account of his application of the method of doubt, he describes his progress towards a complete overthrow of all received opinions.

His state of mind now is no longer one of proud pleasure in a newly found liberation.

> Je fus triste alors [he says]; je m'étais blessé moi-même dans ce que j'avais de plus cher; j'avais nié l'autorité de cette intelligence que j'estimais tant. Je me trouvais dans le vide et dans le néant, perdu et englouti.

He longs to know but everywhere finds doubts and obscurities, whilst in the philosophers he sees only contradictions and 'puerile or incomprehensible proofs'.

Pantheism brought him 'salvation' (in his own word) from this unhappy scepticism, and this early crisis is so interesting just because it reveals the inner needs which led him to embrace a creed he never thereafter abandoned. His natural bent is towards conviction, not unbelief; he is the contrary of the destructive sceptic and his devotion to pantheism and to science is almost religious in quality, as he himself recognized.[19] Metaphysics becomes 'une ancre qui fixe l'homme', and he declares that there is no joy on earth equal to that given by 'l'absolue, l'indubitable, l'éternelle, l'universelle vérité'.[20] Hence his search for certainty: possessed by 'l'amour de connaître et le goût de la science certaine', he dreams of 'pure metaphysics', '*Magna Mater!*', and he adds: 'Je n'ai d'autre paradis en tête que celui-là.'[21]

He seeks universality in knowledge as well as certainty, a synthetic view of the whole of life. Having declared to his nephew Chevrillon that he is 'the contrary of a sceptic', he goes on to affirm his confidence that all is possible to the human intelligence.

> Je crois, qu'avec des données suffisantes, celles que pourront fournir les instruments perfectionnés et l'observation poursuivie, on pourra tout savoir de l'homme et de la vie. Il n'y a pas de mystère définitif.[22]

This conviction accounts for his lifelong preoccupation with metaphysics and its method. Where the scientist ends, Taine begins his attempt to correlate and synthesize. In his youth,

---

[19] *Corr.*, i. 74–75.   [20] *Corr.*, i. 83, 71.
[21] *Corr.*, i. 46, 197.
[22] A. Chevrillon, 'La Jeunesse de Taine', *Revue de Paris*, 1902, t. iv, p. 30.

studying history and antiquity, he is constantly seeking 'les vérités générales, aspirant à connaître l'ensemble, à savoir ce qu'est l'homme et la société'; having read Guizot's *La Civilisation en Europe*—in a state of 'extraordinary transport'—he sets himself to find 'les lois générales de l'histoire, puis les lois générales de l'art d'écrire'.[23] These traits are characteristic, and they remain after he has adopted pantheism. Now, he declares, he has reached a height from which he can 'embrace the whole philosophical horizon'.[24] Where the individual sciences are incomplete and partial, the new science, metaphysics, will be 'la science complète, . . . le tout posé comme nécessaire'; 'la vraie science est celle qui explique toutes choses par rapport à l'absolu, en montrant qu'elles empruntent leur nécessité de l'absolu'.[25]

This dream of certainty and synthesis persisted all his life. It is far from being merely the fruit of youthful and over-confident enthusiasm. Throughout his maturer work he reaffirms his belief in metaphysics and expounds the method by which it can ultimately subsume all the facts and laws of the particular sciences under one 'universal formula'. It also determines his attitude to English and German philosophy.

(c) The fusion of English positivism and German idealism

Taine singles out as the most significant movements in the philosophy of his age English positivism and German idealism. Both groups have their own merits and their own failings. Although the positivists are admirable in the clarity and reliability of their method, they lack all concern for metaphysics; they are too earth-bound, too preoccupied with experimental data.[26] The idealists, on the other hand, whilst interested above all in metaphysics, have ignored experience and thought wholly in terms of abstractions; their magnificent metaphysical structures have crumbled because they had no foundation in observed reality. The ruins of their systems have a double message for us: they indicate 'le but qu'il faut enfin atteindre et la voie qu'il ne faut point d'abord tenter'.[27] Consequently, since the English seek

[23] *Corr.*, i. 21–22.   [24] *Corr.*, i. 25.
[25] Cited by Chevrillon, op. cit., p. 92.
[26] H. Taine, *Histoire de la littérature anglaise*, 18e éd., Hachette, s.d., 5 vols. [*Litt. angl.*], v. 300.
[27] H. Taine, *Les Philosophes classiques du dix-neuvième siècle en France*, 13e éd., Hachette, s.d. [*Philos.*], p. 370.

certainty but not synthesis and the Germans synthesis without certainty, Taine believes that future philosophy must transcend both schools—by fusing their respective merits. This is the distinctive task of French philosophy, he thinks, for the French have traditionally excelled in teaching Europe how to order ideas. The art of clear expression and the notion of method, first in Descartes but supremely in Condillac and his contemporaries, are France's great contributions to philosophy. Its role is one of mediation: set between these two nations of philosophers, it must try to reconcile them and thereby to offer a new method for European thought. 'Les faits découverts en Angleterre et les théories inventées en Allemagne ont besoin de passer par nos livres pour recevoir en Europe le droit de cité.'[28]

Taine's aim is thus nothing less than a fusion of positivism and idealism, of Mill and Hegel. He will formulate a method derived from positivism that shall be applicable to metaphysics, and he believes this can be done by borrowing certain presuppositions found in Hegel and Spinoza. Hence, it will be argued, the duality in Taine's position as a philosopher: it stems from this effort to have the best of both philosophical worlds, to unite in a higher synthesis positivism, the champion of science, and its antithesis, idealism, the champion of metaphysics.

Although it may seem to us foreordained to failure, Taine's attempt is one to admire none the less. The relation of science and metaphysics is one of the foremost problems of his time, considered in turn by Renan, Vacherot, Ravaisson, Lachelier, Boutroux, Renouvier, and a score of others. Taine is amongst the great protagonists in the dispute around this question, and even his errors helped to clarify the issues involved in it. In a sense, the two opposing sides meet—and conflict—in him, and thus his thinking illustrates a tension in nineteenth-century French philosophy in general.

2. Taine's Positivism

(a) His theory of knowledge

We are following Taine's own practice if we look first at the similarities between his standpoint and positivism. Although, chronologically, he first embraced the idealist assumptions he

---

[28] *Philos.*, p. 20, and *Litt. angl.*, v. 374.

took from Spinoza and Hegel, when he is expounding his own thought in *Les Philosophes classiques* (as he later entitled his book of 1857) the account of the positivist method precedes his idealist emendations of it, and again in the *Histoire de la littérature anglaise* he propounds his own views by reference to his prior account of Mill's theory of knowledge.

Any sketch of his affinities with positivism must begin by remarking his independence of Comte. He appears to have studied him closely only in 1860 or 1861 and again in 1864 when he reviewed the second edition of the *Cours de philosophie positive* in the *Journal des débats*. Chevrillon points out that in Taine's juvenilia, both published and unpublished, no mention of Comte is to be found.[29] Taine himself confirms Chevrillon's finding when he writes in 1864:

La plupart des personnes qui lisent étaient, je suppose, dans le même état que moi à l'endroit de M. Comte. On le connaissait par parcelles: on avait parcouru des extraits ou des comptes-rendus de ses ouvrages, et l'on s'en était tenu là, non sans bonnes raisons, du moins apparentes.[30]

Recently, he continues, the adherence to Comtism of thinkers like Charles Robin, Littré, Buckle, and Mill has prompted a closer study. 'Je l'ai entrepris pour mon compte il y a trois ou quatre ans, et je pense que tout homme amateur de science et de philosophie doit le faire.' Now he can affirm:

pour la première fois, un homme a examiné ce que c'est que la *science*, non pas en général, d'après une idée spéculative, et, pour ainsi dire, en l'air, comme ont fait les autres philosophes, mais d'après des sciences existantes et effectives.

He also points out certain inferiorities, however. Comte's style and the strangeness of his later religious views had dissuaded him from reading Comte earlier, he says, and chief amongst his other faults are his incompetence and dogmatism in metaphysics, literature, history, and psychology (in all Taine's special fields, in short). Taine differs from his predecessor on too many important points, in fact, for there to be any question of discipleship. Where Comte dismissed psychology as a separate science and believed that the

---

[29] Chevrillon, op. cit., p. 223, note 2.
[30] Article on the second edition of the *Cours de philosophie positive*, *Journal des débats*, 6 juillet 1864.

only genuinely scientific parts of it were reducible to physiology and sociology, to Taine it is the queen of the sciences. Where Comte declares metaphysics impossible in a positive age, Taine regards it as the summit of human speculation. Where Comte's chief interest is in the reorganization of society, Taine's aim is to seek truth without any ulterior intention.[31] Where Comte's style is tangled and rebarbative, Taine believes one of the tasks of French philosophy is to express itself lucidly and plainly. It may be—although there is no evidence—that Taine was encouraged by the example of Comte or that occasional minor additions to his views derive from the *Cours*; but Chevrillon has shown that all Taine's major ideas had been developed before he knew Comte by more than hearsay. One cannot claim, therefore, that he took his main concepts or his method from the founder of the positive religion. Taine's positivism is parallel to Comte's; it does not stem from it.

The resemblances between Taine's position and positivism are none the less very close and, in the face of those critics who tend to neglect them, need to be stressed. First and foremost he agrees that the basis of all our knowledge of reality must be sense-experience: 'Toute réalité est perçue expérimentalement par l'homme.' This insistence is found throughout his work: in his youthful criticisms of the ideologues;[32] in the discussion on method which concludes *Les Philosophes classiques*, where the idealist Paul accepts Pierre's positivism as a 'necessary beginning' for his own method; in the two *Préfaces* to the *Essais de critique et d'histoire* (1858 and 1866); and again in his study of Mill, where he even seems at times to be trying to outdo the positivists in his positivism.

Nous allons même plus loin que vous. . . . Nous pensons qu'il n'y a rien au monde que des faits et des lois, c'est-à-dire des événements et leurs rapports, et nous reconnaissons comme vous que toute connaissance consiste d'abord à lier ou à additionner des faits.[33]

De l'intelligence is written from the same experimental stand-

---

[31] Cf. *Philos.*, p. 141: 'Quelle différence y a-t-il entre un philosophe et un orateur? Un philosophe cherche à trouver et à prouver des vérités générales, rien de plus. Il aime la science pure, et ne s'occupe pas de la vie pratique; il ne songe pas à réformer le genre humain.'

[32] Cited by Chevrillon, op. cit., p. 134.

[33] *Philos.*, p. 349, *Essais*, pp. xxi, xxviii, and *Litt. angl.*, v. 357–8.

point: only observation and experiment can establish the new science of psychology. In the *Préface*, in well-known words, he reaffirms this principle:

De tout petits faits bien choisis, importants, significatifs, amplement circonstanciés et minutieusement notés, voilà aujourd'hui la matière de toute science. . . .[34]

This basic tenet leads Taine to further agreement with the positivists. First, he rejects the 'false' abstraction exemplified by the eclectics, Hegel and Spinoza—and for the same reason as the positivists: this is so much the case that his attack on the eclectics in *Les Philosophes classiques* has usually and rightly been thought a significant date in the history of French positivism. All abstracts, he urges, must be extracts from experience if they are to be valid, and we must also beware of concluding that there are any 'abstract entities' which correspond to the abstract words we use. The eclectics ignored these two principles: it was this which ruined Maine de Biran's system and reduced Cousin's philosophy to 'un monceau de phrases inexactes, de raisonnements boiteux et d'équivoques visibles'.[35] The same errors have vitiated German idealism.[36] He himself, he adds in *De l'intelligence*, will treat psychology as 'une science de faits', and throughout the work he insists that we exclude from our study such non-existent entities as *faculté, capacité, pouvoir,* and the like: these are merely convenient names for grouping 'tous les faits d'une espèce distincte'.[37]

Consequently Taine denies that 'the self' and 'substance' have any real existence as separate entities: they are 'des illusions métaphysiques'. In more recent words, there is no 'ghost in the machine'. 'Il n'y a rien de réel dans le moi sauf la file de ses événements', and these 'events' 'sont les mêmes en nature et se ramènent tous à la sensation'.[38] The notion of a 'material substance' is just as illusory as that of a 'spiritual substance'. Even the strictest empiricists have fallen into this error by postulating a primitive substance, 'la matière douée de force', lying behind

[34] H. Taine, *De l'intelligence*, 16ᵉ éd., Hachette, s.d., 2 vols. [*Intell.*], i. 2.
[35] *Philos.*, p. 292.   [36] Cf. *Litt. angl.*, v. 249.
[37] *Intell.*, i. 1–2.
[38] *Intell.*, i. 6–7. In a footnote Taine adds that he had first expressed this view in November 1855. For a still closer resemblance to the author of *The Concept of Mind*, cf. *Intell.*, i. 338–9: 'Ce sont là des êtres métaphysiques, purs fantômes, engendrés par les mots, et qui s'évanouissent dès qu'on examine scrupuleusement le sens des mots.'

our sense-data, and the positivists too are guilty here, for they postulate beyond the phenomenal world 'une région inaccessible, celle des substances'.[39] Spencer is the best example of this: 'l'hypo-thèse scolastique d'une substance inconnaissable' is 'la partie faible et arriérée' of the *First Principles*.[40] But Taine holds that it is a mistake made by all positivists when they allege that we can have no knowledge of causes. His great claim, in contrast, is that causes are an integral part of the facts of sense-experience and can therefore be known by abstraction from them.

Finally, he rejects the notion of *a priori* knowledge. This is implicit in his account of his own method of abstraction, and it is especially evident in his treatment of Cousin's theory of the reason as 'la faculté ou pouvoir qu'a l'esprit de produire les axiomes et les idées des objets infinis'.[41] It likewise prompts his criticisms of the two thinkers to whom he perhaps owed most, Spinoza and Hegel. As early as 1852 he writes to a friend after reading the last volume of Hegel's *Logic*:

Hélas! encore une illusion tombée! Cela est grand, mais cela n'est pas la métaphysique vraie; la méthode est artificielle, et cette construc-tion de l'absolu tant vantée est inutile.[42]

Spinoza commands no more respect, and even in 1849 Taine affirms: 'Il n'est mon maître qu'à moitié. Je crois qu'il a tort sur plusieurs questions fondamentales.'[43] Spinoza's *a priori*, quasi-mathematical method cannot give us any knowledge as to what exists, and it fails to distinguish between 'conceptions' and 'per-ceptions'. Spinoza did not see the real question: he proves that the notion of substance does not imply any contradiction, but that does not prove that substance exists. 'Il démontre des possibilités, non des existences.'[44] Taine will take from Hegel the idea of development (*Entwicklung*), for him 'the fundamental idea of the present age'—but 'not *a priori* as in Hegel, but purely *a posteriori*'.[45] Similarly, his final system may be largely Spinozist,

[39] *Intell.*, i. 8, 348.
[40] H. Taine, *Derniers essais de critique et d'histoire*, 6e éd., Hachette, 1923, p. 199.
[41] *Philos.*, pp. 153-4.   [42] *Corr.*, i. 217.
[43] *Corr.*, i. 75.
[44] Cited by Chevrillon, op. cit., p. 93.
[45] Cf. J. M. Carré, *Les Écrivains français et le mirage allemand (1800-1940)*, 1947, p. 90; and Chevrillon, op. cit., pp. 211-12 and 404-5.

but, as Hommay remarks, his will be 'un spinozisme rajeuni et transformé par le contact de la science moderne'.[46]

(b) The method of abstraction

There is also reason to think that Taine was true to positivism even when he believed he was transcending it. Throughout his work he represents 'true' abstraction as an *addition* to the positivist theory of method. Yet in reality the use of abstraction he advocates is constantly practised by natural scientists (as Taine himself is encouraged to notice) and is wholly consistent with positivism. The explanation of this paradoxical situation lies in a confusion in Taine's mind between the actual method and his understanding of the results it can give.

First, however, we must look at the method itself as Taine expounds it. The first full statement is found in *Les Philosophes classiques*.[47] The scientist or thinker must begin by gathering facts, but for the idealist Paul this is only 'le commencement de la science'. One must now search for the causes which order and determine these facts. 'Every group of facts has its cause', he asserts, and our knowledge is fragmentary and incomplete until we have discovered them. A cause is here defined as 'un fait d'où l'on puisse déduire la nature, les rapports et les changements des autres'. We proceed by abstracting what is common to a whole group of facts in order to form an hypothesis as to what is its 'causal fact'; we then test experimentally whether this hypothesis is justified. 'Abstraction, hypothèse, vérification, tels sont les trois pas de la méthode. Il n'en faut pas davantage, et il les faut tous.'

This method, we can note, is precisely that by which all scientific laws are discovered, provided only that Taine means no more by the terms 'cause' and 'causal fact' than the scientist means by the term 'law', and those who consider him a positivist have understood his use of the terms in this way.[48] The author himself is at pains to emphasize that his procedure is none other than that of the sciences, and he also alleges that he has remained wholly within the field of observed facts and has avoided the false abstraction he criticizes in the eclectics.[49]

The same emphasis on the 'scientific' nature of his method is seen in his later works. The historian and the historian of literature,

---

[46] Cited by Giraud, op. cit., p. 134.
[48] For example, Faguet, op. cit., iii. 248.
[47] *Philos.*, pp. 349–51, 363.
[49] *Philos.*, pp. 367, 362.

he says in 1858, begin by collecting facts which they then group and subject to the method of abstraction in order to discover the *force maîtresse*, the *formule*, the *faculté maîtresse* that will explain them. This process, he insists, is far more than a personal ordering of the facts; it is scientific, and only when history utilizes his method will it cease to be a 'compilation' and become a 'science'.[50] History must 'constater des lois après avoir exposé des faits',[51] and Taine makes his position even plainer by drawing analogies with the biological sciences.

An identical view is found in the *Introduction à l'histoire de la littérature anglaise*. The literary historian gathers facts and studies the personality of the author under discussion, but this is not enough. 'Est-ce une psychologie qu'un cahier de remarques?' Taine's reply is negative: 'La recherche des causes doit venir après la collection des faits.' As is well known, he then discerns the three great causes of *race*, *moment*, and *milieu*. Once again he links his approach with the scientific method:

La seule différence qui sépare ces problèmes moraux des problèmes physiques, c'est que les directions et les grandeurs ne se laissent pas évaluer ni préciser dans les premiers comme dans les seconds.

Despite this minor drawback (in Taine's view), the study of literature has a significant contribution to make to the science of psychology.[52]

His chapter on Mill in the *Histoire* reinforces this position. He agrees with Mill that all knowledge must be built upon facts, but when these have been gathered, a new operation may begin—and at this point Taine believes he is stepping beyond positivism. A new faculty—abstraction—enters, enthusiastically welcomed by Taine.

Une faculté magnifique apparaît, source du langage, interprète de la nature, mère des religions et des philosophies, seule distinction véritable, qui, selon son degré, sépare l'homme de la brute, et les grands hommes des petits.

[50] *Essais*, p. xi.
[51] *Essais*, p. xxiv.
[52] *Litt. angl.*, t. i, pp. xv, xxix. Cf. the parallel with the conception of *philologie* as the basis of a new 'science of man' found in Renan and others. Taine concentrates on more modern literature and is a more scientific psychologist than Renan, but one can note his praise of Renan's philological work (*Litt. angl.*, v. 252).

This faculty he defines as 'le pouvoir d'isoler les éléments des faits et de les considérer à part'. I contemplate a square, for example, and abstract the equality of its sides and angles: thus I seize upon the constituent properties, the 'inner nature' of all squares. All groups of facts can be reduced to their components in this way, and Taine adds that these components or 'abstracts' are what are usually called forces, causes, laws, or essences. They have no existence in themselves, however: 'tout abstrait est un *extrait*, retiré et arraché d'un concret, cas ou individu, dans lequel il réside'. Thus he can stress again that his method is essentially scientific: abstraction, side by side with experiment and observation, is 'la grande opération scientifique'.[53] Unfortunately, whilst this claim is thus far broadly justifiable, he now belies it by the interpretation of the method's results which he puts forward, and here also he unambiguously deserts positivism.

3. Taine's 'Scientific Metaphysics'

This interpretation clearly reflects his search for certainty and universality of knowledge. He begins his *critique* of Mill precisely by pointing to their absence from the body of knowledge positivism admits to be valid. Mill's outlook is 'an abyss of chance' and 'an abyss of ignorance'; if scientists ignore 'la connaissance des premières causes', we are condemned either to scepticism or to the unscientific phantoms of our own feelings and imagination.[54]

How can scientists do other than this, we may wonder? Science may give us 'practical certainty' and its laws may be justified by their predictive utility, but strictly speaking it cannot offer us more than working hypotheses (as Henri Poincaré had to remind Taine's successors early in the following century). And even if we deny the view that causal relationships can never be known to exist outside our own minds, we certainly cannot hold that the same causal relationships which we postulate now will continue to obtain in the future or that they do and will obtain in parts of the universe we cannot observe.[55] The scientific method and the nature of induction are such that we can at best reach a knowledge

[53] *Litt. angl.*, v. 358–9, 363; and *Corr.*, iv. 332.
[54] *Litt. angl.*, v. 355–6.
[55] Cf. the passages from Mill cited by Taine himself, *Litt. angl.*, v. 352–3.

that is probable and that applies only to that small section of the universe which we have been able to study scientifically.[56]

Taine denies that our knowledge is subject to these limitations: abstraction allows us to surmount them. The contrast between his attitude and positivism may be seen in his account of the nature of definitions in his chapter on Mill.[57] One may define a sphere as the solid generated by the revolution of a semicircle about its diameter. For Mill this is merely a definition of a name, of our use of the word 'sphere'; there is no definition of things. Taine agrees that it defines a name, but it also defines the 'generating formula' from which all the properties of every sphere are derived. It expresses 'la cause intérieure et primordiale de toutes ses propriétés', and such, he adds, is the nature of every 'true definition'. 'True definitions' are to be distinguished from other possible descriptions. We might describe a sphere by saying that of all bodies having an equal surface it occupies the most space, but this would only give us a property of the sphere which is 'caractéristique et dérivée', not 'génératrice et première'. And since the aim of all science, Taine thinks, should be knowledge of 'causes' and 'inner natures', it follows that the supreme scientific goal is to arrive at 'true definitions'. When it succeeds in doing this a science becomes 'explicative'. Its range is now immensely widened. It is no longer confined to the 'how' of phenomena; it can grasp the 'why' of reality. For every fact and every 'law' (understood in the more limited sense used by the natural scientist) we can discover 'la raison explicative' and thus build up 'notre trésor de raisons explicatives'. In his confidence Taine proclaims:

Nous ne sommes plus capables seulement de connaissances relatives et bornées; nous sommes capables aussi de *connaissances absolues et sans limites....*[58]

The way is also opened for the creation of a scientific metaphysics. Having discovered the 'causes' governing particular groups of facts, we may then seek by abstraction for the 'raisons explicatives' from which they in their turn are derived. Having reached the all-inclusive 'definition' of each particular science in this way, we may advance still farther and, again by abstraction,

[56] Taine believes that induction rightly used can give certain knowledge, and here again he distinguishes his position from Mill's. Cf. *Intell.*, i. 5, note.

[57] *Litt. angl.*, v. 359–62.

[58] *Essais*, p. viii, and *Intell.*, ii. 444, 383–4 (my italics). Cf. *Litt. angl.*, v. 365.

seize the supreme and primary causes from which everything else in Nature springs. We shall at last have uncovered those first causes with which metaphysics is concerned and be able to contemplate in rapture 'ces définitions souveraines', 'ces créatrices immortelles, seules stables à travers l'infinité du temps . . . , seules indivisibles à travers l'infinité de l'étendue'. And we may 'dare' to go even further than this and subsume even these definitions under 'le fait primitif et unique d'où elles se déduisent et qui les engendre'. Now we shall have discovered 'the unity of the universe', conquered the summit of the pyramid of knowledge, and achieved the final aim of science. Now, at last, we shall be transported to the very 'bosom' of Nature and watch 'comme d'une source, se dérouler, par des canaux distincts et ramifiés, le torrent éternel des événements et la mer infinie des choses'.[59]

As Taine views this future achievement of his method, he not only mixes his metaphors, but the cautious, careful attitude of the scientist yields to the exaltation of the pantheist. Man is overwhelmed by an almost religious awe; his mind is elevated above the mortality and insignificance of the human condition; he sees the completed pattern of the tapestry of Nature, not merely its reverse side.[60]

C'est à ce moment que l'on sent naître en soi la notion de la Nature. . . . Au suprême sommet des choses, au plus haut de l'éther lumineux et inaccessible, se prononce l'axiome éternel, et le retentissement prolongé de cette formule créatrice compose, par ces ondulations inépuisables, l'immensité de l'univers.[61]

This pantheistic vision is the ultimate reward of a scientific metaphysics, of this 'science des premières causes' whose results, won through the method of abstraction, will possess both certainty and universality. We have come a long way from positivism; how far we must now attempt to judge.

4. Taine's Idealism

The assumptions underlying his conception of abstraction are taken from Hegel and Spinoza, from the latter in particular, and here his 'idealism' is far more in evidence than the positivist emphases that have been noticed previously. It is these

[59] *Philos.*, pp. 368-9.   [60] *Philos.*, p. 371, and *Litt. angl.*, v. 368.
[61] *Philos.*, p. 370.

assumptions—and the features of Taine's philosophy resulting from them—which validate Rosca's conclusion:

Hippolyte Taine comprend Hegel à travers le Spinoza hégélien, Spinoza mathématicien et mécaniste, et bâtit, avec des matériaux qu'il puise des deux mains dans les écrits de Hegel, un système qui, dans ses assises fondamentales, n'est qu'un système spinoziste.[62]

It is thus worth while to remember his youthful intellectual crisis, in which all his previous beliefs were undermined by doubt, and to recall that it was his discovery of Spinoza which ended this period of unhappy scepticism. Spinoza's pantheism, he says, was his salvation, and he goes on to describe the liberation and re-direction of mind that resulted from this contact. His account captures precisely the vision of a universal and absolute science just outlined.

En effet, dès lors, la métaphysique me parut intelligible et la science sérieuse. J'arrivai, à force de chercher, à une hauteur d'où je pouvais embrasser tout l'horizon philosophique, comprendre l'opposition des systèmes, voir la naissance des opinions, découvrir le nœud des divergences et la solution des difficultés. Je sus ce qu'il fallait examiner pour trouver le faux ou le vrai. Je vis le point où je devais porter toutes mes recherches. Je possédais d'ailleurs la méthode; je l'avais étudiée par curiosité et amusement. Dès lors je me mis avec ardeur au travail; les nuages se dissipèrent; je compris l'origine de mes erreurs; j'aperçus l'enchaînement et l'ensemble.[63]

This remarkable passage, written shortly before he was twenty, expresses a view that never deserted him and that dictated the better-known pantheistic passages found at the end of *Les Philosophes classiques*, in 'Sainte-Odile', and elsewhere. This vision of the world as a necessary and determined unity is far from being the conclusion of Taine's metaphysical thinking, as it might sometimes seem when he speaks as if it were derived from the workings of abstraction. Its priority is not only chronological but also rational. It inspires his belief in the validity of his search for a scientific metaphysics and is assumed behind his interpretation of the method of abstraction.[64]

---

[62] Rosca, op. cit., p. 414.   [63] *Corr.*, i. 25.

[64] The same would seem to be true of Taine's master, Spinoza. Cf. S. Hampshire, *Spinoza*, Harmondsworth, 1951, p. 218: 'Spinoza's whole metaphysics is substantially contained in his notion of Nature, as a whole, as the unique substance; as soon as he is granted the use of this notion, together with the tradi-

The principal assumptions he makes relate to the notion of causality, a notion whose importance in his whole system one could hardly overestimate. Our knowledge of objects is defined as knowledge of their causes.[65] Hence the aim of all science becomes the discovery of causes, and metaphysics is seen as 'la recherche des premières causes', for that, in his view, is exactly equivalent to the study of the nature of being or reality.[66] Again he remarks:

Il y a toute une classe de choses, substances, essences, causes, natures, forces, qu'on nomme êtres métaphysiques, et qui, en effet, sont la matière de la métaphysique. Tous ces noms se réduisent à un, qui est celui de cause. . . .[67]

In the *Préface* to *Les Philosophes classiques* he openly declares: 'On vient de voir que cette philosophie a pour origine une certaine notion des causes.' And he adds: 'J'ai tâché ici de justifier et d'appliquer cette notion. Je n'ai point cherché autre chose *ici ni ailleurs*.'[68] Not surprisingly, therefore, the assumptions he makes concerning causality are at the foundation of his entire method.

The two reigning philosophies, eclecticism and positivism, both have an unsatisfactory theory of causation in his opinion. Eclecticism gives an independent existence to causes and regards them as entities that are distinct from their effects. Positivism, on the other hand, refuses to say anything about the causal realm: we can search only for the laws of coexistence and succession of phenomena. 'Les spiritualistes relèguent les causes hors des objets, les positivistes relèguent les causes hors de la science.'[69] The first group transgresses Taine's view that all our knowledge must be grounded in experience. The second group, as he rightly saw, introduces the possibility of chance into the world and condemns us to a purely relative, hypothetical knowledge.

Spinoza and Hegel offered him the elements of an alternative account of causation which he adopted as a young man and retained for the rest of his life. It is the idea of cause held by the idealist philosophers, it may be recalled, which he undertakes to

tional connotations of the word "substance", he is already launched on his way to his final conclusions. What must we suppose if Nature as a whole is to be regarded as completely intelligible? This is the question from which Spinozism begins.'

[65] *Essais*, p. iv.
[66] *Philos.*, p. vi, and *Litt. angl.*, v. 373.
[67] *Philos.*, p. vi.
[68] *Philos.*, p. x (my italics).
[69] *Philos.*, pp. vi–vii.

defend against the Oxonian disciple of Mill's philosophy.[70] He takes from Spinoza, first, the assumption of a rigorous determinism in the world, the belief that 'nothing in the universe is contingent'. Secondly, he accepts his assertion that 'the order and connexion of ideas is the same as the order and connexion of things'—that reality is rational and therefore rationally comprehensible.[71] Hegel, whom he studied a little later than Spinoza, confirmed him in these assumptions. His interpretation of the concept of 'evolution' in the German philosopher, for example, is in terms of the notion of a universal determinism.

Toutes les idées élaborées depuis cinquante ans en Allemagne se réduisent à une seule, celle du *développement* (*Entwicklung*), qui consiste à représenter toutes les parties d'un groupe comme solidaires et complémentaires, en sorte que chacune d'elles nécessite le reste, et que toutes réunies, elles manifestent, par leur succession et leurs contrastes, la qualité intérieure qui les assemble et les produit.[72]

Hegel, he declares in his first enthusiasm, 'c'est Spinoza agrandi par Aristote, et debout sur cette pyramide de sciences que l'expérience moderne construit depuis trois cents ans'.[73] The effect of these two doctrines upon Taine's theory of knowledge is far-reaching. The postulation of absolute determinism banishes the possibility of chance in the universe. We are perceiving relationships that are necessary, not merely contingent, when we discern a linking of cause and effect. Where the positivist's 'law' amounts to no more than a statement that two facts are apparently linked, a 'law' as Taine now conceives it posits that these two facts really are and necessarily must be linked. Furthermore, this type of determinism guarantees the unity of the whole of Nature, each and every part of it causally related to the rest. Nature is 'une hiérarchie de nécessités' and therefore 'un être unique, indivisible, dont tous les êtres sont les membres'.[74] The second assumption allows Taine to discount Kant's relativism. The real and the rational are identified; causal

[70] *Litt. angl.*, v. 356.
[71] Spinoza, *Ethics*, Part I, Proposition xxix, and Part II, Proposition vii (*Opera*, recog. J. van Vloten et J. P. N. Land, The Hague, 1913–14, 4 vols., i. 60 and 77).
[72] *Litt. angl.*, v. 247.
[73] *Philos.*, p. 133. His admiration persisted despite the reservations he makes; in 1870 he joins with Renan in trying to raise a subscription for a Hegel monument.
[74] *Philos.*, p. 370; cf. *Intell.*, ii. 383–4.

necessity is not imposed by our mind upon the world—perhaps illegitimately—but resides in the 'things in themselves'. It is not we who project intelligibility upon the world; the world itself is intelligible. He remarks in *De l'intelligence* that our need to suppose that there are necessary relations and a necessary order in the universe no doubt possesses (with a passing concession to Kant) 'pour cause première notre structure mentale'—but it also possesses 'pour cause dernière l'ajustement de notre esprit à la structure des choses'.[75] The same conviction also allows him to surmount the phenomenalism of the positivists. The correlation between reality and our minds vouches for the reliability of our perceptions. Perception is 'une hallucination *vraie*'.[76] Thus Descartes's 'malignant demon', which has plagued empiricist philosophy, is effectively banished!

The differences between these presuppositions and the working assumptions made by positivism and the natural sciences may seem small, but they are all-important. Where the latter accept the notions of universal determinism and of the rationality of the universe as hypotheses, Taine is asserting that they are certainties. Where they consequently claim no more than a high degree of probability for their conclusions, he holds that his method can give absolute and certain knowledge. Equally important, whilst they believe that causes in Taine's sense are never the data of experience and can therefore never be known by us, Taine, on the basis of his assumptions, is able to contend that by abstraction from the data of experience we can move beyond phenomena to study the 'causes', the 'essential natures', of everything in Nature, the human mind included, and that thereby a scientific metaphysics becomes possible.

5. *The Fusion of Positivism and Idealism*

Has Taine's attempt to unite science and metaphysics succeeded? It is highly doubtful. The very undertaking seems to presuppose a misunderstanding of the limits of the scientific approach, and the outcome is a method whose confusions—verbal confusions in particular—suffice to invalidate it.

One can begin from his use of the word 'fact'. For positivism a 'fact' is equivalent to a sensation, a phenomenon, and at times

[75] *Intell.*, ii. 456.   [76] *Intell.*, ii. 10 (my italics) and *passim*.

Taine accepts this.[77] More commonly, however, he adopts a wider meaning whilst still contending that his is the scientific usage. A good instance is seen in the *Préface* to the second edition of the *Essais de critique et d'histoire*. Talking about factual evidence he declares:

> Que ce fait soit une formation de tissus observés au microscope, un chiffre d'équivalent constaté par la balance, une concordance de facultés et de sentiments démêlés par la critique, sa valeur est la même. . . .[78]

The final example of a fact given here is not a fact in the sense that applies to the first two examples. To take a different case, Taine always maintains that the causes discovered by abstraction are themselves facts; they are not metaphysical entities of the kind postulated by the eclectics. Thus he claims that nutrition and decomposition are 'causal facts' which explain the structure and organization of animals.[79] But again these are not facts in the scientific sense; they are convenient names used to summarize such facts. Similarly, he elsewhere refers to gravitation as a 'fact',[80] whereas for the scientist it accounts for many observed facts but is not itself observed.

It is clear that Taine had to consider 'causes' as 'facts' if he were to sustain his claim that in discovering them we are not merely ordering phenomena but revealing the 'generating facts' of Nature. He even maintains on occasion that the 'facts of sensation' are less real than the laws and general causes behind them. Phenomena have an *apparent* reality: 'au fond il n'existe que des abstraits, des universaux, des choses générales, lesquelles nous apparaissent comme particulières'.[81] This is one especially acute symptom of what has really happened—which is that after alleging that his method is scientific because it works always with 'facts', he then interprets 'facts' in an Hegelian sense. It is this verbal sleight of hand that permits him to contend that the method can be both scientific and metaphysical.

---

[77] Cf. *Litt. angl.*, v. 357.   [78] *Essais*, p. xxi.
[79] *Philos.*, p. 358.   [80] *Philos.*, pp. viii–ix.
[81] *Corr.*, ii. 257–8. Cf. *Intell.*, i. 11, where he even revokes his previous refusal to regard substance as anything other than a word: speaking of energy as 'une quantité constante dans la nature', he says: 'On saisit là quelque chose d'éternel; le fond immuable des êtres est atteint; on a touché la substance permanente.' Contrast, however, *Corr.*, ii. 244, where he declares, talking of himself, Renan, and Berthelot: 'Des trois, je suis le plus positiviste, le moins mystique. J'admets que les causes ne sont que les abstraits ou universaux.'

There is a parallel confusion in his use of the term 'cause'. Having claimed to use it in its scientific meaning,[82] he proceeds to attribute quite different senses to it. First, he confuses efficient and final causes, as Lachelier, Caro, and others have often pointed out, and despite Chevrillon's disclaimer it is difficult to deny that the charge is well founded.[83] He alleges, for instance, that the species to which an animal belongs is a cause and not just the sum total of certain individual animals.[84] Secondly, as has been seen, where the scientist's 'law' is an empirically tested hypothesis which can never have more than great probability, Taine's 'law' or causal relationship is claimed to be necessary and absolute. Here again Taine has accepted an Hegelian usage whilst pretending to accept a scientific usage.

The terms 'fact', 'cause', and also 'law' thus have in Taine's system, as Rosca concludes, 'une valeur profondément différente de celle qu'ils possèdent dans la conception positiviste'.

Ils ont [he adds] . . . une signification hégélienne et non pas positiviste ou empiriste. C'est donc en ce qu'elle a de plus profond que la doctrine de Taine diffère de celle d'Auguste Comte et de Stuart Mill.

We can also agree with Rosca that positivism is no more the starting-point, in a sense, than the conclusion of Taine's philosophy.[85] The pantheistic vision of Nature which Taine suggests will await us at the summit of the pyramid of knowledge is in reality presupposed in the assumptions of universal determinism and the identity of the real and the rational, and it is upon these assumptions that he builds his method. Unlike Rosca, however, we have stressed that Taine's allegiance is not to idealism alone, as Rosca sometimes seems to imply, but also to positivism—not only to Spinoza and Hegel but also to Mill, a master amongst dull mediocrities, whose equal has not been seen since Hegel, as Taine describes him in the preface to Le Positivisme anglais. This analysis is perhaps psychologically more faithful to Taine's case, and it also helps to account for the divergence between critics concerning Taine's philosophical standpoint.

Taine's divided loyalty accounts in part for the weakness of

---

[82] *Philos.*, p. 367.
[83] J. Lachelier, 'Fragments d'un article sur Taine', cited by Giraud, op. cit., pp. 297–8; Caro, op. cit., pp. 222–3; Chevrillon, op. cit., p. 272.
[84] *Philos.*, p. 136.
[85] Rosca, op. cit., pp. 276, 259 note.

his system but it equally helps to explain its interest. In him two of the three major currents of the century's philosophy seek to intermingle. Only the stream of Kantian *criticisme* is missing. He had a warm regard for Renouvier and Cournot, the leading neo-criticists of his day,[86] but he is less a critical philosopher in the Kantian sense than a reincarnation of the geometric spirit of the seventeenth century. Like Spinoza, Taine aspires to found a method that shall be mathematical; he is seeking for certainty and universality in other spheres of knowledge because he has already found them in mathematics. Already in 1849 we find him minimizing the differences between mathematics and the natural sciences,[87] and it may be that certain of his errors would have been avoided—as he himself perhaps realized at the very last—if he had been more sympathetic to Kant—the philosopher who began his thinking from the question: 'How is mathematical knowledge possible?' Kantianism apart, however, Lenoir's comment on Taine is justified:

> Plus proche des éclectiques qu'il ne le pense, il fait l'inventaire des idées contemporaines pour les rapprocher et, lorsqu'elles lui paraissent opposées, les concilier.[88]

6. *Taine's Views on Religion, Metaphysics, and Ethics*

Taine's philosophical speculation is largely confined to the elaboration of his method. He applies it to the fields of history, literature, art, and psychology but not to the various branches of philosophy itself or to the study of religions.

Some critics have seen Taine as irreligious by temperament, whilst others, like Giraud, see in him 'un fond d'exaltation mys-

[86] Cf. *Corr.*, ii. 353, and a review cited by Giraud, op. cit., p. 243, in which he refers to Renouvier as 'un philosophe, celui-là de la grande espèce, je veux dire indépendant, solitaire, créateur systématique . . .'. He also reviews Cournot's *Traité de l'enchaînement des idées fondamentales* with equal warmth: cf. V. Giraud, *H. Taine—Études et documents*, 1928, p. 253.

[87] Cited by Chevrillon, op. cit., pp. 104–5.

[88] Lenoir, 'L'Idéalisme de Taine', loc. cit., p. 862. His attitude to Kant is always marked by half-heartedness and reserve: cf. *Corr.*, iv. 11, 152, and Barzellotti, op. cit., p. 144. But it may be that at the end of his life he realized that it was Kant who presented the strongest objections to his method. In the notes on *Les Éléments derniers des choses* published by Barzellotti (pp. 407 ff., and cf. pp. 54, 181) he even seems to be attempting to reconcile his thought with Kant; see in particular the note written in June 1892, cited pp. 418–20, where his admissions seem to invalidate much in his method for metaphysics.

tique'.[89] Both views have some validity. We have noted that where Renan seeks a religion, Taine is mainly concerned with metaphysics. Yet his attachment to metaphysics is almost religious in its intensity, as is also his adherence to pantheism. In his youth he writes to Prévost-Paradol: 'Mon bon ami, que tu as raison de trouver la science mystique! La nature est Dieu, le vrai Dieu, . . . parfaitement belle, éternellement vivante, absolument une et nécessaire.'[90] He never loses this feeling for Nature: as the same friend remarked, he is a 'panthéiste spiritualiste'.[91] Equally, it is well known that he would refer to the work of Marcus Aurelius as his 'gospel'.[92]

Yet he never claims more than a personal authority for any religious opinion he holds. Religion, unlike metaphysics, he usually argues, cannot be scientifically established: every attempt to mingle science and religion is contrary to both. Religion for Taine is 'une sorte de poème tenu pour vrai', founded upon inspiration and faith.[93] Hence, whatever religious belief he adopted, it could not be open to positivist criticism or approval since it would never be presented as more than a personal affirmation.

Likewise—and more surprisingly—Taine offers a method for metaphysics, not a metaphysical system itself. It is certainly true that the method rests upon certain metaphysical assumptions, as we saw, but Taine goes no further. In the concluding pages of *De l'intelligence* he remarks: 'Ici, nous sommes au seuil de la métaphysique. Nous n'y entrons pas; nous n'avions à étudier que la connaissance. . . .'[94] He never advances beyond this point.

No more does he erect an ethical system, although he leaves open the way for it. He is not a materialistic determinist for whom moral judgement is irrelevant, as has sometimes been alleged, especially by his contemporaries. Universal determinism, far from invalidating moral praise and blame, is their very foundation. Replying to Bourget's portrayal of him in *Le Disciple* as Adrien Sixte, he urges that it is 'impossible sans le déterminisme de fonder le droit de punir, la justice du châtiment'.[95] If chance

[89] Giraud, *Essai sur Taine*, p. 19; cf. M. Leroy, *Taine*, 1933, p. 184.
[90] *Corr.*, i. 150.
[91] Cited by Giraud, ibid., p. 132.
[92] For example, *Corr.*, i. 175 and iv. 274.
[93] *Litt. angl.*, t. i, p. xxxiii, and *Essais*, p. 22.
[94] *Intell.*, ii. 462.
[95] *Corr.*, iv. 333, 292.

affected human decisions, moral responsibility would be undermined. Determinism, by insisting that all our decisions are caused and never the product of chance, safeguards the validity of our moral judgements. He also points out as early as 1851 that 'determined' actions are not necessarily 'constrained'—that is, wholly caused by factors outside the moral agent's control.[96] Nor, finally, can it be sustained that he is a thoroughgoing materialist. He does hold that many psychological events are the effect of prior physiological events, but not all of them. Taine's very opposition to Comte's equation of scientific psychology with the study of physiological processes indicates his true standpoint. In 1858 he affirms that the forces which govern man are 'tout humaines'.[97] And his notorious declaration that 'le vice et la vertu sont des produits comme le vitriol et le sucre' should not be understood to mean that they are physically caused; Taine believes that they are 'des produits moraux'.[98] Determinism and responsibility are thus compatible on all these counts, and in his own works Taine does not hesitate to pass moral judgements on the Jacobins, Robespierre, and Napoleon, for example, and he also assesses works of art and literature by both moral and non-moral criteria.

Taine here seems to be contradicting one of the principles he had embraced to found his method for metaphysics. If Nature is a hierarchy of necessities, as he claims in order to validate the method, it would seem that our acts are subject to very considerable external constraint—to such an extent that we can no longer be held morally responsible for them. However this may be, Taine none the less believes that moral judgements are valid and that the way is clear for the construction of an ethical system.

Yet it is most doubtful whether he would claim that the majority of his own judgements were more than 'moral recommendations' or were any more amenable to verification than religious beliefs. Morality is a social creation, and the task of the scientist is to explain a moral code not by seeking philosophical justification for it but by uncovering the causes which led to its enforcement in any particular society. Hence he can write: 'Séparons . . . la science de la poésie et de la morale pratique, comme nous l'avons séparée de la religion. . . .'[99]

---

[96] Cited by Chevrillon, op. cit., p. 117.
[97] Essais, p. xi.   [98] Litt. angl., t. i, p. xv, and Corr., iii. 214.
[99] Essais, p. 48.

Religious, metaphysical, and ethical doctrine is thus absent from Taine's work, and he himself pointed to this fact when he insisted that his task had been to devise a method of discovery and to apply it over a limited field. Answering critics who had attacked what they called his 'system', he says:

Je n'ai point tant de prétention que d'avoir un système: j'essaye tout au plus de suivre une méthode. Un système est une explication de l'ensemble, et indique une œuvre faite; une méthode est une manière de travailler et indique une œuvre à faire.[1]

These views represent only one side of an ambiguous attitude, however. They are certainly the beliefs that guide most of his work and help to give a positivistic colouring to his individual monographs. Yet at the same time he cherishes the dream that in the future we may attain not only a scientific metaphysics but also a scientific religion and ethics—and a political theory and an aesthetic that are scientific also. Our age is limited by its ignorance but we have the right to entertain hopes for future generations which we cannot admit for ourselves.

La science approche enfin, et approche de l'homme [he somewhat menacingly declares]; . . . c'est à l'âme qu'elle se prend, munie des instruments exacts et perçants dont trois cents ans d'expérience ont prouvé la justesse et mesuré la portée.

But he goes farther than this anticipation of a scientific psychology. Having summarized the past achievements of the scientific method, he concludes with a celebrated expression of faith in its future:

Dans cet emploi de la science et dans cette conception des choses il y a un art, une morale, une politique, une religion nouvelles, et c'est notre affaire aujourd'hui de les chercher.[2]

The contrast between these declarations on the future of religion and ethics and his views on their present status offers a final illustration of the tension in his thought between idealism, with its belief in the possibility of an objective religious, metaphysical, ethical, aesthetic, and political philosophy, and positivism which denies this possibility on epistemological grounds. The fact that Taine, unlike Renan, does not try to anticipate the discoveries of

[1] *Essais*, p. xiii.   [2] *Litt. angl.*, iv. 388, 390.

these new 'sciences' may save him from some of Renan's difficulties, but it cannot obscure the extent of his divergence at this
point from the positivist philosophy.

7. Conclusion

The famous passages from the conclusion of his study on Byron
just quoted have often been used by critics as examples of Taine's
scientism, and rightly so for such is the conclusion of his thought.
He illustrates with especial clarity one of the most significant dis-
tortions of positivism in the mid-nineteenth century, a distortion
arising from the intermingling of German idealism and Anglo-
French positivism. The addition of Hegel and positivism produces
scientism: this is the equation demonstrated in the philosophies
of Taine and Renan alike.

Here is a phenomenon of the utmost interest in the history of
Hegelianism as well as of French positivism. Hegel's fortunes in
France have still to be fully sketched, but even a casual inspection
reveals a double-sidedness in his impact, corresponding partially
but far from entirely with two different periods in time. On the
one hand he is presented as an idealist—in Cousin's celebrated
lectures, for example. This view is current about 1830, but it
persists to a much later date, and whilst Caro, Nourrisson, and
others are attacking Hegel as a materialist,[3] others are still interpreting him as a spiritualist—Véra in his *Introduction à la philosophie de Hegel* (1864) and Paul Janet, for example. Janet denies
that Taine and Renan are true Hegelians or that Scherer gives an
accurate account of Hegel's philosophy: positivism and German
idealism are inflexibly opposed, and he even argues that the latter
can be 'le salut du spiritualisme'.[4] On the other hand, and particularly in the period after 1850, Hegel is presented as a positivist or
as a materialist. Earlier, in a letter, Comte had praised him as 'le
plus capable de pousser la philosophie positive'.[5] After 1850 Taine,
Renan, and Scherer discover and utilize Hegelian philosophy,

---

[3] Caro, op. cit., p. 52, and E. Nourrisson, *Spinoza et le matérialisme contemporain*, 1866.

[4] P. Janet, 'Le Spiritualisme français au dix-neuvième siècle', *R.D.M.*, 15 mai
1868, p. 370. Scherer's article, 'Hégel et l'hégélianisme', appeared in the *R.D.M.*,
15 fév. 1861, pp. 812–56.

[5] Cited by E. Littré, *Auguste Comte et la philosophie positive*, 2ᵉ éd., 1864,
p. 160.

and it is now that anti-positivist critics cease to see Hegel as an ally and come more and more to identify him with positivism. Thus, in 1861, one of its Protestant antagonists, Eugène Bersier, reviewing Scherer's famous article, says of Hegel's ideas: 'En serrant de près ces idées, nous y avons vu l'expression d'une tendance qui ne diffère en rien de celle de l'école positiviste française', whilst Secrétan asserts likewise that 'le positivisme nous ramène à Hegel, comme Hegel aboutit au positivisme'.[6] This identification is commonly made at this time, and Reynaud argues, though too sweepingly, that as a result of the popularization of Hegel, 'une telle vague de naturalisme et de matérialisme déferle sur la pensée française que les représentants de la tradition catholique et spiritualiste s'émeuvent et essaient de résister'.[7] The causes of these differing interpretations require fuller study. Yet the fusion Taine effects suggests one of the reasons. Where earlier critics are surveying Hegel's thought without preconceptions, later critics bring to it very marked expectations. Hegel is now associated in their minds with the materialism (as they often believed) of contemporary positivists.

Taine contributes to a no less significant change in the notion of positivism held by his contemporaries. It comes to be connected with scientism, and writers overlook the fact that there is a wide difference between them, as great as that between Hegel's idealism and the empiricism of Condillac or Mill. Hence late-nineteenth-century critics tended to proclaim *la faillite du scientisme* as though it involved *la faillite de la science* as well, and of positivism with it. Yet many of the arguments advanced in the so-called 'reaction against positivism' of the last two or three decades of the century are in fact arguments that are effective only against scientism, against the pretentions of Taine and Renan, and do not at all challenge the positivist position or the legitimate procedures of the sciences. Nor are these arguments relevant to the more strictly scientific work of Taine himself. It is far truer to suggest—even though to do so has the appearance of paradox—that many allegedly anti-positivist contentions were valid only against those elements in the thought of Taine and Renan which

---

[6] E. Bersier, 'Revue du mois', *Revue chrétienne*, 1861, p. 225; and C. Secrétan, *La Philosophie de la liberté*, 2e éd., 1866, p. xlviii.

[7] L. Reynaud, *L'Influence allemande en France au 18e et au 19e siècles*, 1922, p. 240.

were a betrayal of positivism. Poincaré's view—a view that was often taken as supporting an anti-positivist position—that the laws of science are merely useful hypotheses coincides with the positivist standpoint; the assertion this claim contradicts and effectively destroys is Taine's theory that the scientific method can give *certain* knowledge—and in making this assertion, we have seen, he is differing from positivism itself. Likewise, the positivist is unaffected by Boutroux's submission that there is a principle of indeterminacy, an element of contingency, at work in Nature, and he is equally untouched by the belief of Boutroux and Bergson that the laws of science are abstractions imposed upon Nature. In sharp contrast, these arguments do directly challenge Taine's assertion of universal determinism and of the identity of the real and the rational; they challenge, that is to say, precisely those Spinozist assumptions which underlie his theory of method and separate it so firmly from positivism.

Consequently—however surprising it may seem—Bergson and Boutroux are at one with the positivists in the criticisms they make of Taine's conclusions. Needless to say, Mill finds more to praise in Taine than an anti-positivist might. Reviewing *De l'in-telligence*, he welcomes it as 'the first serious attempt to supply the want of a better than the official psychology', and he praises Taine for rejecting Comte's prejudice against psychology. But when he considers the final two chapters of the work, his objections are in substance precisely those that Boutroux and his fellow anti-positivists were to make. These two chapters, Mill contends,

overleap the bounds of really scientific inference and, without even the warrant of supposed intuition *a priori*, claim absolute validity through all space and time for generalisations of human thought, which we can only admit under the inherent limitations of human experience.

Taine has been misled by the clarity and sureness of the results gained in the study of mathematics.

When M. Taine goes on to claim for the first principles of other sciences—for instance, of mechanics—a similar origin and evidence to what he claims for those of geometry, and on the strength of that evidence attributes to them an absolute truth, valid for the entire universe, and independent of the limits of experience, he falls into what seem to us still greater fallacies. . . .[8]

8 Mill, op. cit., iv. 112–13, 118.

Here is the very kernel of Taine's philosophical hopes, of the impressiveness of his attempt to build a method for metaphysics and of his final failure as a philosopher. He wished, in Mill's words, to reject 'the inherent limitations of human experience', to reach up to 'an absolute truth, valid for the entire universe, and independent of the limits of experience'. His search was for a method that should yield what has been termed 'angelic knowledge', certain and universal, untainted by confusion and doubt. It is therefore not surprising if his attempt to fuse positivism and idealism and thus to perfect such a method should seem, although not ignoble, ultimately unconvincing.

VIII

POSITIVISM AND THE PARNASSIANS (1)

'UN POÈTE POSITIVISTE'—LOUISE ACKERMANN

1. Positivism and the Parnassians

OUR study so far has been restricted to philosophers. Yet positivism affected men's sensibilities as well as their intellect, and it is commonly argued, for example, that the literature of the Second Empire is overshadowed by an *état d'esprit positiviste*. Lack of space and the very intangibility of this influence, of which conclusive evidence is often hard to find, prevent a detailed discussion here: only explicit positivism can be included. But, however, historians of literature have often alleged a more definite connexion with the positivist outlook; for instance, Van Tieghem, amongst many others, can assert: 'Ce que les purs artistes de 1830–35 refusèrent aux Saint-Simoniens, les poètes de 1850–60 l'accordèrent au positivisme.'[1] A brief elaboration is thus necessary.

Such claims as Van Tieghem's need severe qualification, I believe, not least (as noted earlier[2]) because the definition of positivism they presuppose is sometimes inexact or even erroneous. Still more important, they tend to disregard or greatly to underestimate the intensity of anti-positivist aspiration in Second Empire writers and to imply that they are far less disturbed by religious and metaphysical longings than is the case. Leconte de Lisle and Louis Ménard, his friend and fellow Parnassian, offer good illustrations. Leconte de Lisle's ideas on poetry have been discussed more fully in this regard elsewhere.[3] The poet seeks to reveal 'the ideal' in his portrayal of visible beauty. He claims that poetry affords knowledge that can be gained in no other way and credits poets with a type of 'extra-human' 'vision' that can

---

[1] P. Van Tieghem, *Petite histoire des grandes doctrines littéraires en France*, 1946, p. 242. For other examples, cf. p. 1, note 1, above.

[2] Cf. p. 8 above.

[3] Cf. D. G. Charlton, 'Positivism and Leconte de Lisle's Ideas on Poetry', *French Studies*, Oxford, xi, 1957, pp. 246–59.

have no validity for the positivist. And far from believing that the poet should confine himself to naturalistic observation and description, he holds that poetic creation must involve all our faculties and a total reaction of the poet to his object. Similar aspiration is evident in the themes of religious desire and despair which resound through his actual poetry and also in his concern for 'the ideal': this determines alike his judgements on other poets, his own aesthetic, and his contemptuous reaction against his own age, against spiritual heedlessness, 'l'égoïsme de notre siècle qui ne reconnaît que l'or pour dieu', 'l'indifférence et le mépris de l'Idéal'.[4] He himself longs with his Brahma for knowledge of man's final end:

> Qui suis-je? Réponds-moi, Raison des Origines!;

and for religious faith:

> Pour quel Dieu désormais brûler l'orge et le sel?
> Sur quel autel détruit verser les vins mystiques?[5]

One can also remark the frequency in his poems of the seer, absorbed in contemplation of the metaphysical unknown—the philosopher-poet in *Les Sandales d'Empédocle*, the ascetics of *La Ravine Saint-Gilles* and *Les Ascètes*, the poet Valmiki, the Centaur in *Khirôn*, the Sachem in *Le Calumet du Sachem*.

Anti-positivist tendencies are even more marked in Ménard. After a youthful but evanescent enthusiasm for science, well seen in *Prométhée délivré* (1843), his first work, he comes to emphasize less its possibilities than its self-imposed limitations. 'Ce qui m'intéresse est hors de sa sphère. Il est inutile de l'interroger sur la destinée de l'homme, elle ne la connaît pas.'[6] He turns to *philologie*, and his attitude to *la symbolique des religions* and to Ancient Greece (of which he became a highly respected if somewhat immoderate student), as well as to poetry, reveals the strong religious impetus behind his thought. As he tries to interpret the

---

[4] C. M. Leconte de Lisle, *Premières poésies et lettres intimes*, edited by B. Guinaudeau, Fasquelle, 1902, pp. 64–65, and *Derniers poèmes*, Lemerre, 1926, p. 244. On the idealism of his Breton period, see I. Putter, *The Pessimism of Leconte de Lisle: Sources and Evolution*, Berkeley and Los Angeles, 1954, pp. 60 ff. On his religious aspiration and despair, see in particular H. Elsenberg, *Le Sentiment religieux chez Leconte de Lisle*, 1909.

[5] C. M. Leconte de Lisle, *Poèmes antiques*, Lemerre, s.d., p. 60, *La Vision de Brahma* (1857), and *Poèmes barbares*, Lemerre, s.d., p. 354, *L'Anathème* (1855).

[6] L. Ménard, *Rêveries d'un païen mystique*, éd. définitive, Crès, 1911, p. 146.

symbolic language of past mythologies, 'interrogeant la langue des symboles, cette langue mystérieuse que parlaient nos pères et que nous ne comprenons plus', he is seeking to learn 'le secret de notre destinée', to reveal the common substratum of truth contained in all religions, to discern 'un idéal mystérieux que nos rêves poursuivent toujours plus haut dans les profondeurs de l'inconnu'.[7] His goal is nothing less than a religious and ethical syncretism:

> Le temple idéal où vont mes prières
> Renferme tous les Dieux que le monde a connus

—an ambition recalling Gourmont's neat stricture upon '[ceux qui] admettent tous les dieux, n'étant pas sûrs de croire en Dieu'.[8] Likewise, his principal works as *philologue*, *De la morale avant les philosophes* (1860) and *Du polythéisme hellénique* (1863), show that his admiration goes to the religion and ethics of Greece even more than to its cult of beauty and love of liberty, and he borrows from them to formulate his own *paganisme mystique* and his *religion des morts*.[9] And in poetry he seeks to unite beauty and 'la recherche de l'idéal', his aim being that of his own Euphorion:

> Je veux de l'Idéal traduire le mystère,
> Et montrer à la terre
> Des formes de beauté dont Dieu sera jaloux.[10]

His simple but fervently held ethic is equally at variance with positivism. There is an objective moral law revealed through the conscience of each individual, and each individual possesses free will and thus moral responsibility: these are the views he defends in his *Rêveries d'un païen mystique* and allies himself with the neo-criticists to propound.[11] The core of his anti-positivism is

---

[7] L. Ménard, *Rêveries*, p. 129, and 'Les Études d'histoire religieuse d'Ernest Renan', *Revue philosophique et religieuse*, vii, 1857, p. 185. Cf. his *Lettres d'un mort*, Librairie de l'Art indépendant, 1895, p. 115.

[8] *Rêveries*, p. 206, *Panthéon*; and R. de Gourmont, *Promenades littéraires*, 4e série, 8e éd., 1920, p. 161.

[9] Cf. especially L. Ménard, *De la morale avant les philosophes*, 2e éd., Charpentier, 1863, pp. 4, 13, 157.

[10] L. Ménard, *Poèmes et rêveries d'un païen mystique*, Librairie de l'Art indépendant, 1895 (normal spelling restored), pp. 6, 219.

[11] Cf. in particular *Eschatologie* and *Lettres d'un mythologue*, *Rêveries*, pp. 154, 158, 222. Cf. *De la morale*, pp. 89, 102. For an assessment of his relation to the thought of Renouvier, to whose two reviews he contributed from their inception

here, and in his *Catéchisme religieux des libres penseurs* (1875) and elsewhere he openly denies that scientific methods provide the only road to knowledge.[12]

If we turn for a final example to the greatest novelist of the age, Flaubert, we meet parallel aspirations, however overlaid by scepticism in his mature thought. As a youth he longs for metaphysical insight, stimulated by Le Poittevin, admirer of Spinoza, Kant, Hegel, and Descartes. His earliest works—*Agonies, Novembre,* and *Mémoires d'un fou*—clearly reveal his questionings as to the purpose of life, and their mark is still visible in Saint Antoine's struggle for intellectual certainty, the discussions of Bouvard and Pécuchet, and his own studies of Spinoza and Goethe and their pantheism. Religious yearning is still more apparent in him. One need not accept Guillemin's thesis that he is unwittingly a Christian to acknowledge this, although his argument highlights it.[13] However much Flaubert satirizes the Church and its priests, he is in no doubt as to the sadness and emptiness of religious unbelief. He despises both the *voltairiens*, 'des gens qui rient sur les grandes choses', and the nineteenth-century materialists for their light-hearted rejection of God. His reactions during his visit to the Holy Sepulchre are well known, and equally symptomatic of his desire for faith are his admiration for Creuzer's *Symbolik,* his recurrent preoccupation with *La Tentation de Saint Antoine,* his reverence for Spinoza, 'le plus religieux des hommes', and his interest in Spencer's *First Principles.* For all his hatred of dogma, he never hid his respect for the 'religious sentiment', 'le plus naturel et le plus poétique de l'humanité', nor does he mock the sincere piety of Saint Julien or Félicité or, towards the end of *Bouvard et Pécuchet,* the elevation felt by the two men at the sight of a Midnight Mass.[14]

Examples could be multiplied, and to look more widely at, for instance, Second Empire poetry is to realize that most writers are either non-philosophical or opposed to positivism. In the first category come Banville, Gautier, Heredia, Glatigny, Dierx, and Coppée—and even Bouilhet, for *Mélaenis* is no more than a *conte*

in 1872 and 1878 respectively, see J. Wahl, *The Pluralist Philosophies of England and America,* translated Rothwell, London, 1925, pp. 62–72.

[12] *La Critique philosophique,* 15 juillet 1875, p. 383.

[13] H. Guillemin, *Flaubert devant la vie et devant Dieu,* 1939.

[14] For further illustration, cf. also R. Dumesnil, *Gustave Flaubert,* 1947, p. 465 and *passim.*

archéologique and *Les Fossiles* is a *poème scientifique,* an historical evocation and not a *poème philosophique.* In the second group come Hugo and Baudelaire above all, Victor de Laprade, Lafenestre, and Emmanuel des Essarts, all three Christians, and Thalès Bernard. The only writers in the 'philosophic genre' remaining, apart from Isabelle Guyon and De Ricard, both very minor figures, are Leconte de Lisle, Ménard, Madame Ackermann, and Sully Prudhomme.[15] Only they could give support to the assertion that the young poets of 1850 'furent, pour la plupart, atteints par la contagion de l'esprit positiviste'.[16] Even of these four, only the latter two have an explicit allegiance to positivist ideas, and they too, we shall see, are often as ardent as Leconte de Lisle and Ménard in their search for a non-positivist belief.

This is not at all to deny that the thought of certain writers during these years does have at times a positivistic colouring; it is to warn against over-simple and one-sided generalization and to suggest that one must look more for affinities with positivism than for clear-cut loyalties to it. An analysis of these affinities could also profitably include writers like Vigny, in whom one finds, Canat suggests, the 'moral crisis' which resulted when Comte 'succeeded in ruining the Romantic faith';[17] like Sainte-Beuve, observer rather than participant in some ways, yet sensitively reflecting the ideological life of his day; or like Dumas *fils,* soon to be a leader of *la réaction idéaliste au théâtre,* yet to a limited extent suggesting a positivist attitude in his earliest plays.[18] Zola and the Goncourts, too, are writing prior to 1870.

How far do these affinities extend? Each individual will differ, but the cases of Leconte de Lisle and Ménard are perhaps typical. In the former's thought they are discernible, first, in his rejection of religious faith—his denial of a supernatural world, of the possibility of religious knowledge through revelation and of immortality—and, secondly, in the phenomenalism of *Bhagavat, La Vision de Brahma, La Maya,* and other poems which assert our imprisonment within the circle of sense-experience. However

<hr/>

[15] Cf. A. Schaffer, *The Genres of Parnassian Poetry—A Study of the Parnassian Minors,* Baltimore, 1944, ch. ii.

[16] P. Martino, *Parnasse et symbolisme,* 1947, p. 31.

[17] R. Canat, *Du sentiment de la solitude morale chez les romantiques et les parnassiens,* 1904, p. 231. Cf. D. O. Evans, 'Alfred de Vigny and Positivism', *Romanic Review,* New York, xxxv, 1944, pp. 288–98.

[18] Cf. D. Knowles, *La Réaction idéaliste au théâtre depuis 1890,* 1934.

reluctantly, he is forced to adopt a wholly naturalistic philosophy. When he praises Greek polytheism, it is for its moral code, its respect for human dignity, its love of beauty, and its social and political consequences—not, significantly, for any supernatural element. And when he turns to Buddhism for consolation, it is to 'une manière de bouddhisme scientifique' in which even 'Nirvana' is shorn of any transcendental meaning.[19] His Indian poems evoke for preference the teaching of the Vedanta, most naturalistic of the Eastern creeds, whose main tenets are that the universe is a tissue of appearances and that death is final extinction bringing release from a life of inevitable suffering and evil. He excludes the more mystical doctrines of orthodox Buddhism —the conception of the Supreme Being, Brahma, into whom the believer may be absorbed, the 'paradise' of 'Lower Buddhism', the 'Nirvana' of 'Higher Buddhism'.[20] Here his outlook is close to positivism. Yet he never openly links them, and, more important, he also goes beyond the positivist standpoint: he slips from strict agnosticism into the assertiveness of the atheist, and instead of declaring our ignorance about the supernatural, the future life, and the 'unknowable', he proclaims their non-existence. His final moral nihilism and his fatalism are likewise aberrations that the positivist condemns. Lastly, even the coincidences that exist extend over a relatively limited area of his pessimistic thought: his is a pessimism that stems far more from moral disgust with both man and Nature, the heritage of the Romantic *mal du siècle*, political disillusion, and financial hardship, and above all from his reserved, solitary, rather misanthropic temperament.[21]

A similar metaphysical scepticism is found in Ménard—most obviously in *Le Diable au café* (1864), but underlying even his ethical affirmations and especially his religious thinking. And as early as *Prométhée délivré* this is linked with the impact of the scientific spirit:

> ... l'âge nouveau commence.
> Adieu, divine foi! l'homme a fermé son cœur;
> Il a sacrifié l'amour à la science.[22]

---

[19] C. A. Fusil, *La Poésie scientifique de 1750 à nos jours*, 1918, p. 64.

[20] Cf. the most useful article by E. Carcassonne, 'Leconte de Lisle et la philosophie indienne', *R.L.C.* xi, 1931, pp. 618–46. Leconte de Lisle's main source, E. Burnouf, *Introduction à l'histoire du bouddhisme indien*, 1844, presents both the theistic and the atheistic views (p. 18).

[21] Cf. Putter, op. cit., especially pp. 34, 65, 142. [22] *Poèmes et rêveries*, p. 36.

His epic poem *Euphorion* (1855) tells of 'un pèlerinage à la recherche de l'idéal'[23]—that ends in disappointed failure. Likewise he never achieves the reconciliation of Protestantism and free-thought to which he aspires in such *rêveries* as the *Commentaire d'un républicain* (1872) and *Alliance de la religion et de la philosophie* (1878), and that primarily because he cannot achieve a coherent 'translation' of Christian supernatural dogma into a scientifically acceptable equivalent. Again, he argues that religion is essentially an ethical code: what is not ethical is *metaphorical*, and thus he interprets the Christian 'union with God' as union with 'l'ensemble des choses', 'la loi de justice', 'le Dieu intérieur [de la conscience]', and 'le bien absolu'.[24] Elsewhere he tries to 'demythologize' Christianity—equating the Resurrection story and the myth of Dionysus, interpreting the doctrine of the Incarnation as no more than '[une] apothéose de la vertu de l'homme', linking the Passion with his own belief in the redemptive power of suffering.[25] All these uneasy intellectual devices stem from his inability to accept the reality of the supernatural and miraculous, and here an affinity with positivism is clear. Yet, as with Leconte de Lisle, it is not openly developed or acknowledged. Nor does he ever suggest that his own beliefs should be empirically verified, or try to meet positivist arguments against his postulation of an objective moral law apprehended by the individual conscience: here he thinks and concludes as if wholly unresponsive to the positivist position. Even the scepticism which reduces his *paganisme mystique* to an ethical creed with at best a hope of genuine supernatural faith in the future is never attributed to positivist influence, and it more probably derives from a wider agnostic atmosphere.[26] Ménard evokes in one of his *rêveries* a banquet of ancient prophets and teachers; one might say that the role of positivism in his thought—and in that of many of his fellow scholars of religion—is at most the role of spectral visitant at the philological feast.

Louise Ackermann and Sully Prudhomme, by contrast, are explicitly indebted to positivist thought: for this reason they are more fully studied here, whilst writers with more tenuous and

---

[23] *Poèmes et rêveries*, p. 6.   [24] *Rêveries*, p. 189; cf. pp. 161–2.
[25] In *Le Banquet d'Alexandrie*, *Rêveries*, pp. 71, 74, 82.
[26] Cf. in particular *Sacra Privata* and *Le Jour des Morts*, *Rêveries*, pp. 201, 224.

ambiguous loyalties have to be omitted. Of the two Sully Prud-homme is undoubtedly the more original: if his reputation as a poet has deservedly fallen, as a thinker it ought to be higher than it is. Madame Ackermann is less important, yet she was renowned in her day as 'un poète positiviste' (the title of Caro's article in 1874 which helped to establish her fame). Her mature poetry is philosophical in the strictest sense, the product of long, solitary study and speculation, of intellection rather than poetic imagina-tion. This may lend a certain bookish abstraction to her verse, but it also makes it to an unusual degree, as Caro remarked, 'le témoi-gnage de la crise morale et religieuse que nous traversons'.[27] For this alone she would be worth study. Her thought moves through Comte's three states with a tidiness that cannot but gratify the historian of ideas. From her youthful acceptance of Christianity she passes to pessimism and antagonistic unbelief. A little later, under the impact of Hegel and his French expositors, she evolves a pantheistic system that recalls Renan, Taine, and all those honest doubters for whom pantheism was a 'last-ditch meta-physics'. Finally, after a period during which pantheism and positivism are uneasily combined in her thought, she enters Comte's third state and remains to the end of her life its some-what sombre protagonist. She also offers an interesting example of one facet of positivism's fortunes at this time which has not yet been mentioned: its fusion with pessimism. How far, we must ask, is the former responsible for the latter, as is sometimes alleged more generally of nineteenth-century thought? Perhaps surprisingly at first sight, she also unites with them a tentative humanism, and her final word expresses pride in man. Believing that 'tout est pour le pire dans le plus mauvais des mondes pos-sibles',[28] this fiery spirit—described by Lalo as 'cette furieuse, tragique et hautaine sybille du malheur', by Haussonville as 'la Sapho de l'athéisme'[29]—yet avoids nihilism and seeks in her final thought to exalt human life.

[27] E. Caro, 'La Poésie philosophique dans les nouvelles écoles—Un Poète positiviste', *R.D.M.*, 15 mai 1874, p. 248.

[28] L. Ackermann, *Pensées d'une solitaire*, Lemerre, 1882 [*Pens.*], p. 63.

[29] C. Lalo, *L'Art et la vie: L'Économie des passions*, 1947, p. 153; and O. B. P. G. de C. D'Haussonville, 'Madame Ackermann, d'après des lettres et des papiers inédits', *R.D.M.*, 15 nov. 1891, p. 319.

2. 'La Sapho de l'athéisme'

(a) The growth of unbelief

Madame Ackermann was born in Paris in 1813, and in a brief survey of her life written in 1874 she recounts that her childhood was sad, sombre, and for the most part emotionally starved. 'Aussi haut que remontent mes souvenirs, je n'aperçois qu'un lointain sombre. Il me semble que le soleil n'a jamais lui dans ce temps-là.' Of an essentially solitary disposition, avoiding the company of other children, she seems to have found her greatest pleasure in browsing amongst the volumes of her father's library—Molière, Racine, La Fontaine, and above all Corneille, in her own copy, a present that gave her 'une des joies les plus vives de ma vie'.[30] Thus began her life-long habit of reading. 'Je lisais de tout et pêle-mêle', she says when describing her adolescence, and whilst at boarding-school in Paris between 1829 and 1832 she devours the works of the Romantic poets—Senancour, Musset, Hugo, and Vigny above all—and of the most fashionable foreign authors of the day—Shakespeare, Byron, Goethe, and Schiller.[31] By this time she herself had started to write poetry, and for a period after her return to her home in the country she appears to have led a quiet, intellectually satisfying life with her parents and two sisters, marred only by her mother's attempts to introduce her into the local 'society'. Whilst her father tended his flowers, her mother her crops, and her sisters their needlework, she would devote herself to study and poetic composition. Then each evening the family would sit together and read aloud to one another—no longer from the classics, but from the new writers whose works Louise had brought back from Paris. Shortly afterwards, however, came the death of her father, 'le meilleur des pères', and in 1838 she was allowed to go for a year to live with the Schubart family in Berlin, then one of the European centres of philosophical and literary controversy. When she left to return home, she says, she was 'complètement germanisée'.[32] Two years later her mother died, and her sisters having married, she went back to the Schubarts. It was during this second visit that she met a serious,

---

[30] Œuvres de Louise Ackermann — Ma Vie; Premières poésies; Poésies philosophiques, Lemerre, 1885 [Œuv.], pp. iv–v.

[31] Œuv., pp. vi–x.

[32] Œuv., p. xii.

ascetic young man who had abandoned his intention of entering the Protestant ministry after losing his faith and who was now engaged in philological study. This was Paul Ackermann, whom she married in 1844. Despite the fact that she entered upon married life 'sans entraînement aucun', regarding it as 'simplement un mariage de convenance morale', she enjoyed two extremely happy years with her husband, helping him in his work, meeting many of the distinguished intellectuals in Berlin— Alexander von Humboldt, Varnhagen, Müller, and others—and living a life of 'intimate and tranquil happiness'.[33] Tragically, her husband died in mid-1846 at the age of thirty-four. The rest of her life was spent in solitary retirement. She bought a small estate on the outskirts of Nice, where one of her sisters lived, and here she remained, cultivating her land, voraciously reading—books, reviews, papers—interesting herself above all in science and philosophy, from time to time composing the poems that were eventually to be collected as the *Poèmes philosophiques* (1874). The story of this second part of her life is in fact the story of her studies and her poems. For the rest, she led an existence of ordered, industrious serenity, bourgeoise in outward respects— so that Paul Desjardins could exclaim in disappointment that she looked like 'une loueuse de chaises'—interesting to us only in virtue of her lonely and intense intellectual life.

Her father was a 'voltairien de vieille roche' and her childhood passed without her receiving any religious education. It was only later that her mother, motivated according to her daughter by 'un sentiment très vif des convenances mondaines', insisted that Louise should have some instruction in religion and should take her first communion, and she was sent to a *pension* for this purpose. The impact of the Christian faith upon the sensitive girl was considerable: it had 'un effet foudroyant'. She recounts this experience in her autobiographical essay:

> Sérieuse à la fois et crédule, je pris au pied de la lettre les histoires de péché et de rédemption qui me furent débitées; je les embrassai même avec une passion qu'on n'aurait guère attendue d'une enfant de mon âge.

For a time it almost seemed as if she were destined to enter a convent: 'j'étais pour mon entourage pieux un objet d'édification,

---

[33] *Œuv.*, pp. xv–xvi.

quelque chose comme une sainte future'. Upon her return, her father (she tells us) 'fut effrayé des ravages que la foi avait exercés sur ma jeune âme'. Hurriedly he gave her Voltaire and Buffon to read! Yet she was of a religious disposition, as she herself says,[34] and for some time she remains a Christian. This period, which Citoleux places between 1826 and 1832, is represented in her earlier verse by such poems as *Une Autre Vie, Adieux d'une religieuse à la France* (both written in 1826), *Adieu de Jeanne d'Arc* and *Mort de Jeanne d'Arc* (both 1830), none of which she included in her later selection of the *Premières poésies*.[35] This time of religious faith is only reflected in this volume by *Élan mystique*, dated 1832, in which she confesses:

> Un immense besoin de divine harmonie
> M'entraînait malgré moi vers la sphère infinie . . .

Turning from the sadness of the world she cries to Christ, 'comme un enfant en pleurs':

> Prends-moi!
> Prends-moi, car j'ai besoin, par delà toute chose,
> D'un grand et saint espoir où mon cœur se repose,
> D'une idée où mon âme, à qui l'avenir ment,
> S'enferme et trouve enfin un terme à son tourment.[36]

Already, none the less, signs of a growing incredulity are apparent in the nihilistic opening of *Une Autre Vie* and, even more strikingly, in *L'Homme*, written in 1830. Madame Ackermann herself cites this poem in an appendix to *Ma Vie* to rebut any suggestion that her pessimism derived from Schopenhauer.[37] Man is a 'vil atome animé',

> Léger grain de poussière
> Que le néant a rejeté . . . ,

doomed to suffering and unhappiness amidst an insensible universe;

> Ta vie est un jour sur la terre,
> Tu n'es rien dans l'immensité!

Death brings man his first and only happiness.[38]

---

[34] *Œuv.*, pp. v–vi.

[35] These poems are cited by Haussonville and by Madame Ackermann herself (in *Ma Vie*). The manuscript collection of them was made by her sister. Cf. M. Citoleux, *La Poésie philosophique au dix-neuvième siècle — Madame Ackermann*, 1906 (to which I am greatly indebted throughout this chapter), pp. 186–95.

[36] *Œuv.*, pp. 5, 7.   [37] *Œuv.*, p. xxiii.

[38] Cited by Citoleux, op. cit., pp. 188–90.

To judge from her own account, these despairing lines are a symptom of the loss of faith which took place whilst she was at school in Paris. The Abbé Daubrée, son of the *directrice*, sought to bolster up her belief by lending her his own theological note-books, she tells us. But this well-meaning act only had the effect of bringing her to the point of intellectual decision—a decision against the Christian doctrines. 'Ces dogmes, que je n'acceptais ni ne rejetais,... m'apparurent tout à coup dans leur monstrueuse absurdité. Je ne pus que les repousser en bloc.' The desire to believe persists, and she recalls that later she experienced 'des rechutes de mysticisme'. But belief itself never returned: 'Quant à la foi proprement dite, elle m'était devenue à tout jamais impossible.'[39] She may invoke God on rare occasions, as in *Le Départ* (1838), or speak as if she believed the soul to be immortal, as in *A une artiste* (1840). Although the evidence is slight, it may even be that until about 1840 she retains a certain 'vague religion'.[40] But for the greater part of her adult life her attitude to Christianity is one of indifference or else, more commonly later, of outspoken anta-gonism. In all probability she was indifferent and nothing more for a substantial period from about 1840 or earlier until well after the death of her husband, and this personal tragedy does not appear to have affected her views on religion at all. In the *Contes*, written between 1852 and 1853, and *In Memoriam* (1850–2) there are no traces of any philosophical or religious preoccupation, unless it be in the conception of Nature as consoler:

> Car la nature est vraiment souveraine
> Contre nos maux qu'elle calme et guérit. . . .[41]

It is only in 1862, in *Les Malheureux*, that her revolt against the Christian religion is finally declared in poetic form.

Meanwhile, this violent outburst was being prepared in the long meditations whose results she noted down in her diary, and throughout the eighteen-fifties her personal pessimism was deepening. About 1858, moreover, she turns from predominantly literary studies and begins to delve into contemporary science and philosophy, and already in 1855 she had begun the corre-spondence with Ernest Havet which, intensified after 1863, was

[39] *Œuv.*, pp. viii–ix.
[40] Citoleux, op. cit., p. 197.
[41] L. Ackermann, *Contes et poésies*, Hachette, 1863, p. 43, *Sakountala*.

to be an important factor in her intellectual development—certainly in encouraging her scepticism, possibly in an even more forceful fashion.[42] Anti-religious references appear with increasing frequency from about 1860 in the journal and from 1862 in her poetry, and the years between 1860 and 1866 are perhaps the time when she was most vehemently opposed to Christianity. It is only in her final poems like *L'Homme* (written 1877, published 1879) and *Le Christ délivré* that her positive antagonism has been softened into a confession of sceptical ignorance and of the impossibility of all belief, either in the Christian faith or in atheistic opposition to it.

(b) *The sources of her unbelief*

The reasons for Madame Ackermann's original rejection of the Christian faith are hard to discern, for adequate evidence is lacking for this period between 1829 and 1832. She finds its dogmas 'absurd', but she does not reveal her grounds for this view, and her dissent may not have been logically argued at all: she more probably reacted at a less conscious level. Positivism, in the guise of Voltaire and her father, may have its place in this rejection, but only in its most vague and imprecise form, less as an ordered theory of knowledge than as an assumption that science and religion are somehow incompatible. Other considerations seem to have been equally or more important, considerations stemming from her pessimism and her sense of man's insignificance. In poems like *Une Autre Vie* and *L'Homme* (1830) the dominant themes are the cruelty and unhappiness of life and her awareness of *le néant de l'homme*. It may be—though most of what can be said here is conjecture—that her pessimistic view of life clashed in her mind with the doctrine of God's goodness, and her sense of man's unimportance in Nature with the status which Christianity gives to man in the eyes of God. In themselves these are totally inadequate reasons for rejecting the Christian faith—as Pascal might well have reminded her—but it can perhaps be said that these disparities impose a certain strain upon credulity.

This interpretation is perhaps confirmed by the fact that it is broadly these same problems which are taken up and developed

[42] For two estimates of Havet's influence, cf. Haussonville, loc. cit., and Citoleux, op. cit., p. 125. Cf. Louis Havet's protest against the former's views, *R.D.M.*, 15 déc. 1891, pp. 941–3.

in Madame Ackermann's later, better-documented attack on Christianity. The very first criticisms she transfers from her journal to the *Pensées d'une solitaire* are directed against the cruelty of death—we are all *condamnés à mort*—and of the Christian conception of Hell. Again and again in the *Pensées* these two allied accusations are brought against Christianity—the cruelty and immorality of both the natural world and the Christian teachings. If God exists, Nature and theology alike testify to His wickedness.

Il semble vraiment qu'une volonté méchante préside aux événements humains. . . . Le hasard seul n'aurait ni cette perspicacité ni cette persistance dans le choix des combinaisons mauvaises.[43]

In *Les Malheureux*, likewise, her emphasis is upon the torments of life:

Nous n'avions rencontré que désespoir et doute,
Perdus parmi les flots d'un monde indifférent. . . .[44]

And in *Prométhée* (1865) her hatred of the God who inflicts this unhappy existence upon man reaches its climax. Here God is portrayed as a tyrannical villain who has allowed men to suffer even though He had the power to create a happier world. He is 'un Dieu jaloux qui frappe et qui déteste', and Prometheus cries in despair and outraged horror:

'Celui qui pouvait tout a voulu la douleur.'

God is judged by the human conscience and condemned:

Elle ne peut t'absoudre et va te rejeter.[45]

A similar accusation is made in *Pascal* (1871), accompanied by the same disdainful rejection of God's claim to be worshipped by man.

Qu'importe qu'il soit Dieu si son œuvre est impie?
Quoi! c'est son propre fils qu'il a crucifié?
Il pouvait pardonner, mais il veut qu'on expie;
Il immole, et cela s'appelle avoir pitié!

Even as we die, we shall cast our curse upon this despot who amuses Himself by inflicting pain and death, who uses His infinite power to impose anguish and torment.[46]

It has sometimes been deduced from *Prométhée* and *Pascal*

[43] *Pens.*, pp. 4, 5, 32.
[44] *Œuv.*, p. 76.
[45] *Œuv.*, p. 101.
[46] *Œuv.*, pp. 156, 158.

that Madame Ackermann believes in the existence of God, even though she thinks of him as *un Dieu-bourreau*, and Lalo suggests that her pessimism is not atheist but anti-deist. Haussonville likewise alleges that there is an opposition between her atheism and her expressions of hatred for God and points to 'l'étrange contradiction qui fait le fond de sa philosophie: la haine contre un Dieu qu'elle nie et qu'elle rend cependant responsable des maux de l'humanité'.[47] Yet these judgements perhaps take too seriously what is basically a rhetorical device. She employs the *fiction* that God exists in order to present the more vividly her belief that the cruelty of the natural order renders His existence completely incredible. Even in 1865, when she wrote *Prométhée*, she remarks that the age is near when it will be impossible to understand how anyone could have believed in God.[48] The closest she comes to the view attributed to her by these critics is in a comment made in the same year: 'Si Dieu existait, ce serait un monstre. Il vaut mieux pour lui qu'il ne soit pas. C'est surtout plus moral.'[49]

Other Christian doctrines are no less repugnant to her moral sense. She is repelled by the Christian conception of Hell, by the story of God's treatment of His Son, by the Christian notion of Heaven in which she detects a strong element of bribery, and by the 'préceptes impitoyables' to be found in the teaching of Christ Himself and which explain how He can be at the same time 'le Dieu des cœurs tendres et des fanatiques'.[50] These immoral doctrines have, not surprisingly, had immoral consequences. Christianity has worsened an already appalling situation; its explanation of the world has only brought man 'un surcroît de ténèbres, de luttes et de tortures'. Religious faith, as Prometheus says, has been 'un mauvais rêve'.[51] The illusory hope of immortality in particular has drawn out man's moral cowardice and succeeded in debasing even Pascal:

> Hélas! tant que la Foi l'aveugle et le mutile,
> Il ne peut que trembler, gémir et supplier;
> L'être faible devient alors un être lâche.[52]

---

[47] Lalo, op. cit., p. 151, and Haussonville, loc. cit., p. 347; cf. Caro, loc. cit., p. 248.   [48] *Pens.*, p. 42.
[49] Cited by Citoleux, op. cit., p. 168.
[50] *Pens.*, pp. 53, 59, 63, and *Œuv.*, p. 79, *Les Malheureux*.
[51] *Œuv.*, pp. xxii, 102.
[52] *Œuv.*, p. 152, *Pascal*.

Religion thrives in fact on ignorance and fear. Men are not driven to belief by love of the truth but in order to calm their terror; 'ils ferment les yeux et s'abandonnent'. With a quite excessive contempt she declares in her *Pensées*:

Les dévots sont des poltrons, les dévots sont des lâches. Prosternés devant un Dieu inique et capricieux, ils n'ont qu'un but, qu'une pensée: le fléchir à tout prix.[53]

Her reaction against Christianity thus derives basically from an outraged moral conscience; she yields to her hatred for religion all the more readily, she claims, in that she feels that it springs from the most generous and elevated parts of her nature.[54]

This conclusion helps one to delimit the influence of positivism on her unbelief. Her moral revulsion has nothing to do with the positivist philosophy: it involves an ethical judgement that positivism, by its very premisses, is unable to make. On the contrary, the case of Madame Ackermann helps to justify the view that much of the nineteenth-century unbelief that has been laid at the door of the scientific and positivist attitudes arises more from a moral rejection of the Christian faith and Church. This is so true of Madame Ackermann at least that Citoleux can declare that positivism *restrained* her anti-Christian dogmatism;[55] it forced her to abandon in the end the metaphysical doctrine of atheism and to replace positive disbelief by a more cautious scepticism.

Her attitude is perhaps strengthened by the sense of *le néant de l'homme* which can be detected even in the poems of 1830. This awareness must have seemed to her at variance with the Christian claim that man has a central place in God's plan for His universe. Even when optimistic enough to believe that Nature is moving slowly towards an ideal, she nevertheless remarks that its goal far transcends humanity. The mature woman holds the same opinion as the girl of seventeen who wrote *L'Homme*. Man is only 'un simple atome emporté dans le mouvement universel', and she is unable to imagine how an astronomer could ever be a Christian, as he surveys the infinities of the sky and is possessed by 'le sentiment de son propre néant qui saisit l'homme en face de ces espaces sans bornes'.[56] Here the connexion between her

[53] *Pens.*, pp. 22, 64.
[54] *Pens.*, p. 21.
[55] Citoleux, op. cit., p. 112.
[56] *Pens.*, pp. 6, 29.

unbelief and her awareness of man's insignificance is explicitly declared.

The themes of the sufferings and unimportance of human life are fused in her constant references to the forces dominating all our activity. Man is the plaything of fate, the slave of a rigidly determined world.

> Fatalité! voilà le mot de l'univers, depuis l'atome invisible jusqu'à l'homme; prononcer celui de Liberté, c'est n'avoir aucune idée des lois inflexibles qui enchaînent toutes les manifestations de l'être.

Madame Ackermann even identifies her view with the doctrine of predestination, characteristically attributing to Christianity one of the cruellest heresies in its history.[57] Her outlook, expressed in such poems as *Les Malheureux, Prométhée, La Nature à l'homme* (1867), and *Le Cri* (1871), is unfortunately not altogether coherent. In particular, she combines belief in universal determinism with belief in the intervention of chance—a union that is philosophically unusual, to say the least, even though almost a commonplace of a good deal of nineteenth-century poetry. We are the victims of an implacable destiny and also of 'l'aveugle Hasard'; the universe is controlled by

> un couple aveugle et morne,
> La Force et le Hasard.[58]

Once again, as in her moral rejection of Christianity, it is not positivism that is the deciding influence. Her feeling here springs from her personal pessimism, from what Citoleux calls *le pessimisme du cœur*, born of the misfortunes and loneliness of her own life, rather than from any philosophical or scientific tenet. It is true that she believed her fatalism was confirmed by science and positivism, that is, that she misunderstood the hypothetical, working determinism of the scientific method. But this idea merely strengthens an attitude whose roots lie in her own knowledge of life rather than her reading and to which she gives voice in early poems like *Une Autre Vie* and *L'Homme* (1830), long before she had any real contact with the positivist philosophy. She certainly repudiates the existence of miracles and the supernatural; there is a constant suggestion that science and religion

---

[57] *Pens.*, pp. 51, 26–27.
[58] *Œuv.*, p. 77, *Les Malheureux*, and p. 102, *Prométhée*.

are incompatible. Yet these are not the decisive factors. Even in
Les Malheureux (1862) her reaction against the doctrine of immortality is determined by moral anger primarily. The hope of
an after-life is an immoral bribe and brings into our existence
a cruel and tormenting uncertainty, whilst for the lover, for instance, the possibility that his beloved still exists in another world
induces despair, not consolation:

> C'est assez d'un tombeau, je ne veux pas d'un monde
> Se dressant entre nous.[59]

Later, in *L'Amour et la mort* (1863–4), she will assert that the
notion of an after-life is an illusion, a fantasy, 'mensonge de
l'amour et de l'orgueil humain'.[60] But even if she held this view
in 1862, it is the moral repudiation that is primary.

It is also doubtful whether the actual discoveries of science
were of any great importance in her intellectual development,
and she reveals none of the detailed scientific knowledge seen
in Sully Prudhomme. She may write in one of her *pensées*:
'L'élément des religions, c'est l'ignorance. La foi disparaît devant
la science.'[61] Yet it is questionable whether she could have sub-
stantiated this assertion in detail. Indeed, the effect of contemporary scientific theories on her was probably much less disruptive
than in the case of many others of her generation. She herself
remarks: 'Quant aux résultats récents de la science, ils ne m'ont
jamais personnellement troublée; j'y étais préparée d'avance.'[62]
Biology's revelations of the savageries of Nature, for instance,
come merely as added reasons for her existing gloom. In some
ways such scientific discoveries as she knew about even helped to
lighten her pessimism. She claims to have found her more optimistic pantheist ideas supported by the theories of evolution and
of the transformation of energy. Or again, she thinks that scientific investigation has opened up new vistas for poetry and created
'un nouvel état d'âme'.[63]

The real impact of the scientific spirit on her religious views
operates at a later stage, one may thus conclude. She was an unbeliever before she became a positivist.

Positivism merely confirms her dissent, and the theme she

[59] *Œuv.*, p. 77, and p. 106, *Paroles d'un amant.*
[60] *Œuv.*, p. 86.   [61] *Pens.*, p. 33.
[62] *Œuv.*, p. xxi.   [63] *Œuv.*, p. xix.

borrows from it is that of man's inevitable ignorance about religious and metaphysical problems. Man is confronted by the unknown, 'un être qui ne sait rien et ne peut rien affirmer'. The folly of religions is to try to describe a realm wholly inaccessible to us. The religious sentiment itself—awe before the mysteries around us—is natural enough; it is even a sign of man's greatness.[64] But to dictate rigid and exclusive doctrines about these mysteries, as faith proudly does, is absurd. The only wise and noble attitude is utter doubt; it is cowardly (again the moral judgement intervenes) to sacrifice one's reason and integrity in order to escape the torments of scepticism. This was Pascal's error when he exchanged reason and science for the illusions of faith:

> La foi t'a pris, Pascal, et ne t'a plus rendu.
> Que ta raison résiste, aussitôt tu l'accables.[65]

Madame Ackermann proceeds to banish religion in the name of the unknowable—in sharp contrast to Spencer during these same years. The classic statement of her attitude is in the first part of *Le Positivisme*, written in 1864, and it indicates the strongest arm against religion she took from the positivist philosophy.

> Il s'ouvre par delà toute science humaine
> Un vide dont la Foi fut prompte à s'emparer.
> De cet abîme obscur elle a fait son domaine;
> En s'y précipitant elle a cru l'éclairer.
> Eh bien! nous t'expulsons de tes divins royaumes,
> Dominatrice ardente, et l'instant est venu:
> Tu ne vas plus savoir où loger tes fantômes;
>   Nous fermons l'Inconnu.[66]

In this way positivism reinforces the more personal reasons that had already led Madame Ackermann to religious unbelief, and this is also the theme which will have priority in her later thought.

[64] *Pens.*, pp. 10–11, and *Œuv.*, p. 137, *De la lumière!*
[65] *Œuv.*, p. 164, *L'Idéal*; cf. pp. 140, 144, 147, 151, *Pascal*.
[66] *Œuv.*, p. 91.

3. *Louise Ackermann and Pantheism*

During the eighteen-sixties Madame Ackermann passed through an intermediate and complex stage in her transition from the Christian belief of her youth to the positivist creed of her final years. In this period, stretching very roughly from 1860 to 1867, a militant pantheism exists side by side with her irreligion and her increasing positivism. She was always to profess a kind of hesitant, hypothetical pantheism in later life, but at this time she is committed to a more absolute faith in it. Inspired by her reading of Goethe, Hegel, and Spinoza, she comes to believe that there is a 'divine principle' at work in the universe, driving life towards an ideal. In 1861 she admits in her journal that the order of the world suggests to her the idea of a 'great law'. And by 1863 she can assert: 'Je suis plus que personne persuadée de la présence d'un principe divin dans l'univers'—though she is careful to add: 'mais mon esprit se refuse à lui prêter une existence distincte'. At several points this pantheistic view coincided with her established opinions. It confirmed her acceptance of determinism and her opposition to dualism, and it encouraged her denial of personal immortality. It also went some way towards contenting her inner need for an ideal, whilst banishing what she felt to be the crude anthropomorphism of the Christian doctrines of Creation and Providence. Pantheism was almost a form of atheism for her in fact, and in 1867 she notes with satisfaction: 'Dans le système de Spinoza, Dieu existe si peu que ce n'est pas la peine de l'adorer.'[67] Its effect was thus to strengthen her existing views, but to give her as well a basis for qualified optimism. Negative for the most part, her pantheism was positive in its adherence to the idea of progress. In mid-1864 she sketches in her journal the plan for her poem *La Nature à l'homme*, dated 1867, in which her belief in progress is most fervently expressed. 'Quel est cet idéal [she asks herself], vers lequel la Nature s'achemine à travers le temps éternel et les formes infinies?' She dismisses the notion that man is the realization of this ideal; 'non [she says of man in relation to Nature], nous ne serons qu'un échelon rompu sous ses pas'.[68] And in the poem itself she looks forward to the creation of

---

[67] Cited by Citoleux, op. cit., pp. 167, 90; cf. p. 222.
[68] Ibid., p. 182; cf. *Pens.*, pp. 6, 45.

N

'un être libre et souverain'—the superman of the future. As for man, in Nature's eyes he is only

> l'ébauche imparfaite
> Du chef-d'œuvre que j'ai rêvé . . .[69]

In this way meaning is given to the apparently pointless change and movement which she evokes in such poems as *Le Nuage*. Her phenomenalism, relativism, and determinism are related after all to a transcending purpose.

> L'éternel mouvement n'est que l'élan des choses
> Vers l'idéal sacré qu'entrevoit mon désir.

Even the cruelty of Nature is transformed when viewed through pantheist eyes. It is no longer seen as a purposeless curse destined to continue to the end of time but as the labour-pains of Nature as she brings to birth the ideal being whose creation has always been her purpose. Man is sacrificed, but for a great end. Nature is not a harsh, unfeeling force, but a mother tenderly longing for the birth of her son.

> J'ai déjà trop longtemps fait œuvre de marâtre,
> J'ai trop enseveli, j'ai trop exterminé,
> Moi qui ne suis au fond que la mère idolâtre
> D'un seul enfant qui n'est pas né.

And although mankind lives under the dominance of fate, its laws will be shattered by this supreme creation: 'il met les lois au joug', 'Fatalité, sa main rompt tes anneaux d'airain!'[70]

This philosophy comes strangely from one who was at the same time, in poems like *Prométhée*, cursing the God of Christianity because of man's pointless sufferings. As an anti-Christian Madame Ackermann sees Nature as a tyrannical, merciless power whose very existence orders out of court the Christian theory of God. As a pantheist she sees it as a loving mother whose cruelties are necessary and justified. As an anti-Christian she believes the world is ruled by a ruthless determinism. As a pantheist she posits a future in which its inescapable laws shall be overthrown. As an anti-Christian she mocks the notion of a supernatural, of a divine order. As a pantheist she happily accepts the idea of a 'divine principle' active in Nature. As an anti-Christian she

---

[69] *Œuv.*, pp. 112–13.   [70] *Œuv.*, pp. 111–12.

thunders at the meaninglessness of life. As a pantheist she finds purpose even in its unhappiest aspects. The contradictions are glaring, and they are not untypical of the nineteenth-century unbeliever turned pantheist.

The divergence between these two conceptions may even have proved a strain upon Madame Ackermann's own credulity, for only four years later, in *L'Homme à la nature* (1871), she repudiates her belief in cosmic advance. After 1871 she may entertain pantheism as an hypothesis, but for the most part the cautious hope of progress which she retains is centred upon man. Nature is excluded from the forward movement and is once again regarded, in *L'Homme* (1877) for example, as pitiless and without aim. From 1867 onwards she also seems to have realized that the absolute pantheism of *La Nature à l'homme* conflicted with the positivist principles she had adopted during the very same years. The results of this realization were its rejection as anything more than a purely conjectural theory and, secondly, a more coherent development of her positivist contentions. After the period between 1867 and 1870 during which she wrote nothing, she has at last moved altogether into the third of Comte's states.

4. *Louise Ackermann as a Positivist*

Madame Ackermann's systematic study of religion dates from 1857 and of science and philosophy from 1858. At the first her attention seems to have been given chiefly to religious questions. She reads the articles in the *Revue des Deux Mondes* by Charles de Rémusat on English Unitarianism (15 sept. 1856) and by Saint-René Taillandier on the history of religious ideas in the nineteenth century (15 sept. 1857)—from both of which she extracts the arguments injurious to Christianity whilst ignoring the counter-arguments which the authors themselves wished to advocate. She summarizes Renan's *Études d'histoire religieuse* (1857) and the standpoint held by Strauss, for example; but she omits the objections against the two thinkers advanced by Saint-René Taillandier.[71] Her principal aim is apparently to find support for her unbelief, and the same approach is evident in her summaries of Havet's *Le Christianisme et ses origines*, Renan's *Vie*

---

[71] Cf. Citoleux, op. cit., pp. 114 ff.

de Jésus (which she finds too uncritical of Christianity), and of
the thought of Proudhon and Scherer. Gradually, however, now
reinforced in her views on religion, she gives more time to science
and philosophy. The first scientific article she resumes in her
journal is by Charles Lévêque and dates from 1858, and throughout the following decade the references to science are steadily
multiplied. One can only conjecture as to how far these religious
and scientific studies implanted a positivistic attitude in her mind.
Their role was probably preparatory rather than decisive. More
important are the philosophical works and articles she refers to.
The first of these is Berthelot's article in reply to Renan published
in the *Revue des Deux Mondes* in November 1863 on 'La Science
idéale et la science positive'. She makes a long summary of it and
in particular copies in full Berthelot's declaration of his positivist
position. She also notes his rejection of *a priori* knowledge: 'Les
philosophes n'ont jamais retrouvé au moyen d'un *à priori* prétendu que les connaissances de leurs temps.' Prior to her reading
of this article there is a reference in the journal in 1861 that is
quasi-positivist in tone—when she speaks of man as 'un être qui
ne sait rien et ne peut rien affirmer'; and again in January 1863
she declares: 'J'ai cessé de chercher la vérité, car je sais que je ne
la trouverais pas.'[72] Yet the very fullness of her summary of
Berthelot's article suggests that it held a special significance for
her and that from this time she became aware of her real affiliations. In the years following she makes extracts from other positivist or quasi-positivist writers—from Laugel's *Les Problèmes
de la nature* (1864), from Littré's views on liberty, from an article
by Albert Réville which referred in particular to T. H. Huxley,
from Littré's *La Science au point de vue philosophique* (1873),
and from Jules Soury's *Bréviaire de l'histoire du matérialisme*
(1881). Already in 1866, moreover, she appears to be familiar with
Taine's works, for she writes in her journal:

> Le système de Taine est vrai. La penséé humaine est soumise à des
> lois inflexibles, comme tout autre phénomène; seulement nous ne
> pouvons pas les déterminer avec autant de rigueur.

(Here, it appears, she is again falling into the mistake of confusing
fatalism and the working determinism of the scientific method—
not that this is surprising in view of Taine's own ambiguities on

---

[72] Cited by Citoleux, ibid., pp. 102, 173; cf. *Pens.*, p. 11.

the point.) And again in 1872 she writes to Havet about Taine's concept of 'l'hallucination vraie' in *De l'intelligence*. It is suggested by Haussonville that Comte and Spencer also directed her thought,[73] but it is worth remarking that he offers no evidence that she ever read either author and that no evidence is forthcoming in Citoleux's study of the thinkers she admired. It seems likely, in short, that her positivist views were developed above all by her reading of Berthelot, Littré, and perhaps Taine, in so far as he was faithful to positivism, and by the influence of Havet upon her. Her study of the sciences was probably a factor also, both in predisposing her to accept the positivist theory and in strengthening her conviction after she had done so.

One can be far more precise about positivism's effects on her thought. She is little interested in its relations with psychology, biology, sociology, and logic or even in its detailed theory of knowledge. Her chief concern, both now and throughout her life, is with more metaphysical, moral, and religious questions, and she regards positivism almost exclusively from the standpoint of these interests. Its most important tenet for her is, we saw, that our knowledge is strictly circumscribed by the limits of observation and that we are surrounded by an 'unknowable' which we can in principle never penetrate. Secondly, positivism seemed to her to support her beliefs that the supernatural is nonexistent and that all life is rigidly determined. Neither of these views is in fact a legitimate deduction from the positivist position strictly defined: yet these conclusions were drawn by philosophers of the time, and Madame Ackermann is less to blame than thinkers like Havet (and Littré on occasion), who, better tutored than she in philosophy, ought not to have given currency to these errors.

However that may be, the upshot of her adoption of positivism was to shut the door even more firmly against religious faith, and in this its primary importance consists. But unhappily, unlike Littré, she is not content merely to survey the mysterious sea which man can never chart. She is the reverse of the happy sceptic or even of the reconciled sceptic. Citoleux implies on several occasions that she adopted the positivist philosophy in order to provide herself with new grounds for pessimism. 'Le positivisme lui fournissait un motif de plainte: l'ignorance finale', he asserts; it

[73] Haussonville, loc. cit., p. 336.

undermined her belief in progress, 'et favorisait davantage le pessimisme de la pensée'.[74] These suggestions seem improper, and he provides no evidence to justify them. Nor does his thesis that Madame Ackermann's pessimism is first of all emotional and only secondarily and later intellectual require the insinuation that there is a certain insincerity in her philosophical pessimism. (Nor is it necessary to link the priority of emotional pessimism in her to the fact that she was a woman and to say with Citoleux 'elle fut femme jusque dans sa philosophie'.[75]) To accept his interpretation is to underestimate the gravity of her dilemma.

This dilemma lies in the opposition between her aspiration towards an ideal and a knowledge of the 'Infinite' and her conviction, on the other hand, that we are all condemned to ignorance. It is religious doctrine she criticizes, not the religious feeling of awe before life's mystery, and unbelief did not come altogether naturally to her. She possessed a 'religious nature', as she says, and she also remarks, somewhat inelegantly: 'Les croyances sont comme les vieilles dents: cela branle, mais cela tient.'[76] Man longs to know the 'unknowable': this is the theme she develops in the second part of *Le Positivisme*:

> Nous restons sans espoir, sans recours, sans asile,
> Tandis qu'obstinément le Désir qu'on exile
> Revient errer autour du gouffre défendu.[77]

In about 1866 Madame Ackermann received from Havet his edition of *Les Pensées de Pascal*. This was a momentous event in her intellectual life, for Pascal comes to symbolize for her *le tourment de l'idéal* in the religious realm, just as Musset and Don Juan represented in her eyes the same torment in the realm of love. 'Je n'en aurai jamais fini avec lui', she writes of Pascal in 1871; 'Pascal et Don Juan sont deux fantômes qui depuis longtemps me hantaient de concert.'[78]

She takes her interpretation very largely from Havet's preface and emphasizes three aspects of the Apology in particular. She follows Havet in stressing the irrationality and the moral weakness of Pascal's submission to Christianity; for both of them his main strength lies in the critical and negative elements in his

---

[74] Citoleux, op. cit., p. 167; cf. pp. 173, 236.
[75] Ibid., p. 2.   [76] *Pens.*, pp. 8–9.
[77] *Œuv.*, p. 92.   [78] Cited by Citoleux, op. cit., pp. 51–52.

thought and not in his defence of the Christian faith. Pascal sacrificed his mind by becoming a believer.[79] The theology he adopted,
moreover, was precisely Christianity in its most cruel form,
Jansenism (or so Madame Ackermann believed, at least), and
there is a sense in which Pascal thus confirmed her in her worst
suspicions about the immorality and savagery of the Christian
doctrines. Secondly, she welcomes the sceptical sections of the
Apology and turns them against Pascal's own faith. The Pyr-
rhonism of the *Pensées* thus reinforces her own positivist scepticism, all the more so since she rejects as absurd the author's
reply to the free-thinker's doubts. Thirdly and perhaps most
important, she found in him her own separation of mind between
religious hope and incredulity. At an intenser level he had lived
her own dilemmas, and she returns to this feature in his thought
again and again. 'Ce qui m'intéresse dans Pascal [she writes],
c'est une âme aux prises et qui combat. . . . En tous sens, cet esprit
courait à l'infini.' His conflicts are the conflicts of us all: 'C'est
l'homme qui parle par sa bouche. Soif de bonheur, invincible
besoin de rattacher au ciel la chaîne de nos misères, quoi de plus
humain?'[80] Pascal becomes (both in *Pascal* and *L'Idéal*) a symbol
of her own divided allegiance, and his despair is identified with
hers.

> Oui, tout est vrai, Pascal, nous le reconnaissons:
> Voilà nos désespoirs, nos doutes, nos tortures,
> Et devant l'Infini ce sont là nos frissons.

Only the conclusion that emerges from their torment is different,
and to the argument of the *Pari* Madame Ackermann replies:

> Et s'il faut accepter ta sombre alternative,
> Croire ou désespérer, nous désespérerons.[81]

The outlooks of Littré and Pascal, of positivism and Christian
pessimism (if one can so call it) are thus blended in the theme
which she develops in her later poems—that of *le tourment de
l'idéal*.

> Et l'homme est là, devant une obscurité vide,
> Sans guide désormais, et tout au désespoir
> De n'avoir pu forcer, en sa poursuite avide,
> L'Invisible à se laisser voir.

---

[79] *Œuv.*, p. 148, *Pascal*, and *Pens.*, p. 61.   [80] *Pens.*, pp. 60–61.
[81] *Œuv.*, pp. 155, 157, *Pascal*.

Man's longing to know is 'un désir qui va s'exaspérant'; obsessed by 'le rêve divin de la lumière', we are yet born blind.[82] Of the poems written around 1871, *Pascal, De la lumière!*, and *L'Idéal* all reiterate this notion of the fruitless search for the 'Implacable Idéal', 'L'Idéal qu'ardemment poursuit notre désir':

> Idéal! Idéal! sur tes traces divines,
> Combien déjà se sont égarés et perdus!
> Les meilleurs d'entre nous sont ceux que tu fascines. . . .[83]

Thus positivism reveals in her poetry its Pyrrhonic reverse face, and the cry of *J'ignore* replaces fatalism and atheism as the chief ground of her philosophical pessimism. On occasions it gives her a further reason for regret. In *Le Nuage* (1864) she affirms that reality consists of nothing more than the ceaseless succession and variation of phenomena:

> Partout le mouvement incessant et divers,
> Dans le cercle éternel des formes fugitives,
> Agitant l'immense univers.[84]

At such moments she is impressed more by the operations of chance in the universe than by the inflexible rule of natural law, and in a passage in her journal in 1866—with which she concludes her *Pensées d'une solitaire*—she even advances the strangely unpositivist view that life is no more than a dream.[85]

Madame Ackermann misuses the positivist philosophy, we saw, to justify fatalism and atheism, but she does not follow some of her contemporaries by making the equally illegitimate jumps to materialism and scientism. Though she spurns spiritualism, she dismisses no less firmly its antithesis. One of the merits of pantheism in her eyes was that it rejected materialism, and in a letter to her nephew she affirms quite dogmatically: 'Je déteste le pur matérialisme.' She continues:

Le philosophe que je te recommande, puisque tu fais tes études philosophiques, est Spinoza. J'y mêle un peu d'Hegel et j'en compose un ragoût philosophique très sain et très fortifiant. Il a l'extrême avantage de me permettre de me passer de la nourriture vulgaire d'un Dieu personnel, sans m'enfoncer dans la matière.[86]

[82] *Œuv.*, p. 137, *De la lumière!*
[83] *Œuv.*, pp. 165, 159, *L'Idéal*, and p. 177, *Le Déluge*.
[84] *Œuv.*, p. 96.
[85] *Pens.*, p. 66.
[86] Cited by Haussonville, loc. cit., pp. 337–8.

Her opposition was also justified—and more effectively so—by an appeal to the phenomenalism which she took from both Kant and positivism. After reading Kant she comments that the materialists cannot, in the face of his critique, 'affirmer une matière qu'ils ne perçoivent pas'. Again after reading Tyndall, she notes in her journal that they cannot establish the existence of a logical continuity between molecular activity and the phenomena of consciousness. 'C'est là un écueil [she adds with satisfaction] contre lequel le matérialisme viendra inévitablement échouer toutes les fois qu'il prétendra être une philosophie complète de l'esprit humain.' And yet again towards the end of her life she asks her friend, Louise Read, to send a copy of *L'Homme* to M. Bazile Bernstein, who had accused her of materialism. 'Il y trouvera la preuve [she writes] que je ne suis pas aussi matérialiste qu'il se l'imagine. Comment! moi, une ennemie de l'Idéal et de l'Infini?' On the contrary, she holds that man's greatness lies in the qualities by which he transcends mere animality.[87]

Her rejection of scientism is no less convinced. On rare occasions she is tempted to think that science may be able to yield the knowledge of the ideal to which she aspires. Science will deliver us from ignorance, 'cet horrible supplice', she claims in *Pascal*. But the view she usually held is found in *De la lumière!*, written in the same year as *Pascal*. Science may cast a few fitful gleams of light upon the unknown, but it can do no more than that:

Un peu de jour s'est fait où ses rayons portaient;
Mais son pouvoir ne va qu'à chasser des ténèbres
Les fantômes qui les hantaient.[88]

Nor, finally, does Madame Ackermann make the improper transition from positivism to nihilism. Although she is a pessimist, she is not a nihilist. Human life is not entirely without purpose even though it is enacted against a sombre background. She even adopts a kind of humanism and a tentative ethical creed.

[87] Cf. Citoleux, op. cit., pp. 87, 103, 239. On Bernstein, see Citoleux, 'Madame Ackermann et les étrangers', *R.L.C.* xi, 1931, p. 471.
[88] *Œuv.*, pp. 152, 137.

5. *The Humanism of Louise Ackermann*

Her humanistic conception of man resembles Pascal's picture of
la grandeur de l'homme, albeit combined—and thereby strikingly
modified—with positivism, and was probably developed by her
study of the *Pensées.* Like Pascal she attributes the greatness and
uniqueness of man above all to his self-awareness and his powers
of thought. In *L'Homme* she depicts Nature as awaiting human
beings in order to become conscious of itself—perhaps a remini-
scence of Hegel as well as of Pascal. Man declares in this poem:

> L'Inconscience encor sur la nature entière
> Étendait tristement son voile épais et lourd.
> J'apparus; aussitôt à travers la matière
> L'Esprit se faisait jour.

Man gives meaning to what had previously been meaningless,
and taking up the theme of 'le roseau pensant' she roundly
asserts:

> Tout l'infini du temps ne vaut pas, ô Nature!
> La minute où j'aurai pensé.[89]

The very ethical subjectivism of the positivist is also turned to
man's glory. Man has himself created moral values and thereby
opposed his will to the amoral blindness of Nature's laws. By an
unexpected reversal, moreover, even those aspirations that have
led him into religious and metaphysical speculation are a symptom of his greatness; although fated to frustration, they endow
him with a splendour of his own. His longing for the 'Invisible'
is 'un désir sans espoir', but for that very reason it is also '[un]
cri sacré'.[90]

This notion of man is the foundation of her ethical assertions.
'J'ai trois faibles et je les confesse sans honte [she once wrote in
her journal]: la nature, la poésie et la vertu.' And Haussonville
confirms from his personal knowledge that she was of unwavering
moral rectitude.[91] She claims that, though a religious unbeliever,
she is never an ethical unbeliever. 'Je repousse le nom d'incré-
dule. . . . Je crois à la loi morale. Ma conscience me tient lieu de

---

[89] *Œuv.,* pp. 168, 171; cf. *Pens.,* pp. 46, 65.
[90] *Œuv.,* pp. 168–9, *L'Homme,* and p. 137, *De la lumière!*
[91] Citoleux, op. cit., p. 169, and Haussonville, loc. cit., p. 349.

foi, la confiance d'espérance. C'est la religion moins Dieu.'[92] One can abandon all religious and metaphysical sanctions and still retain a moral code, *une morale indépendante*.[93] She believes that the existence of sanctions would empty virtuous action of its merit. The Christian acts for ulterior motives—to save his soul, to placate his God—whereas the unbeliever acts out of a disinterested love of what he conceives to be virtuous. To reject religion and accept the ethical subjectivism of positivist philosophy is, however unexpected it may seem at first glance, to open the way to the highest type of moral action, a virtue that is utterly unselfish and completely human. It is not surprising that she should therefore have praised Kant's separation of ethics and religion—even though she cannot forgive his postulation of free will, immortality, and God.[94] Not God but man created justice, and each successive generation of men re-creates it. 'Il n'y a rien d'absolu ni d'arrêté dans la morale.'[95] Morality at a given time reflects the stage which the human conscience and human cultivation have reached. During her pantheistic period she links this developing ethical awareness to the movement of progress in the universe as a whole. But this Hegelian evolution towards the ideal is not the justification of her ethic; she is not smuggling in a new sanction, as Renan does, for example. Consequently her abandonment of pantheism leaves the moral code untouched. Having first believed man and Nature are working hand in hand, she later holds that man is working against Nature—but in either case her ethic is as peremptory. Positivism poses no ethical dilemma for Madame Ackermann, and in this she is somewhat unusual in an age when so many felt that it called ethics into question.

C'est nous, libres penseurs, qui sommes les désintéressés, les

---

[92] Cited by Citoleux, ibid., p. 71 (dated Jan. 1863).

[93] She was a friend of that minor but indefatigable and talented disciple of Kant, Madame C. Coignet, editor of the weekly journal *La Morale indépendante*, begun in 1865, and author in particular of *De Kant à Bergson—Réconciliation de la religion et de la science dans un spiritualisme nouveau*, 1911. Here (p. 9) she reiterates her unchanged view: 'La morale indépendante est une loi conforme à la raison, nous dictant nos droits et nos devoirs avec une autorité absolue, puisée dans la personnalité libre qui revêt l'homme d'une dignité unique et constitue l'unité supérieure de sa race.' Madame Ackermann's ideas are very similar.

[94] Cf. Citoleux, op. cit., p. 88.

[95] *Pens.*, p. 22.

généreux; nous faisons de la vertu pour rien. Nous ne la vendrions pas, dût-elle même nous être payée en monnaie de paradis.[96]

This is not to imply that her ethical beliefs are satisfactory from a philosophical point of view. In particular, it is very doubtful whether she ever resolved the opposition between her fatalism and her ethics. On the one hand, she can dogmatically declare: 'Nous ne sommes pas maîtres de nos actions. Nous les jugeons, mais elles nous sont imposées par notre nature.'[97] On the other hand, she can claim that the moral action of the unbeliever is a disinterested choice. In fact her fatalism completely precludes the possibility of the type of action she has in mind when she argues that 'le bien doit être fait gratis'.

None the less, although this contradiction remains, to abandon pantheism for positivism saved her from certain difficulties. She is now defending a more limited position. Man's ethical assertions are purely personal, his own protestations against an alien world. Provided one does not feel troubled by the seeming oddity that so amoral a universe should have produced by the operation of its blind laws so moral a consciousness, no other ethical position perhaps is more impregnable.

And since this moral awareness is attributed wholly to man's self-development, its existence permits a certain legitimate pride and a qualified hope. Haussonville tells us that towards the end of her life she became more sensitive of the merits even of Christian morality, and in one of her last poems, Le Christ délivré, she looks forward to the time when Christian charity and Christian ethics shall be freed from their baneful union with the Church.[98] This is characteristic of her increased hopefulness. Human life, she still believes, will ultimately be wiped out by the destruction portrayed in Le Déluge, but until then our life can perhaps take on a further dignity and yield a fuller satisfaction than in the past.

Positivism thus brought her reconciliation as well as division of mind, for she found in it added reasons for a tentative confidence in man. As this minute creature scans the world around him he can even feel a certain Promethean pride:

[96] Pens., pp. 16–17.
[97] Pens., p. 8.
[98] Published in the second edition of the Pensées d'une solitaire. Cf. Haussonville, loc. cit., p. 350.

Je puis avec orgueil, au sein des nuits profondes,
De l'éther étoilé contempler la splendeur.
Gardez votre infini, cieux lointains, vastes mondes,
   J'ai le mien dans mon cœur![99]

Life appears to her, she writes in 1874, as 'un drame lamentable
qui se joue dans un coin perdu de l'univers, en vertu de lois
aveugles, devant une nature indifférente, avec le néant pour
dénouement'.[1] But in this sombre drama man is cast as hero.

---

[99] *Œuv.*, p. 169, *L'Homme.*   [1] *Œuv.*, p. xxii.

IX

POSITIVISM AND THE PARNASSIANS (2)

THE PHILOSOPHY OF SULLY PRUDHOMME

1. *Introduction*

SULLY PRUDHOMME (1839–1907) illustrates above all else the mortality of fame. Throughout the last thirty years or more of the nineteenth century he was amongst the most celebrated of contemporary French poets, a leader of the Parnassian group and an admired friend of eminent scholars, philosophers, poets, and critics of his day—Boutroux, Scherer, Gautier, Sainte-Beuve, Jules Lemaître, Gaston Paris, Anatole France, Heredia, amongst many others. Today, despite the studies of Estève (1925) and Flottes (1930), he is little read. His earlier *poésie sentimentale* —from *Stances et poèmes* (1865) onwards—his later *poésie philosophique*—*Les Destins* (1872), *La Justice* (1878), *Le Bonheur* (1888)—the prose works, on the arts and philosophy, written in the last fifteen or twenty years of his life, all are now neglected except by the historian of literature.

For the student of nineteenth-century thought, however, his work retains its interest, for the writer who deservedly impressed professional philosophers like Boutroux and Hémon[1] epitomizes, as we shall see, a great deal in the intellectual life of his age. He himself gave first place to philosophy and to the life-long speculations whose results he set down in his notebooks and letters and in published works, from the *Préface* to his translation of Lucretius (started in 1859) to his final philosophical works, *Que sais-je?*, *Le Crédit de la science*, *La Vraie Religion selon Pascal*, *Le Problème des causes finales*, and *Psychologie du libre arbitre*. 'La philosophie a rapetissé à mes yeux [he remarks in 1868] toutes

---

[1] E. Boutroux, 'Un Poète philosophe, M. Sully Prudhomme', *Revue politique et littéraire*, 4 sept. 1875, pp. 227–31; C. Hémon, *La Philosophie de Sully Prudhomme*, Alcan, 1907. Cf. E. Scherer, *Études sur la littérature contemporaine*, 1863–95, 10 vols., ix. 307–20; C. Spiess, *Le Penseur chez Sully Prudhomme*, 1908; E. Zyromski, *Sully Prudhomme*, 1907; and the laudatory review by F. Pillon in *L'Année philosophique — Deuxième Année (1868)*, 1869.

les affaires humaines.'[2] Gaston Paris discerns in him 'un profond
sérieux, un perpétuel reploiement sur lui-même, une préoccupa-
tion constante des choses religieuses', whilst Bourget speaks of
'le scrupule d'une pensée toujours en quête de vérité'.[3] The priority
he gives to philosophy also accounts for his desire to fuse poetry
and thought, and this in turn helps to explain the unsatisfactori-
ness of many of his poems, in particular those which are explicitly
philosophical. Yet this intellectual self-consciousness and his wide
knowledge of the history of philosophy make him an unusually
valuable witness to the ideological disputes of his time.

He is also better informed on the discoveries of contemporary
science than most other poets of his day. Where Ménard and
Leconte de Lisle are thinking chiefly of *philologie* when they
refer to 'la science', he is familiar with the natural sciences themselves, and where they unite poetry and philology, he tries to
link poetry and the sciences properly speaking. Even as a youth
he felt drawn to scientific study—'par une direction supérieure
qu'accepta ma curiosité, en dépit de mon penchant marqué déjà
pour les vers'.[4] He graduated (in 1856) as *bachelier ès sciences*,
and only illness prevented him from taking a course in mathematics at the École Polytechnique. Later, whilst working for a year
(1860) at the Schneider works at Le Creusot, he also saw the
practical application of scientific discovery, and even as a law
student he continued to interest himself in it. He gives us through
his *Journal intime* a typical if youthfully proud glimpse of his
attitude at this time.

> Je passe ma journée à rédiger ma théorie de la mémoire. . . . Ainsi
> à la veille d'un examen dont je ne sais pas un mot, je fais de la psycho-
> logie pendant cinq heures. Ô passion![5]

His thorough knowledge of the natural sciences and their methods
is in fact one of the primary sources of his work in both philosophy
and poetry. Only a writer with an informed interest in them could
have written the section on *Les Sciences* in *Le Bonheur* and the
first six vigils of *La Justice*, for example, and so knowledgeable a

---

[2] R. F. A. Sully Prudhomme, *Journal intime: Lettres — Pensées*, Lemerre, 1922
[*J. Int.*], p. 101.
[3] G. Paris, *Penseurs et poètes*, 1896, p. 171; and P. Bourget, *Pages de critique
et de doctrine*, s.d. (Plon-Nourrit), 2 vols., ii. 174.
[4] R. F. A. Sully Prudhomme, *Préface* to Hémon, op. cit. [*Hémon Préf.*], p. iii.
[5] *J. Int.*, p. 50; the examination was, of course, in law.

student of the century's literature as Estève can comment: 'Parmi nos poètes du dix-neuvième siècle, il est le seul, à ma connaissance, qui ait joint au bénéfice d'une culture littéraire étendue celui d'une culture scientifique approfondie.'[6] One side of him always ranked the sciences more highly than the arts, and if his sensitivity and feeling for literature had not attracted him to poetry, he might well have made his name as a scientist. In a most revealing letter he summarizes this leaning towards science.

Certainement la littérature a produit des ouvrages merveilleux, mais je vous avoue que c'est par l'expression de la vérité qu'elle me semble le plus digne d'intérêt; les ouvrages de science sont, à mes yeux, bien supérieurs aux œuvres d'imagination; je ne connais pas une œuvre littéraire qui approche pour moi des découvertes de Newton. . . . L'Iliade et l'Odyssée ne me paraissent être que des jeux d'enfant, comparés à la découverte du carré de l'hypoténuse et de la rotation de la terre.[7]

He adds in the same letter: 'c'est que je ne suis pas assez artiste...', and one may well feel that his scientific erudition mars a good deal of his poetry and that his earlier elegiac poems are preferable to the poèmes philosophiques.[8]

'Il a su traduire, mieux que personne en ses vers, les rêves, les aspirations et les plus nobles inquiétudes de ses contemporains', Giraud testifies.[9] In particular he suffered, more intensely than any of his fellow poets, from the conflict between his anti-positivist yearnings and his positivist convictions. Naturally indecisive, so that his friend Gaston Paris could describe him as 'toujours incertain et irrésolu', a man in whom intellectual rigour and emotional sensitivity were equally balanced, he became the prey of an uncertainty that sterilized his will.[10] Hence his never-ending re-examinations of the relation of science and religion, so that

---

[6] E. Estève, Sully Prudhomme, poète sentimental et poète philosophe, 1925, p. 12.

[7] J. Int., p. 193, letter to Mme Amiel dated Dec. 1877.

[8] Cf. Estève, op. cit., pp. 222, 234; Bourget, op. cit., ii. 200; and H. J. Hunt's judgement on La Justice in The Epic in Nineteenth-Century France, Oxford, 1941, p. 394.

[9] V. Giraud, Maîtres d'autrefois et d'aujourd'hui, 1914, p. 258.

[10] Paris, op. cit., pp. 208–9. Cf. J. Int., p. 42: 'L'irrésolution est un dissolvant de la volonté qui la rend fluide et propre à tous canaux. La vie de l'irrésolu est à tous: tout le monde vit pour lui, à sa place; il est mollement malheureux, mollement heureux, annulé.'

many of his works are in the nature of philosophical balance-sheets, even his poems.

La science froide et sûre en face d'un spectre religieux qui ne veut pas lui céder la place, voilà le *drame* moderne de la pensée humaine.[11]

2. *Sully Prudhomme as a Positivist*

His views confront us at the outset with a seeming paradox: throughout his career he accepts the truth of the positivist position and yet aspires to transcend the limitations of human knowledge that it imposes. Does this aspiration imply an abandonment of positivism? He did not think so. The uncompromisingly positivist attitude to metaphysics which he expressed in the preface to *De la nature des choses* is reaffirmed when he publishes the work in 1869 and again in 1878 when *La Justice* appeared, for which, as he points out, this early preface is the background.[12] The same conviction persists in later works such as *Que sais-je?* (1896) and *Le Problème des causes finales* (1903).

After his brief period of Christian belief at the age of eighteen, he tells us, he carried out an investigation of our ways of knowledge. His conclusion was that they were 'bien insuffisants pour instituer la science de l'objet métaphysique'.[13] This attitude is expanded in the preface to *De la nature des choses*, a long philosophical essay which has been unduly neglected, for its clarity and freedom from current confusions are arresting, particularly in a youth in his twenties, and he also expresses here the theory of knowledge which, despite uncertainties and occasional defections, he retained for the rest of his life.

He begins by distinguishing two stages in our acquisition of knowledge—first, sense-experience and, secondly, reflection upon it—and, already opposed to any *a priori* approach, he insists that the task of reflection is never to replace observation but to order and judge 'le témoignage indispensable' it offers.[14] Nor does he fall into the error illustrated in Taine's thought by claiming that reason applied to experience can give us knowledge of 'the external

[11] *J. Int.*, pp. 186–7.
[12] R. F. A. Sully Prudhomme, *Œuvres—Poésies*, Lemerre, 1925–6, 6 vols. [*Œuv.*], t. iv, p. iii.   [13] *Hémon Préf.*, p. vii.
[14] R. F. A. Sully Prudhomme, *Préface* to his translation of Lucretius, *De natura rerum*, in *Œuv.*, t. iv [*Préf.*], p. xxiv.

world in itself' or the causes determining it. Science is confined to exploring the relations between phenomena. No positivist could develop the point more forcefully. First, he asserts, we must differentiate between our sensation and the 'object' to which we attribute the sensation. It is false to speak of 'matter' or 'substance', as though we still lived in the time of Epicurus, or to 'exteriorize' our sensations. These errors, only too natural in spontaneous experience, were committed in Aristotle's physics and are still committed at the present day, and by a skilful analysis of physics, chemistry, and physiology he shows the ways in which scientists have projected on to non-human data characteristics that are in reality human. We can never know 'the thing in itself' and, reminiscent of the author of the *Critique of Pure Reason,* he declares that to perceive is necessarily to 'subjectivize': 'c'est voir la chose à travers soi-même et non en elle-même, c'est y mêler du moi'.[15]

When we consider our inner experience, we again meet with inevitable barriers, and in discussing these Sully Prudhomme is explicitly criticizing the eclectic doctrines. 'Nous croyons . . . qu'il n'y a pas d'aperception immédiate interne.' The notion of the 'self' as a unity is never directly validated: it is merely inferred from our experiences of sensation, emotion, desire, and thought. Even *De l'intelligence* does not put the matter more bluntly.

Nous pouvons nous apercevoir sentant, désirant, pensant, mais non point dans notre substance, indépendamment de toute modification de nous-même. . . . L'être du moi est pour l'esprit qui l'étudie un inconnu objectif au même titre que les choses extérieures.[16]

The writer is now in a position to attack the separation of 'external reality' into two 'substances', mind and matter. We cannot say whether there are two or a thousand different 'substances', and indeed the notion of a single 'substance' is not easily to be dismissed, 'car tout se lie et se tient solidairement dans nos perceptions'. Our sense-experience distinguishes neither mind nor matter: 'elle fait concevoir seulement un tout indivisible qui se manifeste par des groupes de phénomènes d'ordre différent'.[17]

---

[15] *Préf.,* p. lxvii. Cf. Pillon's comment on this *Préface,* cited *Œuv.,* iv. 54; after quoting Sully Prudhomme's views on perception he declares: 'La conclusion de ce remarquable passage est nettement criticiste.'

[16] *Préf.,* p. lxxiii.

[17] *Préf.,* p. lxx.

Thus both materialism and spiritualism arise from ignoring the limits inherent in the act of experiencing: to affirm either view is 'hypothétique et téméraire'. He concedes to the materialists that we can show that 'physical phenomena' are accompanied by 'mental phenomena' according to constant laws, but whilst we may say that a particular physiological state *determines* a particular mental state, that does not mean that the former *produces* the latter—a distinction that recalls Claude Bernard's separation of 'conditions' and 'causes'.

La différence entre déterminer et produire est capitale: produire, c'est fournir les matériaux de la chose qui naît; déterminer, c'est simplement fournir les conditions de la naissance.[18]

He recalls Bernard again and also Mill's opposition to Taine's notion of abstraction when he speaks of causality. Explicitly contrasting the materialists and the positivists—at a time when they were too often confused—he sides with the latter. Unlike Lefèvre in his *Épopée terrestre*, the positivist abstains from making any judgements about substances and first causes[19]—and rightly, for all we can conclude from our sense-experience, he stresses,

c'est que tels groupes de sensations sont toujours précédés, accompagnés ou suivis de tels autres, mais il n'en résulte en aucune façon qu'ils soient raison d'être, c'est-à-dire cause et fin les uns des autres.[20]

Materialists and spiritualists alike have been misled by the 'categories' which are the very conditions of our knowing into imagining that every phenomenon presupposes a substance, a cause, an aim, and space and time: thus they have been led to pose 'des questions absurdes', he adds in terms that recall the strictures of later positivists about 'meaningless questions' and 'philosophical puzzles'. The truth is that 'toute application de nos propres catégories à l'univers entier est arbitraire et n'offre aucun caractère scientifique'.[21] And if we ask what, in that case, is the purpose of science, Sully Prudhomme's reply is very like that of Poincaré later:

[18] *Préf.*, pp. lxxviii and lxxx.
[19] *J. Int.*, p. 103.
[20] *Préf.*, p. lxxxv.
[21] *Préf.*, pp. xci, cii. To erect a metaphysical system would presuppose, he always contends, 'l'adaptation de l'intelligence humaine à l'objet métaphysique'. 'Or celui-ci répugne à cette adaptation' (*Hémon Préf.*, p. i).

la fin de toute science est un système de rapports que la réflexion découvre dans ces données et qui les rend *intelligibles*.[22]

Nor is he tempted (except in a moment of inconsistency) to pass from these strictly positivist views to a scientism of the kind advanced by Taine or Renan. The scientific method, 'cette méthode lente et sûre', is as powerless as any other to erect a metaphysics. Despite its superiority, he concludes,

la science . . . ne peut, non plus que la philosophie, espérer d'étendre ses conquêtes au delà d'un domaine relativement restreint dont l'essence humaine, qui est bornée, donne exactement la mesure.[23]

Sully Prudhomme may have little originality as a thinker, but the contrast between this position and the 'scientific metaphysics' of Taine or the 'religion of science' of Renan shows the clear-sightedness of his acceptance of positivism. 'Sachons plutôt ne pas savoir [he adds], ce n'est pas la moindre vertu du vrai philosophe.'[24]

These beliefs recur throughout Sully Prudhomme's later works: although unpromising poetic material, they even inspire a number of his shorter poems—his verses *Après la lecture de Kant*, regretting the subjectivism imposed by Kant's analysis of pure reason, the sonnet *A Kant*, the poem on Descartes's notion of intuitive knowledge, amongst others.[25] And above all they provide the background for the many poems and the many passages of philosophical speculation in which he deplores the limits of our knowledge.

3. *Sully Prudhomme's Metaphysical Search*

'Je suis bien convaincu de la vanité de l'ontologie', he writes to Boutroux in 1875, reaffirming the outlook we have just studied; '. . . il n'y a qu'un objet d'étude, le monde *phénoménal*.'[26] Yet he longs to resolve the metaphysical mysteries that preoccupy him, he seeks to answer questions which the positivist in him believes unanswerable. This is Sully Prudhomme's persistent dilemma: to believe that 'le *comment* est la question scientifique et seule féconde' but to be obsessed by 'le *pourquoi*', 'problème formidable

[22] *Préf.*, p. xxiv.   [23] *Préf.*, pp. xci, xciii.
[24] *Préf.*, p. cvii.
[25] *Œuv.*, vi. 109, 95, *Épaves*, and ii. 43, *Les Épreuves*.
[26] *J. Int.*, pp. 198, 200.

que je n'ai pas l'outrecuidant espoir de résoudre et que néanmoins je n'ai jamais pu m'interdire d'agiter'. Science knows none
of the truths he most wishes to know, yet outside science there
can be no knowledge.[27] This situation provokes both the theme
of desolating ignorance expressed in many poems, especially in
the section of *Les Épreuves* entitled *Doute,* and the conflict of
head and heart which underlies so much of his thought. '*Il y a
en moi conflit entre l'intuition qui affirme et la déduction qui
nie.*'[28] This conflict may, as Sainte-Beuve suggests,[29] have been
a fashionable pose in the mid-nineteenth century, but for Sully
Prudhomme it was sincerely felt to the point of anguish.

> En moi-même se livre un combat sans vainqueur
> Entre la foi sans preuve et la raison sans charme.[30]

The voice of intuition and of his personal aspirations protests
against the barren, sceptical affirmations of the intellect; the
intellect mocks and dismisses its complaints.

So ardent is his wish for metaphysical knowledge that at
moments he can argue that future poets will attain it, although
we cannot, or anticipate the coming of a Newton of metaphysics,
'un Newton pour l'âme de l'homme'.[31] But his exclamations here
express the desires of the heart, not the pondered conclusions of
the intellect. Only at one point does he appear to abandon positivism—in his belief that in one's conscience, in that 'intuition
of the heart' of which Pascal reminded him, one can find 'une
autre source de certitude que la raison'.[32] But, significantly, this
view is maintained only in regard to ethics, and then hesitantly,
as we shall see later, and is finally renounced. Speaking of 'les
révélations immédiates et spontanées de la conscience' he reluctantly admits their *metaphysical* barrenness: they teach him
nothing about 'the first cause', his 'fate', or the 'meaning' of his
life.[33]

This does not imply that we cannot speculate about metaphysical questions. We can each entertain our own hopes and
undertake our 'personal investigation'. But we can never gain

---

[27] *J. Int.,* pp. 41, 205, and *Hémon Préf.,* p. viii.
[28] *J. Int.,* p. 207.
[29] C. A. Sainte-Beuve, *Nouveaux Lundis,* 1863–70, 13 vols., v. 14.
[30] *Œuv.,* iv. 80, *La Justice.*
[31] *Œuv.,* iii. 147, *Les Vaines Tendresses,* and i. 44–45, *Stances et poèmes.*
[32] *Hémon Préf.,* p. xiv; cf. p. xv.   [33] *Hémon Préf.,* p. ix.

knowledge, nor can one conjecture be more probable, philosophically speaking, than any other. And although Sully Prudhomme himself constantly ponders on the problems posed by 'man's excessive curiosity', he never offers more than his private 'beliefs'.[34] This speculative side of his thought does not consist of a systematic construction but, as Hémon remarks, of 'un perpétuel examen de conscience'.[35] His attitude to metaphysics from 1859 onwards is that affirmed in the letter he wrote to Hémon in 1906 and especially in the allegory of the blind man moving towards an unknown and undiscoverable destination:

> Peut-être à mon insu ma carrière est-elle ensoleillée et ascendante. Ah! je ne m'y suis pas engagé moi-même; ce n'est pas moi qui ai bâti et appareillé mon esquif et le dirige. Qui est-ce? Je l'ignore; ce constructeur-pilote reste muet. Je ne sais pas davantage où il me conduit, mais je ne peux me défendre d'espérer, plus exactement d'aspirer....[36]

The affirmations he makes thus never claim more than an emotional and speculative validity for the individual himself; they are openly presented as unverifiable. Giving his views on God, for instance, he adds: 'mon sentiment m'est tout personnel'.[37] Again, he suggests that physical and mental phenomena may be two manifestations of a single substance that one might describe as 'l'Être universel, c'est ce que nous appellerions Dieu'. But, unlike Spinoza and Taine, he points out categorically that this is 'une simple conjecture': 'on donne provisoirement audience à toutes les aspirations de l'esprit humain, depuis l'idéalisme jusqu'au positivisme'[38]—a remark that illustrates his constant search to reconcile opposing positions, as well as the diffidence with which he puts forward his personal ideas.

It follows from his standpoint that these private conjectures can never contradict positivism, even though in its eyes they may be 'literally nonsensical', since they cannot possibly be empirically verified. Strictly speaking, therefore, they are irrelevant for an estimate of Sully Prudhomme's relation to the positivist philosophy. Yet they not only reveal more fully the conflict of head and heart within him; they also have a special interest at this stage in our history in that almost all the philosophical

---

[34] *Hémon Préf.*, pp. xix, xvi.
[35] Hémon, op. cit., p. 42; cf. his own assertion in *Hémon Préf.*, p. i.
[36] *Hémon Préf.*, p. xviii.   [37] *Hémon Préf.*, p. xi.
[38] *Préf.*, p. lxxxii.

influences we have encountered left a mark upon them. One can see this clearly in studying various manifestations of the conflict.

4. 'The Conflict of Head and Heart'

(a) Sully Prudhomme and Pascal

The division of mind from which he suffered is itself indicative of the widely varying influences reflected in his thought. On the one side stands an unrelenting, agnostic positivism, reinforced in its scepticism by Kant's *Critique of Pure Reason*. On the other there are the desires and 'intimations' of the 'heart', protesting against the restricted range of scientific knowledge, earnestly seeking a metaphysical faith, and in the realm of ethics occasionally invoking those intuitive reasons which the reason fails to comprehend. Here, by virtue of his aspirations, if no further, he joins the tradition of an anti-positivism based on the notion of an 'inner light', whether in the form Rousseau embraced—an inner light of conscience, 'instinct divin, immortelle et céleste voix, guide assuré . . .'—or in the late-nineteenth-century guise of an 'intellectual intuition' that enables us to grasp realities in their living entirety. There are fairly clear reminiscences of Rousseau in his treatment of the notion of *le cœur*, particularly in the *Huitième Veille* of *La Justice* ('La Conscience'), and he is also referred to—with somewhat cryptic brevity—in *Le Bonheur*:

> Rousseau pour sûr asile ouvre la conscience,
> Temple unique d'un Dieu qui se passe d'encens. . . .[39]

One can even find prefigurations of Bergsonism—in his views on freedom, as we shall note later, and also in an isolated comment in the *Préface* of 1869 on chemical analysis:

> En somme [he writes], analyser un corps, c'est le détruire, et c'est par conséquent laisser échapper le principe même de son unité pour ne mettre en évidence que les résultats de cette destruction.[40]

Yet his conception of *le cœur* is principally taken from Pascal—and he rightly finds a place in the history of Pascal's 'revival' in the later nineteenth century. He may not belong to that 'Idealist reaction' surveyed by Eastwood,[41] but his prolonged concern with

---

[39] *Œuv.*, v. 248. [40] *Préf.*, p. lxi.
[41] D. M. Eastwood, *The Revival of Pascal—A study of his relation to modern French thought*, Oxford, 1936.

Pascal is symptomatic of a wish to transcend positivism; in him the influence of Pascal goes as far as is consistent with retaining a positivist outlook.

He first read the *Pensées* as a young man, and for the rest of his life he carried on a kind of intimate intellectual dialogue with their author. As early as 1862 he notes in his *Journal intime*:

Pascal, je t'admire, tu es mien, je te pénètre comme si je pensais en toi. . . . Sois mon maître, adopte-moi, je souffre infiniment, je gravite autour de la vérité, je ne l'atteins jamais.[42]

From the *Stances et poèmes* (1865) onwards there are numerous allusions to Pascal in his poetry, and in the last twenty years of his life he published articles on him and his longest prose work, *La Vraie Religion selon Pascal* (1905).

Pascal's fascination for Sully Prudhomme derives first and foremost from the combination he illustrates of scientific genius and religious belief.[43] How can one be believer and scientist at the same time, satisfy the heart without betraying the intellect? This is the central question he addresses to Pascal—a question springing from his own sense of disunity. At first he appears to believe that *la raison raisonnante* and *le cœur* are complementary modes of knowledge for Pascal. Hence the poem *L'Esprit et le cœur*, written in 1862 on the famous *pensée*: 'Le cœur a ses raisons que la raison ne connaît pas', expresses a confidence that was later to desert him.

> C'est qu'il est deux foyers pour éclairer notre âme:
> L'esprit perce la brume avec son rare éclair,
> Mais le cœur la dissipe avec sa chaude flamme
> Comme un ardent midi fait transparent tout l'air.[44]

In his later poems the reminiscences of Pascal are drawn from the more despairing sections of the *Apologie*—as in *Scrupule* (1866) with its theme of the impenetrable mystery of man's destiny; in *La Voie lactée* whose concluding lines:

> Et la solitude immortelle
> Brûle en silence dans la nuit[45]

---

[42] *J. Int.*, p. 5.

[43] Cf. R. F. A. Sully Prudhomme, *La Vraie Religion selon Pascal*, Alcan, 1905, p. 47.

[44] *Œuv.*, vi. 110–11. Reprinted in *Épaves* as *Sur une pensée de Pascal*. At this time he can express his thankfulness to be both philosopher and poet (*J. Int.*, p. 16), whereas later he will feel divided by this duality.

[45] *Œuv.*, ii. 129, *Les Solitudes* (1869).

recall the *pensée*: 'Le silence éternel de ces espaces infinis m'ef-
fraie'; or in *Dernière Solitude* (1869), which reminds us of Pascal's
portrayal of death. He can no longer believe now that even Pascal
succeeded in reconciling head and heart, and the portrait he
presents in his *Sonnet à Mme A. Hayem* is of a man, unmistakably
resembling Sully Prudhomme himself, divided between science
and faith.

> Pascal, qui, tourmentant ton grand cœur attristé,
> En sublimes efforts épuises ton génie
> Pour terrasser le doute et mettre en harmonie
> La misère de l'homme avec sa majesté,
>
> Tu sens par la raison le Credo contesté,
> Et, lutteur isolé dans l'arène infinie,
> Tu combats, une main de ton compas munie,
> L'autre cachant ta plaie où le dogme est resté.[46]

Later still, in *Le Bonheur* (1888), it is Pascal the sceptic who
appears to Faustus and after advising him to return to Stella and
his enjoyment of love and life goes on to counsel a serene acceptance of the limited and relative knowledge which is within man's
grasp.

> 'Homme, dit-il, ta vue est brève.
> Garde-toi d'usurper le lieu
> D'où plonge, sans borne ni trêve
> Et partout, le regard de Dieu.
> Reporte le tien sur les roses;
> Sa lutte avec l'immensité,
> L'origine et la fin des choses
> N'aboutit qu'à la cécité.'[47]

This is the lesson Pascal himself is represented as having learnt:
the search for ultimate truth is vain. It is worth recalling that this
view of Pascal as a sceptic was still widely prevalent when Sully
Prudhomme was writing. One finds it in Cousin and Havet and
it remained strong enough for Droz to think it necessary to refute
it as late as 1886. Even Sainte-Beuve, though opposing this conception, refers to Pascal as a man in whom doubt struggled 'like
a caged lion'.[48]

[46] *Œuv.*, v. 81, *Le Prisme* (1886).
[47] *Œuv.*, v. 285.
[48] Cf. Eastwood, op. cit., ch. i, and especially pp. 5–6.

Yet later, about 1890, when (he tells us[49]) he finally renounced metaphysical speculation, his relationship with Pascal changed once more. In *La Vraie Religion selon Pascal* it is no longer the sceptic whom we meet. He now believes that Pascal's scepticism was not far-reaching enough: it failed to include a critique of the heart as a source of knowledge.

> Pascal n'a jamais été, à proprement parler, pyrrhonien. . . . Nous savons que, loin de là, son doute s'est attaqué uniquement au témoignage des sens et de la raison, qui sont les armes de l'incrédulité religieuse, mais nullement à celui du cœur, qui est le siège de la foi.
>
> Nous ne saurions donc voir dans Pascal le martyr du doute que nous présente une légende fort accréditée.[50]

Pascal is no longer a fellow sufferer! The *Pensées* are finally rejected as inadequate to the demands of the intellect. But it can at least be said that they confirmed him in two of his primary beliefs—first, the idea that *le cœur*, although not an instrument of knowledge, may suggest to each of us personal reasons for choice and action; and secondly, his conviction of the need for personal decision which he found paralleled in the argument of the *Wager*. He adopts the *Pari* even though he sometimes feels its amorality. In *Rouge ou noire*, for example, it forms the theme of the entire poem.

> Parie. A l'infini court la rouge ou la noire.[51]

And later, in the review of modern philosophy in *Le Bonheur*, the argument of the *Wager* is linked with the anguish of the religious seeker:

> La foi n'est dans Pascal qu'une agonie étrange . . .
> Aux dogmes du chrétien le penseur se résigne . . .
> Enfin le géomètre effrayé du problème,
> Ne pouvant ni prouver ni renier son Dieu,
> Risque la vérité dans un pari suprême
> Dont, sur un noir tapis, le bonheur est l'enjeu.[52]

Its influence is visible to the end, as in the concluding words of his study of Pascal:

il faut bien que l'espèce humaine agisse pour vivre et durer; or toutes

---

[49] *Hémon Préf.*, p. ii (written in Nov. 1906): 'Depuis une quinzaine d'années j'ai renoncé à agiter ces questions insolubles.'

[50] *La Vraie Religion*, pp. 33, 46–47.

[51] *Œuv.*, ii. 28, *Les Épreuves* (1866).   [52] *Œuv.*, v. 245–6.

les démarches présupposent des raisons d'agir, lesquelles ne peuvent donc être provisoirement que des actes de foi, religieux ou non.[53]

(b) The problem of the existence of God

Sully Prudhomme's state of philosophical conflict is reflected in a wide variety of themes—in the realm of aesthetics, in which he tries to harmonize art as the description of external experience and art as the expression of a personal apprehension of form and beauty; in the sphere of poetic theory, where he wishes to establish a parallel union of science and poetry; even in the field of political thought in his comments upon the opposition of individualism and the demands of society.[54] But here we may best consider its manifestations in his ideas on three primary metaphysical problems—the existence of a personal God, the reality of free will, and the immortality of the soul.

In a letter written in 1877 he tells his correspondent of the difficulty he experiences in forgetting the serenity he had known as a youthful religious believer. 'On a eu beau détruire et même oublier le dogme, il nous en reste le vague et puissant charme d'une hymne dont on ne se rappelle plus une note, mais dont l'impression lointaine subsiste.'[55] And to François Coppée, a few days before his death, he remarks: 'Oh! que vous êtes heureux de croire!'[56] This longing for a faith he cannot accept provides the theme for many of his poems.

> Je voudrais bien prier, je suis plein de soupirs!
> Ma cruelle raison veut que je les contienne. . . .
> C'est une angoisse impie et sainte que la mienne:
> Mon doute insulte en moi le Dieu de mes désirs.

Like others of his agnostic contemporaries he yearns for assurance that God exists.

> Je vous attends, Seigneur; Seigneur, êtes-vous là?[57]

---

[53] La Vraie Religion, p. 390.
[54] Cf. Hémon's excellent treatment of these aspects of his thought, and H. Morice, La Poésie de Sully Prudhomme, 1920, 'Première Partie', ch. vi, and 'Seconde Partie'.
[55] J. Int., p. 186.
[56] Cited by Morice, op. cit., p. 215.
[57] Œuv., ii. 22, La Prière, Les Épreuves.

Before an old painting of Saint Peter walking on the waters he cries:

> Nous ne demandons point de marcher sur les ondes,
> Mais seulement, ô Dieu! qu'une seule fois tu répondes
> Quand nous crions d'en bas.[58]

He has told of the conversion he underwent at Lyons at the age of eighteen when, despite his scientific training, he awoke in the night filled with the certainty that Christ was divine and that the Christian doctrines were true and asking himself how he could have doubted for a moment a teaching whose validity now appeared so evident to him. His return to Paris and his reading of Strauss quickly dissipated this conviction and the plan he had formed to enter a religious order. Yet the certainty he had possessed then was to preoccupy him for the remainder of his life.[59] He became, as he remarks, 'un chercheur inquiet, désabusé, mais non découragé', examining again and again the evidence for Christianity, and the failure of his search for God explains a good deal of his pessimism and the 'sentiment de la solitude morale' pervading his work.[60] On this religious level the conflict is at its most acute.

> Deux voix s'élèvent tour à tour
> Des profondeurs troubles de l'âme:
> La raison blasphème, et l'amour
> Rêve un dieu juste et le proclame.
>
> Panthéiste, athée ou chrétien,
> Tu connais leurs luttes obscures;
> C'est mon martyre, et c'est le tien,
> De vivre avec ces deux murmures.[61]

The heart aspires to belief in God, but the reason and scientific knowledge remind him of the suffering and evil that dominate the natural world. Drawing upon the discoveries of biology and the evidence for the theory of natural selection, he points to the

---

[58] Œuv., v. 79, Dans une église devant un vieux tableau, Le Prisme. Cf. Œuv., ii. 23, 35.

[59] Hémon Préf., pp. vi–vii.

[60] Cf. J. Int., p. 119: 'Au fond il n'y a qu'une solitude, origine de toutes les autres, c'est l'éloignement où nous sommes de la raison du monde, de Dieu, quel qu'il soit. . . . Il est là et je ne le vois pas; j'appelle, il reste muet, je suis donc horriblement abandonné, je suis seul.'

[61] Œuv., i. 40, Intus, Stances et poèmes.

cruel necessities to which life is subject. Even if a personal God exists, he must be conceived of as an unjust tyrant and not as the beneficent Providence of the Christian theologians. Writing in 1864 of a disastrous fire in a church in Santiago, he asserts: 'La création, considérée d'un regard humain, est une œuvre monstrueuse qui n'est ni révoltante, ni édifiante, mais inconcevable, contradictoire, absurde. . . .'[62] On the Christian hypothesis the smile of a young child and the glare of the tiger are the handiwork of the same Creator. We cannot maintain that the created world is wholly *immoral*, but sooner than 'blaspheme' by believing in a personal God who has established so *amoral* a natural world, he prefers to abandon the notion of a Divine Providence.

> Et quiconque a senti l'ordre du monde inique,
> S'il n'est pas un athée, est un blasphémateur.[63]

He does not entirely reject the idea of an Eternal Being, however, and at different times he adopts as hypotheses the notions of the Divine that have been seen in Taine and in Renan.

He was a friend of Taine,[64] and the Taine-like pantheism he postulates is based, we saw, upon his belief that matter and mind are both appearances of 'un tout indivisible', of a single primary 'substance'. Even in the *Préface* of 1869 he accepts the view that this *Inconnaissable* may be thought of as necessary, absolute, and infinite,[65] and it is this idea he expresses in several of the poems published in 1865 and 1866. Surveying the rising sun he proclaims:

> Nous autres, nous crions: Salut à l'Infini!
> Au grand Tout, à la fois idole, temple et prêtre. . . .

Les Dieux ends with the well-known assertion:

> Dieu n'est pas rien, mais Dieu n'est personne: il est Tout.

---

[62] *J. Int.*, p. 45.

[63] *Œuv.*, iv. 182. In the discussion of Christian dogma towards the end of *La Vraie Religion selon Pascal* he adds a further reason for disbelief: the doctrine of the Creation, in postulating God as a first cause, is based on a misuse of the notion of causality.

[64] He was originally introduced to Taine by Gaston Paris and thereafter they were often in close contact—at Madame Taine's *samedis*, at dinners with Flaubert, Renan, Paris, and others. Cf. Estève, op. cit., pp. 199–200.

[65] *Préf.*, p. xcviii.

In *Scrupule*, describing the natural world's lack of consciousness, he thinks it a strange truth

> Que l'Univers, le Tout, soit Dieu sans le savoir![66]

His God is in fact the God of Spinoza and Taine,

> . . . un Dieu qui jamais n'a frappé ni béni,
> Et dont la majesté dédaigneuse et paisible
> Écrase en souriant l'homme pauvre et fini.[67]

This is the hypothesis he was to revert to in *La Vraie Religion selon Pascal*, for example, where the primary cause is defined as 'la substance unique du monde phénoménal tout entier'.[68] He also takes from Spinozism the distinction between this necessary and absolute realm and the contingent world of phenomena, and his thoughts upon determinism occasionally reflect the ideas of the *Ethics*. But the similarities must not be pressed too far. Unlike Spinoza or Taine, he never claims knowledge of this metaphysical sphere. This conception is 'complètement creuse', 'nous ignorons complètement les catégories du Tout, hormis celles qu'implique notre propre essence'.[69] His pantheism is indeed an expression of the needs of the heart rather than an intellectual system.

Reminding one here of Taine, although without his scientism, he later recalls Renan—and behind him Hegel. The Divine, he sometimes implies, especially in *Le Prisme* (1886), will be realized by the advance of knowledge and moral goodness—a notion he feels encouraged to adopt by the theory of evolution and the idea of *le devenir*. Like Renan and Leconte de Lisle he also looks forward to the coming of a superman who shall bring God into existence, and he yearns for the time when this deity will be visible on earth,

> Quand donc sur la dernière assise enfin gravie,
> Après avoir monté tous les degrés du ciel,
> Trônera la Pensée au faîte de la Vie,
> Conscience du monde et phare universel! . . .
>
> Quand donc aura trouvé sa figure et son lieu
> Le prince et le dernier de la plus haute race,
> Le vivant idéal qu'on doive nommer Dieu!

---

[66] *Œuv.*, i. 135, *Le Lever du soleil, Stances et poèmes*, and ii. 30, 32, *Les Épreuves.*   [67] *Œuv.*, i. 182, *Mon Ciel, Stances et poèmes.*
[68] *La Vraie Religion*, p. 386.   [69] *Préf.*, pp. xcix, ciii.

He proclaims with Hegel-like confidence:

> Le monde entier travaille au suprême cerveau—

although he then adds more soberly:

> Mais l'œuvre à l'infini lentement se prolonge.[70]

(c) The problem of free will

A further difficulty arises when he seeks to establish the reality of human free will in the face of the theory of universal determinism. Unlike Taine, he believes moral responsibility and duty rely upon this freedom. And here again reason and the heart are straining in opposing directions. His observations of the external world (and of himself at times) seemed to demand the adoption of a strict determinism, and his pantheism required the same view, in which 'God' is the source and cause of all. On the other hand, in his view our moral aspiration and indignation imply freedom of the will.

His search to resolve this opposition is best expressed in poetic form in La Justice, in which he reveals (as he remarks in the Dédicace) 'les vicissitudes d'une intelligence et les angoisses d'un cœur, touchant l'essence et le fondement de la justice'.[71] Here the very arrangement of the poem makes the conflict explicit. After the Prologue, in which the poet undertakes his search for the source and nature of morality, there follow eleven Vigils. The first six of these form the first Part of the work and are placed under the title Silence au cœur; the last five, which with the Epilogue comprise the second Part, are entitled Appel au cœur. Within the first seven Vigils, moreover, the same juxtaposition is indicated by their internal ordering. The argument alternates between 'le Chercheur', the reason which seeks evidence and proof and questions the sciences at length in its attempt to find satisfaction, and on the other hand an inner voice which interrupts to protest against the negations of reason but is silenced after each protest by the scientific facts the reason presents.

In the first five Vigils 'le Chercheur' invokes the discoveries of science in order to illustrate the cruelty and amorality of Nature in general and man in particular. The more beautiful and pleasing aspects of the natural world that had been contrasted in Les

---

[70] Œuv., v. 69–70, Le Tourment divin, Le Prisme.
[71] Œuv., iv. 61–62.

Destins (1872) with its evil reverse side are here dismissed by the reason, and a picture is drawn of life dominated by the struggle for survival and by the unrelenting, pitiless victories of the strong over the weak (*Entre espèces*). Human life is no less overshadowed by cruel self-assertion, and he evokes man's brutishness with a force that even Hobbes describing the state of anarchy without the social law might envy (*Dans l'espèce, Entre états*, and *Dans l'état*). Finally, in the sixth Vigil, the reason states yet more forcefully the doctrine of universal fatality which the previous Vigils have been supporting. Our will appears free but is in reality enslaved—by heredity, education, and environment and by all the deeply rooted instincts prompting us in our battle for self-preservation. Even such seemingly noble emotions as maternal love are merely devices of Nature to ensure the continuance of the species, and he also revives a theme often found in his earlier poems, the fatality of love.

> Mais l'amante que j'ai, je ne l'ai pas choisie;
> Je ne pourrais pas plus la changer que ma sœur,

he had declared in *Fatalité* (*Les Épreuves*); and in *Les Amours terrestres* he concludes:

> Le sort a donc tout fait, nous n'avons rien voulu.[72]

It is this same conviction to which the reason is forced at the end of the first Part of *La Justice*. With a pessimism reminiscent of Schopenhauer he claims that our inner sense of liberty is merely 'l'illusion du choix dans la nécessité'.

> Seul le plus fort motif peut enfin prévaloir:
> Fatalement conçu pendant qu'on délibère,
> Fatalement vainqueur, c'est lui qui seul opère
> La fatale option qu'on appelle un vouloir.[73]

Thus the autonomy of human personality, the freedom of the will, and hence ethical responsibility are all no more than deceptive appearances, the creations of human pride and desire.

In the second Part of the poem, however, the heart intervenes

---

[72] *Œuv.*, ii. 16, and iii. 85, *Les Vaines Tendresses* (1875).
[73] *Œuv.*, iv. 178; cf. iii. 134. Although not wholly convincing, A. Baillot argues that Schopenhauer almost certainly exerted a strong influence upon him (*L'Influence de la philosophie de Schopenhauer en France (1860–1900)*, 1927).

to re-establish morality. The error of the reason has been to seek proof and empirical verification for what can only be felt personally through our conscience. This conscience is the source of our longing for the good, of our shame for the evil we have committed, and it prompts our feelings of moral indignation and approbation. He develops this idea in the eighth and ninth Vigils. Now the very fact of his own revolt against the amorality of the universe and the sacrifices men have made to combat human cruelty reassure him that the conscience transcends the egotism of Nature.

> Ô Justice [he cries] . . .
> Le sanglant défilé de tes martyrs proclame
> Qu'il n'est de tribunal sûr et sacré qu'en l'âme;
> Qu'il ne se rend que là des arrêts sans appel,
> Qu'enfin la conscience est ton unique autel! [74]

He firmly rejects Spencer's alternative explanation of these moral sentiments—the view that they are merely the product of ethical conditioning, the accumulated imperatives of our ancestors and our present society. His notion might be likened to Kant's theory of the categorical imperative, although only in part, or, more closely, to Rousseau's conception of conscience. We possess, he thinks, a kind of superior instinct, the moral sense, as infallible as the instincts we observe in action in the animal world and which we may follow with complete confidence. Furthermore, if our conscience is infallible, then duty and responsibility must have reality, and we must therefore possess free will.[75] He is then able to develop in the final sections of the poem his conceptions of justice and dignity (for 'la conscience innée' 'm'enjoint d'être homme et de respecter l'homme'[76]) and to conclude the work with a portrayal of a human city united by its ideals, by sympathy and fraternity, a prophecy which is linked with the ideas of progress and of the world's evolution towards perfection. Renan is now united with Rousseau; science, 'guide et salut de l'équipage', works side by side with love.

[74] *Œuv.*, iv. 216.
[75] He also asserts that he has an inner conviction of freedom. 'Du moins, à tort ou à raison, je me crois libre parce que je me sens libre et, bien que je puisse être logiquement contraint de douter de mon indépendance dans mes résolutions, en fait je ne le peux pas' (*J. Int.*, p. 207). He retains this view to the end of his life; cf. *Hémon Préf.*, p. ix.
[76] *Œuv.*, iv. 236.

> Jour levant, ô Science, ô Conscience, étoile!
> Que, par vous révélé, tout l'homme se dévoile
> Aux yeux de la Justice à peine dessillés![77]

The clash of head and heart is never plainer in his work than here. Reason contends that Nature is amoral; the heart believes that Nature has given us a moral conscience. For the reason, love is determined by the necessity to propagate the human species and even maternal love is egocentric. The heart, however, rejects Spencer's account of our moral emotions which accords so well with this view. It even feels assured of the existence of conscience by the sight of the self-sacrifice shown by maternal love. In fact, his ethic here is a 'natural morality' in which 'Nature' is as ambiguous a term as in the ethical naturalism of the *philosophes*: head and heart form very different pictures of it.

Yet what is again more interesting than a study of his speculations in themselves is to note their similarities to the ideas of more famous thinkers. Resemblances to Rousseau and Kant have already been suggested, and again like Kant he emphasizes the importance of the will in moral action. Moral perfection consists in 'une volonté maîtresse des passions égoïstes', in the willed subordination of individual desires to the general good.[78] Again, we saw him define the good, like Renan, as that which advances man's development in the evolutionary process towards perfection. When we feel remorse,

> C'est la voix de la Nature entière
> Qui dans l'humanité gronde son héritière;

when we know the happiness of virtuous action,

> C'est toute la Nature en nous-même contente,
> Louant l'humanité pour elle militante,
> Laborieuse et souple au frein;
> Elle dit: 'Gloire à toi dont le zèle conspire
> Avec mon vaste règne au bien de mon empire,
> Et m'aide à l'œuvre souverain!'[79]

Sully Prudhomme perhaps had even less excuse than Renan for ignoring Schopenhauer's objection to this view, for earlier he had presented Nature in the same light as the German pessimist.

---

[77] *Œuv.*, iv. 269, 272.
[78] Cf. *Œuv.*, vi. 184 ff., *Pour la fête du travail, Épaves.*
[79] *Œuv.*, iv. 232-3, *La Justice.*

In his later philosophical works—particularly in *Psychologie du libre arbitre*—he offers other arguments in favour of free will, and here again there are resemblances to other thinkers. First and most important, he argues that the doctrine of free will is not incompatible with the regularity of natural laws. He insists again, as earlier in the *Préface* to Lucretius, that science does not assert a necessary connexion between cause and effect.[80] It certainly discerns regular relations between phenomena, but it does not hold that the order of Nature will always remain the same. '*Constance* n'est pas *nécessité*', he affirms. This does not mean that we are thrown into doubt as to whether the sun will rise tomorrow or the law of gravitation cease to apply to our planet. Predictions may be made 'avec toute l'assurance qu'autorise une extrême probabilité'. None the less, there is a vital distinction between 'la nécessité métaphysique' and 'le déterminisme tel que la méthode expérimentale conduit et autorise à le définir'. The latter, he rightly argues, is no more than a useful working assumption. Moreover—and this is a second argument—science is not in a position to say anything about final causes: it leaves completely open the metaphysical question of freedom and necessity. It is noteworthy that both contentions are similar to those of Boutroux, Bergson, and others. He also adds two less persuasive assertions. Since man is free (which is here assumed) and is yet part of a pantheistic unity, 'l'être métaphysique' itself, 'le grand Tout', cannot be less free: we must allow, therefore, for contingency in Nature.[81] And secondly, to those who maintain that the notion of a free, undetermined choice is a contradiction, Sully Prudhomme falls back upon Kant. We are faced by one of those irreducible contradictions Kant termed 'antinomies'—incomprehensible to our fallible human reason. In this situation all that is evident is that science can neither deny nor affirm ultimate human freedom; we must therefore choose, and for himself he chooses to believe in freedom, impelled to do so by the considerations invoked in *La Justice*.[82] Even here, one may add, without

[80] R. F. A. Sully Prudhomme, *Œuvres — Prose*, Lemerre, 1904-8, 2 vols. [*Prose*], ii. 341-5, *Le Problème des causes finales*.
[81] R. F. A. Sully Prudhomme, *Psychologie du libre arbitre*, Alcan, 1907, ch. v.
[82] Cf. *Prose*, ii. 384. He adds another argument. If everything were determined, our belief in our freedom of will would be inexplicable: our belief would itself be caused; but every cause communicates something of itself to its effect; this could not be the case with our belief in freedom if no freedom whatever

implying any direct connexion, his thought is reminiscent of Jules Lequier and Renouvier!

Is one to conclude from Sully Prudhomme's defence of human free will that he is here opposing positivism? The final arguments for freedom just noted might lead one to think that he is, were it not that they are offered as mere subjective conjectures concerning a realm which he has already sharply distinguished from the province of science and therefore of knowledge as a whole. As to the earlier arguments, his contentions about the nature of 'scientific determinism' and the limitation of the scientific approach are very similar to the assertions of Lachelier, Boutroux, Renouvier, Bergson, and their disciples. Yet it is invalid to conclude from this concurrence of arguments that he is abandoning positivism. On the contrary, his ideas coincide with those of John Stuart Mill and Claude Bernard as well as with the view of the anti-positivists. Like Mill he is maintaining (as he asserted in the *Préface* of 1869) that scientific knowledge is limited, confined to the relationships of phenomena and powerless to say anything about any kind of 'ultimate reality'. Here again, indeed, as previously in regard to Mill's criticism of Taine, the impression grows that these arguments of the anti-positivists are only valid against *scientisme* and do not affect the consistently positivist position.

(d) The problem of personal immortality

When one turns in conclusion to study Sully Prudhomme's attitude to the problem of personal immortality, the opposition of the scientific reason and the heart is found to be less acute. He is here far more willing to accept the conclusions of the scientist, for the prospect of an after-life often seems unattractive or even repellent to him. Personal survival would mean, for example, that after death we were bitterly aware of our separation from our friends and those we love.[83] Again, the Christian doctrine of survival confronts us with the terrifying possibility of damnation and imports into this life a haunting uncertainty as to our future. Furthermore, the Christian heaven (which he represents as a society of disembodied spirits) holds out an eternity

existed. Since, therefore, our belief is inexplicable on the determinist theory, that theory must be false.

[83] Cf. *Œuv.*, vi. 81–83, *Sur une tombe, Épaves.*

of boredom, an existence deprived of all passion and all the delights of sensation. Evoking the heaven to which he aspires in *Mon Ciel*, he concludes:

> J'y veux trouver l'automne et sa mélancolie,
> Et l'hiver solennel, et les étés ardents.
>
> Voilà mon paradis, je n'en conçois pas d'autre.
> Il est le plus humain s'il n'est pas le plus beau;
> Ascètes, purs esprits, je vous laisse le vôtre,
> Plus effrayant pour moi que la nuit du tombeau.[84]

Indeed, death often appears to the solitary, unhappy poet as a release from the sufferings of life, as a gateway to the peace of oblivion, and this prompts his frequent poetic yearnings for death: the theme of 'heureux les morts' appears almost as often in his poetry as in that of Leconte de Lisle, although usually in a quieter key.[85]

Yet the poet cannot be wholly resigned to a future of total annihilation, nor, in particular, can he tolerate uncertainty as to his final destiny. As he remarks in the preface to *Le Bonheur*,

> le doute sur l'avenir d'outre-tombe, sur une compensation future des douleurs présentes, sur un règlement final de comptes à rendre, sur la sollicitude enfin et l'existence même d'un Créateur, ce doute . . . devient à la longue très importun.[86]

Consequently he speculates from time to time as to the possibility of a future life, and here there is at least a pale reflection of the conflict that has been seen in more vivid forms: the reason can give no reply to death's enigma, yet the heart longs for assurance.

His meditation after his mother's death, *Sur la mort*, best expresses this opposition.[87] The medical science of his day, he knows, implies that even if the 'soul' is not a wholly illusory concept, it is so inseparable from the body that with the body's disintegration it also must cease to exist. His pantheism, too, combined with this evidence to undermine belief in immortality: only the 'World Soul' has a self-sufficient existence for the pantheist. Nor can science resolve the mystery, for the notion of survival falls completely outside its scope. Science is dumb 'devant l'atroce énigme où la raison succombe',

---

[84] *Œuv.*, i. 184, *Stances et poèmes*.
[85] Cf., in particular, *Les Solitudes*.   [86] *Œuv.*, v. 135-6.
[87] *Œuv.*, iii. 127-32, *Les Vaines Tendresses*.

> Science, qui partout te heurtant au mystère
> Et n'osant l'affronter, l'ajournes seulement.

Philosophy and religion are equally powerless to give us any knowledge of the future.

> Mais vous n'enseignez rien, verbes inanimés!

> Ni vous, dogmes cruels, insensés que vous êtes, . . .
> Ni toi, qui n'es qu'un bruit pour les cerveaux honnêtes
> Vaine philosophie où tout sombre à la fois. . . .

He appeals to the heart and to poetry to give him enlightenment; but still the mystery persists, unsolved and insoluble. Resignation and acceptance are the only possible attitudes we can assume in the face of this total ignorance—and one may note in passing the contrast with Leconte de Lisle, in whom revolt and defiance are so much more common than patient endurance.

> Puisque je n'ai pas pu, disciple de tant d'autres,
> Apprendre ton vrai sort, ô morte que j'aimais,
> Arrière les savants, les docteurs, les apôtres.
> Je n'interroge plus, je subis désormais.

His speculations about immortality do not entirely cease, none the less, and two theories can be found in his writings, both of which he shared with many other thinkers of his time. Firstly, we may live on in the memories of those who loved us. But this is a transitory immortality which ends with their death or even before if they forget us. Standing by his mother's grave, he promises to remember her—

> Mais que suis-je? Et demain quand je t'aurai suivie,
> Quel ami me promet de ne pas t'oublier?[88]

He therefore turns from this type of survival and builds a conception of immortality of the kind already encountered in Renan. By our achievements in the realms of science, art, or moral action, we bequeath to our successors both a noble example and a more advanced starting-point on the road towards perfection. This evolutionary view of immortality forms the moving theme of *Le Zénith* in particular. These intrepid scientists have gained true immortality by their contribution to the progress of science.

[88] *Œuv.*, iii. 130, *Sur la mort.*

Fonder au ciel sa gloire, et dans le grain qu'on sème
Sur terre propager le plus pur de soi-même,
C'est peut-être expirer, mais ce n'est pas finir:
Non! de sa vie à tous léguer l'œuvre et l'exemple,
C'est la revivre en eux plus profonde et plus ample. . . .

We die in the body—'mais pour commencer d'être à la façon d'un dieu'.[89]

At other times Sully Prudhomme anticipates a different kind of immortality and invokes the theories of metempsychosis and interstellar migration—theories that aroused so astonishing a degree of enthusiasm in an age proud of its scientific spirit.[90] Yet it cannot be said that he seriously accepts them; he adopts them merely as vague possibilities. In *Le Bonheur* the migration theory is the starting-point for the poem—but only as a convenient fiction; and the final journey of Faustus and Stella through the ether and beyond the stars to a celestial utopia is no less than avowed fantasy. Nor does the poet claim more than this:

On serait déçu [he warns the reader] si l'on y cherchait une solution rigoureuse des grands problèmes qui s'y posent: l'auteur y caresse seulement un rêve, un souhait que son imagination ne pouvait exaucer avec le plein consentement de sa raison.[91]

The serious conclusion of *Le Bonheur* does not concern the question of personal immortality but consists in the affirmation that happiness comes through self-sacrifice, love, and the pursuit of virtue.

In reality he never finds an answer to this question, apart from the suggestion expressed in *Le Zénith*. Even in late-1906, although he finds great difficulty in imagining the state of a soul that has been deprived of its bodily powers of sensation, the question remains open: 'D'une part, je m'avoue incapable de prouver rigoureusement qu'en moi tout ne meurt pas avec mon corps, mais, d'autre part, je ne suis pas certain que tout en moi meurt avec lui.'[92] In either event the ethic of a base subjective hedonism

---

[89] *Œuv.*, iii. 260.
[90] Following such eighteenth-century writers as Swedenborg and Charles Bonnet, the notion of migration recurs in such illuminists as Ballanche, in Hugo most notably, and in such contemporary works as Reynaud's *Terre et Ciel* (1854) and Flammarion's *Pluralité des mondes habités* (1865). The theory of metempsychosis was more understandably widespread, partly as a result of the impact of Indian religious ideas.
[91] *Œuv.*, v. 136.   [92] *Hémon Préf.*, pp. xiii–xiv.

is to be rejected as unworthy of human dignity. And since we are uncertain of our destiny and as to whether we shall be rewarded and punished in a future life for our actions, he advocates that we should wager as Pascal urges us to do. Moved by an irrational but powerful apprehension concerning a future Judgement, he will gamble in this state of utter doubt 'de manière à risquer mon plaisir plutôt que ma sécurité'.[93] He will live and act *as if* there is to be a future life.

(e) *Summary*

His final conclusion is therefore scepticism concerning all metaphysical and religious questions. In *Le Bonheur*, in order to discover 'la cause et la raison du monde' Faustus interrogates in turn the philosophers of antiquity, the medieval doctors of the Church, and all the greatest philosophers of modern times; to the same end he questions all the sciences one by one. Nowhere does he find the truths he most desires to possess. And Sully Prud-homme himself is no more fortunate in the final years of his life following *Le Bonheur*. He accepts to the last the impossibility of metaphysical knowledge which positivism proclaims.

Mieux vaut donc laisser derrière son voile impénétrable le principe créateur et ordonnateur de l'Univers. Ce n'est pas l'athéisme, c'est la résignation à ne pas interroger l'Univers sur son principe initial.[94]

The conclusion of all the earnest thinking and searching that has been surveyed is the same as the conclusion of his first essay in philosophy: 'Sachons plutôt ne pas savoir, ce n'est pas la moindre vertu du vrai philosophe.'

Sully Prudhomme thus offers a final illustration of the reluctant positivism with which so much of this study has been occupied. And yet his scepticism is not a sterile unbelief that wastes itself in bitterness and recrimination, and in this respect he reminds us less of Leconte de Lisle than of Alfred de Vigny, whose virile stoicism he shares. One can also feel that in the end reason and heart, between which he had so long been divided, were reconciled in a resignation that did not exclude all vestiges of hope.

[93] *Hémon Préf.*, p. xvii. It is of course arguable that this wager is as much a form of subjective hedonism as the pleasure-seeking ethic he rejects, and he himself has moral misgivings about adopting it.

[94] *Hémon Préf.*, p. xii.

Here is the first significant feature of his relationship to positivism: his thought exemplifies a positivism which is reluctant but not embittered. But this chapter has also pointed to more important—and more neglected—facts about his philosophy. First, unlike Comte, Taine, and Renan, he does not link the doctrine of positivism with the very different doctrine of scientism. On the contrary, he insists throughout his work upon the proper limits of the scientific method—in the *Préface* of 1869; in discussing 'la prétendue banqueroute de la science' in *Que sais-je?* (1896); in *Le Crédit de la science* (1902), where he attacks the claim that science has authority outside the realm of phenomena.[95] He has no doubts about the value of the experimental method when it is properly applied, but this can only be in relation to phenomena. Secondly, unlike Louise Ackermann and other writers of the time, he does not confuse the working determinism upon which the scientific approach is based with the doctrine of fatalism. On the contrary, though with occasional misgivings that derive from his own experiences and his pantheistic conjectures, he puts forward the view (as we saw) that 'scientific determinism' leaves open the question of human free will—and here he is more faithful to positivism than the fatalists he opposed. Thirdly, unlike others of his contemporaries, including Littré on occasion, he insists that both materialism and spiritualism are metaphysical theories, arguing in particular that positivism and materialism are far from being synonymous, as many contemporary critics were inclined to assert, that they are in fact mutually exclusive. The modesty of the claims he made for his own philosophical work should not lead one to overlook its significance. Writing to Boutroux in 1875, he quietly comments: 'Tout mon travail établit qu'il n'y a pas lieu, selon moi, de distinguer *substantiellement* la matière et l'esprit. . . .'[96] And he declares to Hémon in 1903: 'Les résultats de mes méditations tendent donc à ébranler les murs dressés par les diverses écoles entre le déterminisme et l'activité libre, entre le matérialisme et le spiritualisme.'[97] 'Ces résultats sont modestes', he adds; but this reticence cannot obscure the fact that he attempted nothing less than to separate positivism from the various metaphysical theories —scientism, fatalism, materialism—which, as earlier chapters

---

[95] *Prose*, ii. 4, and i. 319-21.   [96] *J. Int.*, p. 200.
[97] *J. Int.*, p. 210.

have tried to show, were falsely associated with it during the middle years of the nineteenth century. This was the great contribution which he sought to make to the tradition of positivist thought, and if he was little heeded by many of his contemporaries, this cannot detract from his achievement. By virtue of it, moreover, he looks forward to the more stringent positivism of such late-nineteenth-century thinkers as Mach and Poincaré. They, like him, aimed to cleanse the positivist philosophy of those elements of metaphysical thinking which we have seen associated with it, by Comte, Taine, and Renan above all. He and they alike recall science to its proper and self-appointed limits—the study of the laws of phenomena.

Je regrette [he writes in 1875] ... que tant de savants encore *fassent de l'ontologie sans le vouloir*, quand, par exemple, sous le nom de matière, ils définissent un substratum qu'ils imposent aux phénomènes dont ils n'ont mission que de déterminer les rapports.[98]

In this respect at least he was a truer friend of the positivist philosophy than even he himself perhaps realized.

5. *Sully Prudhomme and Ethics*

Nothing has so far been said of Sully Prudhomme's ethical speculations, except in relation to the problem of free will and to the second Part of *La Justice*. Here again, as in regard to metaphysics, his attitude is of considerable interest. It has been noted again and again during this study that one of the greatest difficulties for the mid-nineteenth-century positivist and quasi-positivist thinkers is to find a place within the body of their philosophy for ethical values. What, we now have to ask, is Sully Prudhomme's reaction to this problem?

On occasion he shares with Comte, Renan, Spencer, Leslie Stephen, and others the dream that it may be possible to construct something like a science of ethics. In his *Journal intime* in mid-1868 he argues that moral action is action which is in accord with the laws of human nature, and he can thus conclude: 'La morale est donc fondée sur la science de la nature humaine.' He is so tempted by this possibility that he goes on to develop the analogy

[98] *J. Int.*, p. 198 (my italics).

between this study and the scientific procedure as it operates in other fields.

La morale est donc *indépendante* au même titre et pour les mêmes raisons que la science dont elle n'est qu'une application. Elle ne relève, comme la science, que de l'expérience et de la réflexion.[99]

But this is an isolated claim and for the most part, in ethics as in metaphysics, he does not stray down the slope that leads from positivism to scientism. More commonly, he maintains that ethics falls ultimately outside the province of reason. Ethical values are not subject to rational proof, demonstration, or empirical verification. This is the view he expresses in *La Justice*, as he himself notes in a letter written to Madame Amiel in 1877: 'L'impuissance de la raison à donner toute l'explication des phénomènes moraux fait le sujet même de mon poème [*La Justice*]. . . .'[1] He wished to insist that duty and ethical obligation remain compelling even though they are without religious or metaphysical sanctions, and it is to this end that he removes ethics from the sphere of ratiocination to the sphere of the 'heart'.

Thus far his attitude is consistent with positivism—ethical statements are not empirically verifiable (except in so far as they are empirical statements in disguise); they are essentially personal affirmations. But Sully Prudhomme does not stop here. Like so many thinkers of his age he is greatly preoccupied by moral questions, determined like George Eliot to retain Duty even though God and immortality have had to be abandoned, and it is as a result of this ethical concern that one finds him prowling somewhat hungrily around the 'objective' moral systems of the past.

The ethic he finally adopted was founded upon the concept of human dignity. He contemptuously dismisses the hedonism of the materialists.

Je crois comme eux [he says in 1868] que la mort aboutit au néant, mais je ne m'en console pas, et toutes les inventions de la science me paraissent de puériles distractions en présence de l'abîme.[2]

The sight of morally fine actions suggests to him a principle of moral obligation. Such actions 'témoignent de la *dignité* humaine',

[99] *J. Int.*, pp. 98–99.
[2] *J. Int.*, p. 103.

[1] *J. Int.*, p. 188.

and he finds in this dignity 'le principe de l'obligation morale qui est l'inévitable alternative d'agir en homme ou de ne l'être même plus du tout, de devenir, au moral, un monstre . . .'.[3] This notion is linked in his mind with the idea of evolution, although it would be wrong to think that his is a system of evolutionary ethics. It would be truer to say that for him evolution operates as a carrot, not as a magnet. Thus he writes in *Que sais-je?*:

> Au fond, ce qui me paraît être objectif dans mes perceptions esthé-tiques, c'est le sentiment qu'elles suscitent en moi de la *dignité humaine*, c'est-à-dire du rang suprême que mon espèce occupe sur un astre et qui paraîtrait justifier son aspiration au grade suivant dans l'ascensionnelle évolution de l'univers.[4]

This particular moral code rests upon a wider notion, however, that of the 'moral conscience'. Although reason cannot guide us we are not condemned to sceptical indecision, for we each have the insights of the 'heart' to follow. He puts forward this belief as early as 1862 in a review of Proudhon's *La Guerre et la paix*, where he affirms in conclusion: 'La vraie justice est identique à la loi de l'amour. Le cœur seul est juste.'[5] The same view, we saw, is consecrated in the second Part of *La Justice*. It is 'la conscience innée', he claims,

> Qui me révèle mon devoir!
> Elle m'enjoint d'être homme et de respecter l'homme . . . ,

and he ends by defining justice as 'l'amour guidé par la lumière'.[6] His standpoint remains the same in his final works, in *Que sais-je?*, for example, where he again ends by stressing the sovereignty of conscience:

> La conscience morale nous oblige, comme une poussée de bas en haut vers cette beauté-là [la beauté morale]; nous pouvons y résister, en rebrousser la direction, mais alors nous nous sentons descendre.[7]

Unfortunately for our purpose, this notion that in our ethical choices we should follow our own 'heart' may cloak either the positivist viewpoint or a very different and anti-positivist belief—and one with which Sully Prudhomme's name has not uncom-

---

[3] *Hémon Préf.*, p. xvi.   [4] *Prose*, ii. 31.
[5] Cited by Estève, op. cit., p. 163.
[6] *Œuv.*, iv. 236, 266; cf. iv. 244–5.
[7] *Prose*, ii. 193.

monly been connected.[8] This belief is that the 'heart' is a means of knowledge of some kind of objective moral good. The positivist claim, by contrast, as it ultimately emerged out of the confused discussions of the mid-nineteenth century, is that in ethical matters we can only follow our personal intimations and that we have no grounds to allege that these intimations are anything more than personal; the 'heart' does not allow us to know the 'unknowable'.

Which of these opposing beliefs does Sully Prudhomme hold? No question is more difficult, and one can only give a tentative reply. At certain times he undoubtedly speaks as if the 'heart' were an instrument of knowledge. In *L'Esprit et le cœur* (1862), for instance, he openly declares:

> L'esprit fait le savant et le cœur fait l'apôtre:
> On ne peut sans les deux saisir la vérité.

In *La Justice* (1878) there is a similar assertion:

> ... Arrière la philosophie:
> Moi, je sais dès que mon cœur sent.[9]

He does seem to be asserting here that the 'heart' gives us a non-empirical kind of knowledge, but one cannot be certain whether he believes this or is merely guilty of a loose use of language. It may be that he is only trying to emphasize that personal ethical action is possible even though ethical philosophy is not. The indications are against this interpretation, however. Rather, he seems to have vacillated in his attitude—and here one finds yet another illustration of the conflict of head and heart within him. In a letter written in December 1877, having emphasized the powerlessness of reason to resolve moral questions by itself, he claims:

> Le cœur est un instrument de connaissance dont les renseigne-
> ments doivent être considérés comme de la même valeur que ceux de
> la raison, bien que les intuitions soient irréductibles aux procédés
> de la raison.[10]

---

[8] Cf., for example, Morice, op. cit., pp. 38–39.

[9] *Œuv.*, iv. 177. See the careful commentary of Gaston Paris (op. cit., p. 237) on this point. Paris even affirms: 'L'idée que le cœur peut n'être pas borné uniquement à sentir, qu'il a peut-être, comme la raison et avec autant d'autorité, le droit d'affirmer, pénètre tout le travail de sa pensée philosophique.'

[10] *J. Int.*, p. 189.

In the light of so explicit an assertion it does seem likely that on occasion he held that the 'Infinite' communicates with man through the medium of the conscience. Later in his life he appears to have resolved this question in the opposite sense. It is doubtful if this change can be precisely dated, but it may well have coincided with the mental upheaval around 1890 when his view of Pascal underwent a marked modification. As was remarked earlier, he now begins to argue that Pascal was too credulous in his conception of *l'esprit de finesse* and *les raisons du cœur*. In criticizing Pascal on this score, he is perhaps also criticizing and repudiating a theory he himself had entertained. However this may be, by 1895 at the latest he has adopted a standpoint very close to that of many twentieth-century positivists. Towards the end of *Le Crédit de la science* in particular he affirms quite emphatically that we can have no knowledge of ethical principles.[11] Such a principle is 'une donnée métaphysique'. At the same time this does not exclude moral action, only ethical philosophizing. 'La métaphysique morale est distincte de la pratique morale. L'homme peut ignorer comment il se sent tenu de sacrifier son intérêt à celui d'autrui, et néanmoins s'y sentir tenu.' He adds that this moral feeling may in part be the legacy of supernatural religion, but it is not dependent upon it. There is no doubt that he still occasionally toyed with the idea that these moral 'suggestions of the heart' might derive from the 'unknowable' itself. Thus he asks himself in 1895:

L'obligation morale a-t-elle pour principe, en moi, un ordre intimé à mon libre vouloir par l'Inconnaissable, qui représenterait dans ce cas *l'impératif catégorique?* Je l'ignore, mais je suis porté à le croire....[12]

He even declares his faith in 'les suggestions profondes que je dois à l'Inconnaissable même...'.[13] But this notion is so hesitantly advanced—as no more than a matter of personal faith—that it cannot be considered a desertion of positivism. Sully Prudhomme's conclusion is the same in this work as in *Le Crédit de la science*. He reiterates the belief that a moral imperative springs from our sense of human dignity: 'Agis en homme, sinon tu seras moins homme.' But he also adds: 'Tout cet édifice de conjectures,

[11] *Prose*, i. 324–5.   [12] *Prose*, ii. 170.
[13] *Prose*, ii. 194.

qui me séduit par son harmonie, est, je le répète, d'ordre poé-tique.'[14]

One can conclude, therefore, that from *Que sais-je?* (1895) onwards, if not intermittently throughout his career, the inter-pretation of his attitude to metaphysics put forward earlier is equally applicable to his approach to ethics. We can attain a personal 'practical certainty', but this certainty can never be philosophically justified or empirically verified. Ethical philo-sophy is banished as metaphysical. Yet this does not condemn Sully Prudhomme to ethical neutrality and inactivity, and this fact differentiates the mood of his final philosophy from that atmosphere of despairing passivity surrounding Leconte de Lisle's later poems and permits the resilient hopefulness, the dignity, the aspiration, that characterize his final works. The impossibility of ethical philosophy does not mean the impossibility of ethical choice and action. Here is another way in which he is compara-tively original in his own age, and at this point he comes very close to the attitude of many twentieth-century positivists. With his views on ethics as with his views on metaphysics we are on the threshold of a further chapter in the history of positivist thought.

[14] *Prose*, ii. 36, 193.

X

CONCLUSION

'TROP d'efforts charmants et puérils . . . pour sauver d'une
main ce qu'il détruit de l'autre', remarked George Sand of
Renan.[1] Her words, with a change of adjectives, might well
be applied to most of the writers we have discussed, whether they
be *esprits mi-positifs et mi-métaphysiques*, in Littré's phrase, or
positivistes à contre-cœur. Littré and Claude Bernard apart, they
are divided minds.

This division is at the source of one intellectual development
of especial moment during these years. Comte, Renan, and Taine
all try to expand the positivist theory of knowledge from which
they begin—Comte in order to establish above all a scientific
social and ethical system, Renan a scientific religion, and Taine
a scientific method for metaphysics. They end by distorting and
misinterpreting the true positivist teaching and identify it with
a quite different philosophy. Scientism: such is the cuckoo's egg
they bring to the positivist nest. And in the light of this fact it
is hardly surprising that scientism came to be regarded as an
integral part of positivism by their common opponents or that,
when science failed to live up to the prophecies erroneously made
on its behalf, its critics should have celebrated not merely *la banqueroute du scientisme* but *la banqueroute de la science*.

In the years following it became imperative to dissociate science
from the metaphysical ways of thought with which they had
linked it. Absolute determinism in Taine and, to some extent, in
Renan's conception of progress; strong Hegelian elements in the
thought of both; materialism in Littré and, perhaps, in Comte:
these are the symptoms which justify Renouvier, the most perceptive student of French philosophy at this time, when he contrasts positivism's claim to proscribe metaphysics with the actual
tendencies visible in these thinkers. Of their treatment of history
he comments: 'l'hypothèse de la nécessité y est partout invoquée,
soit dans les faits, soit dans la théorie, sans y être justifiée nulle

---

[1] Cited by J. Pommier, *Renan, d'après des documents inédits*, 1923, p. 164.

part . . .'. And later he tries to define the philosophy which, under the guise of positivism, is in fact dominant in these years: 'Son esprit, son caractère consistent en une espèce de panthéisme et de fatalisme animés et développés par l'hypothèse du progrès continu et universel'—to which he shrewdly adds: 'C'est comme une religion qu'on essaie de se faire, en feignant qu'on ne se la fait pas, mais qu'elle vous est imposée par l'histoire.' As to the true source of this outlook he says: 'Hegel est incontestablement la plus grande figure philosophique du siècle.'[2] This mingling of Hegel and science, of pantheism and positivism, and the confusions which resulted from it necessitated a critical scrutiny of the methods and assumptions of science. It is this scrutiny which, begun by Renouvier, Cournot, and their disciples, is carried on in the final decades of the century by such thinkers as Poincaré, Duhem, and Milhaud. The story we have surveyed explains much of what was to follow during the years of the Third Republic.

A second, though perhaps minor development has been illustrated in the thought of Madame Ackermann: the alliance of positivism with pessimism. This linking, believed inevitable by many of the following generation, is not a necessary one, however. Agnosticism may certainly distress those who long for religious or metaphysical certainties, who cannot believe unless they already know. But her despair, we saw, derives primarily from her temperament, from her moral condemnation of the world around her, and from a fatalism and an atheism for which positivist philosophy gives no warrant: positivism itself is only a secondary and later factor.

In contrast to his fellow Parnassian, Sully Prudhomme only deserts positivism in isolated ways and thus joins company with Littré and Bernard in his fidelity to it: in this they are arrestingly isolated amongst their French contemporaries. Strange companions, for no positivists were in other ways more dissimilar! Littré and Bernard were on the whole 'born positivists', disturbed but not deeply so by ethical uncertainty and metaphysical ignorance. In Sully Prudhomme philosophical scepticism conflicts with his intensest desires; head is opposed to heart. And if, like Littré, he reaches a state of harmony, the greatest difference between them rests in this: Littré's confidence remains this side of

---

[2] C. Renouvier, 'De la philosophie du dix-neuvième siècle en France', *L'Année philosophique—Première Année (1867)*, 1868, pp. 41, 100-1, 89.

despair; the serenity of Sully Prudhomme's final philosophy lies on its farther shore.

This study began by noting the frequency with which critics have described the Second Empire as an 'age of positivism'. Having considered most of the thinkers who give this generalization whatever validity it may possess, we can now emphasize what an ambiguous justification their outlook offers for it: the conclusion must be that at best this view is a half-truth. It is not merely that it neglects the vitality of anti-positivism, as found in spiritualists and idealists and the neo-criticist group. Just as seriously, it ignores or markedly underestimates the division of allegiance in those whom it cites as positivists, and it largely overlooks the consequences that spring from this division. All these writers have marked affiliations with positivism: to that extent the generalization is valid. But these affiliations alone are very far from summarizing their thought: here it becomes misleading. It over-simplifies their attitude and suggests that it was more confident, less disturbed by religious and metaphysical concern, more superficial also, than it was in fact. It is simply not true that these writers, Comte alone excepted, were indifferent to such non-scientific questions as the nature of man's destiny or the validity of religious beliefs or that they were untroubled by the mystery that lies beyond the reach of science. This was a charge levelled by their contemporaries in the heat of debate, but it ought not to have persisted in the way it has.[3] The positivist does not wish to deny the existence of mystery but to emphasize that a genuine mystery can never be resolved; *l'Inconnaissable*, one can recall, is a positivist notion and not, as often presented, an invention of the idealists. Only at the end of *Le Disciple* does Bourget's imaginary positivist, Adrien Sixte, glimpse and acknowledge the mystery of the universe.[4] These thinkers and poets alike, in sharp opposition, are always conscious of a realm far transcending their knowledge. Even Littré, the least troubled of them, pauses in wonder before that vast ocean of the unknowable 'dont la claire vision est aussi salutaire que formidable', and

[3] Cf., amongst many examples, E. Estève, *Sully Prudhomme*, 1925, pp. 57–58; P. Flottes, *Sully Prudhomme*, 1930, p. 38; R. Jasinski, *Histoire de la littérature française*, 1947, 2 vols., ii. 342; and P. Martino, *Parnasse et symbolisme*, 1947, pp. 138–9.

[4] P. Bourget, *Le Disciple*, 1946 (Fayard), p. 207.

Renan remarked of him: '[il] passa toute sa vie à s'interdire de penser aux problèmes supérieurs et à y penser toujours'.[5] They are in reality far closer than is usually conceded to the nostalgic mood of their English contemporaries—Matthew Arnold, George Eliot, Arthur Hugh Clough, Francis Newman, and, not least, Mill. In both France and England established values and beliefs are being called into question, and whilst a greater anti-religious bitterness may be generated in the predominantly Catholic country, in both the task is accomplished with anxious misgiving.

This work has attempted only one part of a far wider undertaking. The time is ripe for a review of the fortunes and interactions of both positivism and its antagonists during the second half of the nineteenth century. Carried out in the light of a preciser definition of the positivist philosophy than has usually been employed, this might well reveal new features in the history of both groups and in the fields of philosophy and literature alike.

A re-examination of the Second Empire opponents of positivism would be especially valuable. Certain of these writers have been amply studied—Baudelaire, Nerval, Villiers de l'Isle-Adam, Corbière, and Barbey D'Aurevilly, for example, amongst the literary authors of the age and philosophers like Renouvier, Cournot, Ravaisson, and Jules Lequier—but this could be extended to include Secrétan, Janet, Vacherot, Caro, Thalès Bernard, Théodore de Banville, and others. It would be particularly helpful to define the relation between positivism and neo-criticism afresh. Above all an *étude d'ensemble* is lacking. Michaud in particular has already pointed the way towards such a study when he comments upon the apparent suddenness of the reaction against positivism during the Third Republic:

Que s'est-il donc passé? Pour qu'un tel changement pût survenir, il a fallu, sinon un miracle, du moins un concours étonnant de circonstances, et plus encore la convergence de forces puissantes, restées longtemps souterraines, et qui affleurent soudain. Ces forces, un regard très perspicace eût pu les déceler un peu partout, dans le pessimisme de tel maître du Parnasse comme dans l'idéalisme de tel défenseur enthousiaste du progrès, et au cœur du positivisme même, si tant est que chaque être porte son contraire en lui.[6]

[5] E. Renan, *Discours et conférences*, 9e éd., 1928, p. 79.
[6] G. Michaud, *Message poétique du symbolisme*, 1947, 4 vols., i. 200.

This book has tried to indicate certain of these forces—and also to imply that this reaction is less 'miraculous' than Michaud suggests—but a great deal remains to be done. It would be of additional interest to inquire how far the influences which confirmed the next generation in its anti-positivism were already at work during these two decades: illuminism and occultism persisting from the Romantic era, notably in Pierre Leroux, Jean Reynaud, and Victor Hugo; Neo-Buddhism and, linked with it, the impact of Schopenhauer, first felt well before Challemel-Lacour's famous article in 1870;[7] German anti-positivists like Hölderlin and Novalis as well as Wagner; English writers such as Carlyle, Ruskin, Browning, Tennyson, Shelley, and Coleridge as well as Edgar Allan Poe. Most of these foreign *précurseurs du symbolisme* are well known at this time—through literary critics like Montégut, Taine, and Milsand—and one wonders to what extent they are already strengthening the forces of anti-positivism.[8]

Secondly, the fortunes of positivism during the Third Republic might profitably be reconsidered. In many ways, the fifty years or so following 1870, the so-called period of the idealistic reaction, form an age of much more militant positivism than the Second Empire. During this time the positivist outlook is carried into a wide diversity of fields: by Ribot, Dumas, Pierre Janet, and others into psychology; by Richet into physiology; by Le Dantec into biology; by Espinas, Izoulet, Durkheim, and followers like Lévy-Bruhl into sociology; by Charles Lalo into aesthetics; by Henri Berr and Lacombe into the philosophy of history; by Zola into literature. In the realm of philosophy itself, it persists in the generation after Taine, Renan, and Littré in not only these writers but also Abel Rey, Goblot, Cresson, Jules de Gaultier—

[7] *R.D.M.*, 15 mars 1870. Cf. articles by A. Franck (*Journal des débats*, oct. 1850), Saint-René Taillandier (*R.D.M.*, 1er août 1856), Weil (*Revue française*, déc. 1856 and déc. 1857), and books by Foucher de Careil (*Hegel et Schopenhauer*, 1862), Dollfus (*Études sur l'Allemagne*, 1864), and A. de Balche (*Renan et Schopenhauer*, Odessa, 1870). Cf. A. Baillot, *L'Influence de la philosophie de Schopenhauer en France (1860–1900)*, 1927.

[8] In part and for some authors this question has already been considered. On the English writers, cf. A. C. Taylor, *Carlyle et la pensée latine*, 1937; P. Audra, 'Ruskin et la France', *R.C.C.*, 1926; M. Bowden, *Tennyson in France*, Manchester, 1930; H. Peyre, *Shelley et la France*, 1935; L. Seylaz, *Poë et les premiers symbolistes français*, 1923; and C. P. Cambiaire, *The Influence of Poe in France*, New York, 1927. Cf. also F. Baldensperger, *Bibliography of Comparative Literature*, Chapel Hills, 1950.

and, in a different way, in Brunetière and Charles Maurras. These are only some of the thinkers of the period who have commonly been seen as positivists, and there is both need and ample scope for a clarification of their relation to the positivist philosophy: are they true or false friends? This discussion would have to distinguish above all between the tradition of scientism and materialism and that of positivism, and it may be that this latter tradition is to be traced less in certain of them than through the neo-criticists and their successors—those thinkers whom Benrubi groups together as 'critico-epistemological idealists'. Looking back, moreover, one can note that it is these latter writers, Henri Poincaré above all, who seem to have had the greater historical importance in forming contemporary positivist thought.[9]

Thirdly, and closely related to this task, a new evaluation of anti-positivism after 1870 is called for—both in its philosophical and literary manifestations. Much has already been done—by Parodi, Knowles, and Aliotta amongst others.[10] Yet here above all, it seems, new patterns might be revealed by a review which asked how far the 'reaction against positivism' was against positivism in its proper sense or against the scientism of Taine, Renan, Berthelot, and others. A partial answer to this question was suggested earlier: to some extent at least the attacks of Boutroux, Lachelier, and Bergson strike scientism but not positivism, and this is perhaps no less true of Bourget, Fouillée, Brunetière, and other leaders of the 'reaction'.[11] Such a scrutiny might further ask how far these philosophers are original in their attacks and how far they are continuing the work of Renouvier, Cournot, and other Neo-Kantians: they may have taken on a deceptive appearance of isolation. It could also usefully examine those aspects of this revolt which were inspired by aesthetic or moral motives rather than by philosophical arguments properly speaking. In this regard, the 'anti-positivism' of the symbolist writers might well be reviewed. 'La philosophie du symbolisme...

[9] This study might also clarify the apparent contradictions between those who see Poincaré as a precursor of logical positivism and those who link him with the 'reaction against positivism'.

[10] D. Parodi, *Du positivisme à l'idéalisme*, 1930, 2 vols.; D. Knowles, *La Réaction idéaliste au théâtre depuis 1890*, 1934; A. Aliotta, *The Idealistic Reaction against Science*, translated McCaskill, London, 1914. Cf. A. Fouillée, *Le Mouvement idéaliste et la réaction contre la science positive*, 1896; and Abbé de Broglie, *La Réaction contre le positivisme*, 1894.

[11] Cf. pp. 155–6 above.

est essentiellement antipositiviste':[12] this is a common view. Their emotional leanings and their interest in a spiritual world and a metaphysical 'beyond' undoubtedly tend away from positivism, as does their poetic theory. Yet a study of their underlying outlook might lead one to differentiate between their 'emotional anti-positivism' and the 'philosophical anti-positivism' of their aesthetic and, on the other side, the 'philosophical *positivism*' of their religious and metaphysical views.[13] Rimbaud claimed that the poet could become 'le suprême Savant! Car il arrive à *l'inconnu!*'; but he ends by castigating the theory of poetic 'illumination' as 'une de mes folies'. Mallarmé hopes that poetry can become 'un instrument spirituel'; but however suggestive and beautiful his poems may be, do they capture anything of the *Idéal*, are they more than—in his own significant words of 1866— 'glorieux mensonges'?

Lastly—and most difficult task of all—to elucidate these tendencies in nineteenth-century thought would require a thorough study of Kant's influence in France.[14] We have noted the ambiguities of Hegel's impact earlier; the variations in the interpretations of Kant are no less pronounced. Some writers view him in the manner of Heine's famous account of 1835: as the author of the *Critique of Pure Reason* alone, as 'un pur destructeur', 'une sorte d'athée froidement sectaire, qui avait exécuté Dieu en Allemagne'.[15] Others follow in the tradition of Charles de Villers,

[12] G. Lote, 'La Poétique du symbolisme — II: Le Problème de la connaissance et la vérité mystique', *R.C.C.* xxxv, 1934, p. 507.

[13] It may also be a simplification to sum up the Symbolist aesthetic as antipositivist. Cf. A. G. Lehmann, *The Symbolist Aesthetic in France*, Oxford, 1950. Lehmann suggests that the Symbolist movement occupies an intermediate position between 'two contrasting moments of aesthetic history, the contemporary and the positivist' (p. 316).

[14] Certain studies exist but are not specifically concerned with the relation between Neo-Kantianism and positivism. M. Vallois, *La Formation de l'influence kantienne en France*, s.d., only covers the period from 1800 to 1835. J. M. Carré, *Les Écrivains français et le mirage allemand (1800–1940)*, 1947, and L. Reynaud, *L'Influence allemande en France au 18e et au 19e siècles*, 1922, are of some help, as are: V. Delbos, *De Kant aux postkantiens*, 1940, and R. Verneaux, *Les Sources cartésiennes et kantiennes de l'idéalisme français*, 1936 (for the twentieth century in particular). Cf. also J. Laporte, 'Kant et la philosophie française', *Revue de France*, 15 mai 1924, and C. Bouglé, 'Spiritualisme et Kantisme en France', *Revue de Paris*, 1er mai 1934.

[15] Reynaud, op. cit., pp. 222–3. One finds this view as late as E. Caro, *L'Idée de Dieu et ses nouveaux critiques*, 1864, p. 8, and E. Saisset, *Le Scepticisme*, 1865.

who presents him as an opponent of the sensualists and as a defender of free will and moral responsibility: the sub-title of his *Philosophie de Kant* (1801) is *Principes fondamentaux de la philosophie transcendantale*. For Cousin he is a metaphysical idealist; Janet uses him as a stick with which to beat Littré; and Ravaisson asserts of him: 'Nul ne fit plus pour amener à comprendre que l'infini, le parfait, l'absolu, c'est la liberté spirituelle, et que le dernier mot de tout est le principe moral.' Later still, Fouillée declares: 'Le point cardinal de la philosophie kantienne était que, si la science est une fonction de l'esprit, elle n'est ni la seule ni la plus importante.'[16] In part, these divergences are explained if one distinguishes between the *Critique of Pure Reason* and the *Critique of Practical Reason*; each work has its own fortune in France, the former being more influential in the earlier nineteenth century, the latter in its last few decades. It is therefore common to point to Kant's 'double influence' on French thought.[17] Is this adequate? Do not both materialists like Heine and spiritualists like Ravaisson and Fouillée misuse Kant for their own ends? The more faithful Kantian tradition perhaps runs through Cournot, Renouvier, and Lachelier, 'the most distinguished representative of the Kantian movement in France', as Ruggiero describes him[18]—just as in Germany it is seen in Lange and Mach. But what does Kant help them to achieve? Talking of Kantian *criticisme* as he interprets it, Renouvier says: '[L'] exploration du champ et des méthodes de l'esprit humain lui permet d'assigner aux sciences particulières leurs limites, c'est-à-dire les propres conditions sous lesquelles elles parviennent à se constituer. . . .'[19] Is not Kant's most lasting contribution to the controversy of positivism and anti-positivism found here? Rightly viewed, he perhaps offers arms neither to the materialists nor (as was often alleged) to the idealists. His true importance in French philosophy at this time may well lie, first, in the direction he gave for a new review of the limits of science and, secondly, in the impetus he lent to ethical thought. For this latter aspect of

[16] Cf. V. Cousin, *Leçons sur la philosophie de Kant*, 1842; P. Janet, 'La Crise philosophique', *R.D.M.*, 1er août 1864, p. 724; F. Ravaisson, *Rapport sur la philosophie en France au dix-neuvième siècle*, 1904, p. 9; and Fouillée, op. cit., p. xxix.

[17] Cf. Michaud, op. cit., i. 200, for a good summary of this view.

[18] G. Ruggiero, *Modern Philosophy*, translated Hannay and Collingwood, London, 1921, p. 148.

[19] Renouvier, 'De la philosophie du dix-neuvième siècle', loc. cit., p. 106.

his influence one might look first at the libertarian 'wager' of Jules Lequier, developed in Renouvier's ethical work. And again one asks whether Kant is really being used to oppose positivism, or whether this doctrine of ethical choice is not wholly compatible with it. Here, perhaps, in Lequier's theories of choice and belief, which are not unlike the final moral views of Sully Prudhomme later in the century, the positivist can find a resolution of that false ethical dilemma from which others sought escape in scientism or in nihilistic despair. We may have no certainty or knowledge in the scientific and positivist sense of the word concerning religious, metaphysical, and ethical questions, but in these matters we can and must come to our own beliefs in the light of reason and personal experience.

BIBLIOGRAPHY

THE bibliography includes only works quoted above or directly relevant. The works of each author are given in chronological order of date of first publication, except that books precede articles in periodicals and correspondence.

The place of publication is Paris unless otherwise stated.

ACKERMANN, L., *Contes et poésies*, 1863.

—— *Œuvres—Ma Vie; Premières poésies; Poésies philosophiques*, 1885.

—— *Pensées d'une solitaire*, 1882; 2ᵉ éd., edited by L. Read, 1903.

—— 'Lettres inédites pendant ses séjours en Allemagne et en Angleterre', edited by M. Citoleux, *R.L.C.* ix, 1929, pp. 141–62 and 579–89.

—— 'Correspondance pendant son séjour à Nice', edited by M. Citoleux, *R.H.L.F.* xxxvi, 1929, pp. 580–9, and xxxvii, 1930, pp. 81–91, 244–58, and 425–33.

ACTON, H. B., 'Comte's Positivism and the Science of Society', *Philosophy*, London, xxvi, 1951, pp. 291–310.

ADAM, MME A., *Mes Sentiments et nos idées avant 1870*, 1905.

ALIOTTA, A., *The Idealistic Reaction against Science*, translated McCaskill, London, 1914.

ALLIER, R. S. P., *La Philosophie de Renan*, 1894.

ASTIÉ, J. F., 'Examen critique du positivisme', *Revue chrétienne*, 1856, pp. 156 ff., 192 ff., 336 ff., and 461 ff.

BABBITT, I., *The Masters of Modern French Criticism*, Boston and New York, 1912.

BAILLIE, J., *The Belief in Progress*, Oxford, 1950.

BAILLOT, A., *L'Influence de la philosophie de Schopenhauer en France (1860–1900)*, 1927.

BARBEY D'AUREVILLY, J., *Les Œuvres et les hommes: Les Poètes*, 1889.

BARZELLOTTI, G., *La Philosophie de Hippolyte Taine*, 1900.

BAYER, R., *Épistémologie et logique depuis Kant jusqu'à nos jours*, 1954.

BENRUBI, I., *Philosophische Strömungen der Gegenwart in Frankreich*, Leipzig, 1928.

BERGSON, H., *La Pensée et le mouvant*, 3ᵉ éd., 1934.

BERNARD, C., *Introduction à l'étude de la médecine expérimentale*, 1865.

—— *L'Œuvre de Claude Bernard*, Introduction de Duval, Notices par E. Renan, P. Bert, et A. Moreau, 1881.

—— *Pensées, Notes détachées*, 1937.

—— *Philosophie, manuscrit inédit*, edited by Chevalier, 1938.

—— *Principes de médecine expérimentale*, 1947.

—— 'Du progrès dans les sciences physiologiques', *R.D.M.*, 1ᵉʳ août 1865, pp. 640–63.

—— 'Le Problème de la physiologie générale', *R.D.M.*, 15 déc. 1867, pp. 874–92.

BERTHELOT, M., *Science et philosophie*, 1886. (Cf. Renan, E.)

BERTHELOT, P., *Louis Ménard et son œuvre*, 1902.

BERTHELOT, R., 'La Pensée philosophique de Renan', *R.M.M.* xxx, 1923, pp. 365–88.

BEUCHAT, C., *Histoire du naturalisme français*, 1949, 2 vols.

BOAS, G., *French Philosophies of the Romantic Period*, Baltimore, 1925.

BOOSTEN, J. P., *Taine et Renan et l'idée de Dieu*, Nijmegen, 1937.

BOURGET, P., *Essais de psychologie contemporaine*, 1926, 2 vols.

—— *Le Disciple*, 1946 (Fayard).

—— *Études et portraits*, s.d. (Plon-Nourrit), 3 vols.

—— *Pages de critique et de doctrine*, s.d. (Plon-Nourrit), 2 vols.

BOUTMY, E., *Taine, Scherer, Laboulaye*, 1901.

BOUTROUX, E., *De la contingence des lois de la nature*, 1874.

—— *Science et religion dans la philosophie contemporaine*, 1908.

—— 'Un Poète philosophe, M. Sully Prudhomme', *Revue politique et littéraire*, 4 sept. 1875, pp. 227–31.

—— 'Auguste Comte et la métaphysique', *R.C.C.*, 1902, t. x, 1, pp. 769–76, t. x, 2, pp. 206–13, 547–54, and 735–47, t. xi, pp. 57–64 and 145–53.

—— 'La Philosophie en France depuis 1867', *R.M.M.* xvi, 1908, pp. 683–716.

BRÉHIER, E., *Histoire de la philosophie*, t. ii—*La Philosophie moderne*, 1932.

BRIDENNE, J. J., *La Littérature française d'imagination scientifique*, 1950.

BROGLIE, ABBÉ DE, *La Réaction contre le positivisme*, 1894.

BRUNETIÈRE, F., *L'Évolution de la poésie lyrique au dix-neuvième siècle*, 9e éd., s.d., 2 vols.

—— *Discours de combat*, 1900–7, 3 vols.

—— *Sur les chemins de la croyance — Première étape: L'Utilisation du positivisme*, 1905.

BRUNSCHVICG, L., *Les Progrès de la conscience dans la philosophie occidentale*, 1927.

BURNOUF, E., *Introduction à l'histoire du bouddhisme indien*, 1844.

BURY, J. B., *The Idea of Progress*, London, 1920.

CAIRD, E., *The Social Philosophy and Religion of Comte*, Glasgow, 1893.

CANAT, R., *Une Forme du mal du siècle: Du sentiment de la solitude morale chez les romantiques et les parnassiens*, 1904.

CANTECOR, G., *Comte*, nouv. éd., s.d.

CARCASSONNE, E., 'Leconte de Lisle et la philosophie indienne', *R.L.C.* xi, 1931, pp. 618–46.

CARO, E., *L'Idée de Dieu et ses nouveaux critiques*, 1864.

—— 'La Métaphysique et les sciences positives—I: L'École expérimentale', *R.D.M.*, 15 nov. 1866, pp. 421–52.

—— 'La Poésie philosophique dans les nouvelles écoles—Un Poète positiviste', *R.D.M.*, 15 mai 1874, pp. 241–62.

—— 'Émile Littré—Histoire des ses travaux et de ses idées', *R.D.M.*, 1er avril 1882, pp. 516–51 and 1er mai 1882, pp. 5–46. (Cf. Caro, *M. Littré et le positivisme*, 1883.)

CARRÉ, J. M., *Les Écrivains français et le mirage allemand (1800–1940)*, 1947.

CASSAGNE, A., *La Théorie de l'art pour l'art chez les derniers romantiques et les premiers réalistes*, 1906.

CAULLERY, M., *La Science française depuis le dix-septième siècle*, 1933.

CHAIX-RUY, J., *Ernest Renan*, 1956.

CHAUFFARD, E., 'Claude Bernard—Sa Vie et ses œuvres', *R.D.M.*, 15 nov. 1878, pp. 272–310.

CHEVRILLON, A., *Taine—Formation de sa pensée*, 1932.

—— 'La Jeunesse de Taine', *Revue de Paris*, 1902, t. iv, pp. 1–30 and 341–71.

CITOLEUX, M., *La Poésie philosophique au dix-neuvième siècle—Madame Ackermann*, 1906.

—— 'Madame Ackermann et les étrangers', *R.L.C.* xi, 1931, pp. 466–72.

—— 'Le Salon littéraire des Feuillantines: Les Catholiques et les neutres chez Madame Ackermann', *Mercure de France*, t. 233, 1932, pp. 313–31. (Cf. Ackermann, L.)

CLARK, J. G., *La Pensée de Ferdinand Brunetière*, 1954.

CLERC, C., *Le Génie du paganisme*, 1926.

CLOUARD, H., *La Poésie française moderne des romantiques à nos jours*, 1924.

COIGNET, C., *De Kant à Bergson—Réconciliation de la religion et de la science dans un spiritualisme nouveau*, 1911.

COLLINGWOOD, R. G., *The Idea of History*, Oxford, 1946.

COMTE, A., *Plan des travaux scientifiques nécessaires pour réorganiser la société*, in *Opuscules de philosophie sociale*, 1883.

—— *Cours de philosophie positive, augmenté d'une Préface par É. Littré*, 2ᵉ éd., 1864, 6 vols.

—— *Discours sur l'esprit positif*, in *Traité philosophique d'astronomie populaire*, 1844.

—— *Discours sur l'ensemble du positivisme*, in *Système de politique positive*, t. i, 1851.

—— *Système de politique positive*, 1851–4, 4 vols.

—— *Catéchisme positiviste*, 1852.

—— *Synthèse subjective*, t. i, 1856.

—— *Lettres à Valat (1815–1844)*, 1870.

—— *Lettres d'Auguste Comte à J. S. Mill (1841–1846)*, 1877.

—— *Correspondance inédite*, 1901–4, 4 vols.

—— *Lettres et fragments de lettres*, São Paulo, 1926.

—— *Nouvelles lettres inédites*, 1939.

COTARD, H., *La Pensée de Claude Bernard*, Grenoble, 1945.

COUSIN, V., *Leçons sur la philosophie de Kant*, 1842.

CRESSON, A., *Les Courants de la pensée philosophique française*, 1927, 2 vols.

—— *Comte*, 1941.

—— *H. Taine, sa vie, son œuvre*, 1951.

—— *La Philosophie française*, 1951.

DAMPIER, W. C., *A History of Science and its Relations with Philosophy and Religion*, 4th ed., Cambridge, 1948.

DAUDET, A., *Trente ans de Paris*, s.d. (Flammarion).

DELBOS, V., *Le Problème moral dans la philosophie de Spinoza et dans l'histoire du Spinozisme*, 1893.

DELVOLVÉ, J., *Réflexions sur la pensée comtienne*, 1932.

DE ROUVRE, C., *Auguste Comte et le catholicisme*, 1928.

DESCHARMES, R., *Flaubert, sa vie, son caractère, ses idées avant 1857*, 1909.

DESONAY, F., *Le Rêve hellénique chez les poètes parnassiens*, 1928.

D'HAUSSONVILLE, O. B. P. G. de C., 'Madame Ackermann, d'après des lettres et des papiers inédits', *R.D.M.*, 15 nov. 1891, pp. 318–52.

DHURONT, E., *Claude Bernard, sa vie, son œuvre*, 1937.

DOUDAN, X., *Mélanges et lettres*, 1876–7, 4 vols.

DUMAS, G., *Psychologie de deux messies positivistes — Saint-Simon et Auguste Comte*, 1905.

DUMESNIL, R., *Gustave Flaubert, l'homme et l'œuvre*, 3e éd., 1947.

—— *L'Époque réaliste et naturaliste*, 1946.

—— *Le Réalisme et le naturalisme*, s.d. (Gigord).

EASTWOOD, D. M., *The Revival of Pascal—A Study of his relation to modern French thought*, Oxford, 1936.

ELSENBERG, H., *Le Sentiment religieux chez Leconte de Lisle*, 1909.

ERDAN, A., *La France mystique: Tableau des excentricités religieuses de ce temps*, s.d. (Coulon-Pineau), 2 vols.

ESTÈVE, E., *Leconte de Lisle*, 1923.

—— *Sully Prudhomme, poète sentimental et poète philosophe*, 1925.

EVANS, D. O., *Social Romanticism in France, 1830–1848*, Oxford, 1951.

—— 'Alfred de Vigny and Positivism', *Romanic Review*, New York, t. xxxv, 1944, pp. 288–98.

FAGUET, E., *Politiques et moralistes du dix-neuvième siècle*, 5e éd., 1903, 3 vols.

FATH, R., *De l'influence de la science sur la littérature française dans la deuxième moitié du dix-neuvième siècle*, Lausanne, 1901.

FAURE, J. L., *Claude Bernard*, 1926.

FLAUBERT, G., *Œuvres*, 1909–53, 26 vols. (Conard).

FLINT, R., *History of the Philosophy of History*, Edinburgh and London, 1893.

—— *Anti-Theistic Theories*, Edinburgh and London, 1917.

FLOTTES, P., *Le Poète Leconte de Lisle*, 1929.

—— *Sully Prudhomme et sa pensée*, 1930.

—— *Leconte de Lisle, l'homme et l'œuvre*, 1954.

FORT, P. et MANDIN, L., *Histoire de la poésie française depuis 1850*, 1926.

FOUILLÉE, A., *Le Mouvement idéaliste et la réaction contre la science positive*, 1896.

FRANCE, A., *La Vie littéraire*, 1924–5, 4 vols.

FRANCK, A., *Moralistes et philosophes*, 1872.

FUSIL, C. A., *La Poésie scientifique de 1750 à nos jours*, 1918.

GAUTIER, T., *Histoire du romantisme suivie de notices romantiques et d'une étude sur la poésie française (1830–1868)*, 1874.

GINSBERG, M., *The Idea of Progress—A Revaluation*, London, 1953.

GIRAUD, V., *Essai sur Taine*, 6e éd., s.d. (Hachette).

—— *Maîtres d'autrefois et d'aujourd'hui*, 1914.

GIRAUD, V., H. Taine—Études et documents, 1928.
—— Le Problème religieux et l'histoire de la littérature française, 1938.
GONCOURT, E. et J. DE, Journal: Mémoires de la vie littéraire, 1888–1910, 9 vols.
GOOCH, G. P., History and Historians in the Nineteenth Century, London, 1913.
GOUHIER, H., La Vie d'Auguste Comte, 1931.
—— La Jeunesse d'Auguste Comte et la formation du positivisme, 1933–41, 3 vols.
GOURMONT, R. DE, Promenades littéraires, 4e série, 8e éd., 1920.
GRÜBER, H., Le Positivisme depuis Comte jusqu'à nos jours, traduit Mazoyer, 1893.
GUÉRARD, A. L., French Prophets of Yesterday—A Study of Religious Thought under the Second Empire, London, 1913.
GUILLEMIN, H., Flaubert devant la vie et devant Dieu, 1939.
GUNN, J. A., Modern French Philosophy, London, 1922.
HAVET, E., éd., Pascal—Pensées sur la religion, 1866.
HAYEK, F. A., 'The Counter-Revolution of Science', Economica, London, viii, 1941, pp. 9 ff., 119 ff., and 281 ff.
—— 'Scientism and the Study of Society', Economica, London, ix, 1942, pp. 267 ff., x, 1943, pp. 34 ff., and xi, 1944, pp. 27 ff.
HÉMON, C., La Philosophie de Sully Prudhomme, 1907.
HÖFFDING, H., Philosophes contemporains, 1907.
HÜGEL, F. VON, Essays and Addresses on the Philosophy of Religion, London, 1931–3, 2 vols.
HUNT, H. J., The Epic in Nineteenth-Century France, Oxford, 1941.
JANET, PAUL, 'La Crise philosophique et les idées spiritualistes en France', R.D.M., 15 juillet 1864, pp. 459–90, and 1er août 1864, pp. 718–46.
—— 'La Méthode expérimentale et la physiologie à propos des travaux récents de M. Claude Bernard', R.D.M., 15 avril 1866, pp. 908–36.
—— 'Le Spiritualisme français au dix-neuvième siècle', R.D.M., 15 mai 1868, pp. 353–85.
JASINSKI, R., Histoire de la littérature française, 1947, 2 vols.
JAVARY, A., De l'idée de progrès, 1851.
JOERGENSEN, J., The Development of Logical Empiricism, Chicago, 1951.
KAHN, S. J., Science and Aesthetic Judgment—A Study of Taine's Critical Method, London, 1953.
KING, D. L., L'Influence des sciences physiologiques sur la littérature française de 1670 à 1870, 1926.
KNOWLES, D. M., La Réaction idéaliste au théâtre depuis 1890, 1934.
LABORDE-MILÀA, A., Hippolyte Taine: Essai d'une biographie intellectuelle, 1909.
LACOMBE, P., Taine, 1906.
LALANDE, A., Vocabulaire technique et critique de la philosophie, 1951.
LALO, C., L'Art et la vie; L'Économie des passions, 1947.
LAMY, P., Claude Bernard et le matérialisme, 1939.
LANSON, G., Histoire de la littérature française, 9e éd., 1906.

LASSERRE, P., *Renan et nous*, 1923.
—— *La Jeunesse d'Ernest Renan*, 1928, 2 vols.
LAUGEL, A., 'Les Études philosophiques en Angleterre—M. Herbert Spencer', *R.D.M.*, 15 fév. 1864, pp. 930–57.
LEBLOND, M. et A., *Leconte de Lisle*, 1906.
LECONTE DE LISLE, C. M. R., *Œuvres* (*Poèmes antiques*, s.d., *Poèmes barbares*, s.d., *Poèmes tragiques*, s.d., *Derniers poèmes*, 1926), Lemerre, 4 vols.
—— *Premières poésies et lettres intimes*, edited by B. Guinaudeau, 1902.
LEHMANN, A. G., *The Symbolist Aesthetic in France*, Oxford, 1950.
LEMAÎTRE, J., *Les Contemporains*, s.d. (Boivin), 8 vols.
LENOIR, R., 'L'Idéalisme de Taine', *R.M.M.* xxiii, 1916, pp. 859–78.
—— 'Claude Bernard et l'esprit expérimental', *Rev. Philos.*, t. 87, 1919, pp. 72–101.
LEROY, M., *Taine*, 1933.
—— *Histoire des idées sociales en France*, t. ii: *De Babeuf à Tocqueville*, 1950; t. iii: *D'Auguste Comte à P. J. Proudhon*, 1954.
LÉVY-BRUHL, L., *The Philosophy of Auguste Comte*, translated Beaumont-Klein, London, 1903. (Cf. original ed., 1900.)
—— 'Le Centenaire d'Auguste Comte', *R.D.M.*, 15 jan. 1898, pp. 394–423.
LITTRÉ, E., *De la philosophie positive*, 1845.
—— *Conservation, révolution et positivisme*, 2ᵉ éd., 1879.
—— *Auguste Comte et la philosophie positive*, 2ᵉ éd., 1864.
—— 'Préface d'un disciple', in A. Comte, *Cours de philosophie positive*, t. i, 1864.
—— *La Science au point de vue philosophique*, 1873.
—— 'La Philosophie positive; M. Auguste Comte et M. J. Stuart Mill', *R.D.M.*, 15 août 1866, pp. 829–66.
LÖWITH, K., *Meaning in History*, Chicago, 1949.
LOYSON, P. H., 'La Vérité sur la mort de Littré', *La Grande Revue*, t. 62, 1910, pp. 469–83.
—— 'Mémoires inédits de mon père sur la mort de Littré', *La Grande Revue*, t. 101, 1920, pp. 353–62.
LUBAC, H. DE, *The Drama of Atheist Humanism*, translated Riley, London, 1949.
MARTINO, P., *Parnasse et symbolisme*, 7ᵉ éd., 1947.
—— 'Le Second Empire', in *Littérature française*, edited by J. Bédier and P. Hazard, t. ii, 1949, pp. 294–362.
MASSIS, H., *Ernest Renan, ou le romantisme de l'intelligence*, 1923.
MAURIAC, P., *Claude Bernard*, 1941.
—— 'La Figure tourmentée de Claude Bernard', *Mercure de France*, t. 287, 1938, pp. 278–88.
MAYNIAL, E., *Gustave Flaubert*, 1943.
MÉNARD, L., *Lettres d'un mort—Opinions d'un païen sur la société moderne*, 1895.
—— *De la morale avant les philosophes*, 2ᵉ éd., 1863.
—— *Du polythéisme hellénique*, 1863.

MÉNARD, L., *Rêveries d'un païen mystique*, édition définitive, edited by Rioux de Maillou, 1911.
—— *Poèmes et rêveries d'un païen mystique*, 1895.
—— 'Les Études d'histoire religieuse d'Ernest Renan', *Revue philosophique et religieuse*, t. vii, 1857, pp. 178–86.
—— 'Catéchisme religieux des libres penseurs', *La Critique philosophique*, 15 juillet 1875, pp. 375–84, 22 juillet 1875, pp. 391–400, 29 juillet 1875, pp. 407–16, and 12 août 1875, pp. 24–32.
—— 'Lettre à F. Pillon', *La Critique philosophique*, 1887, t. i, pp. 315–20.
MENTRÉ, F., 'Le Hasard dans les découvertes scientifiques d'après Claude Bernard', *Revue de philosophie*, t. iv, 1904, pp. 672–8.
MEYERSON, E., *Identité et réalité*, 1912.
MICHAUD, G., *Message poétique du symbolisme*, 1947, 4 vols.
MILL, J. S., *Auguste Comte and Positivism*, 2nd ed., London, 1866.
—— *Autobiography*, London, 1873.
—— *Dissertations and Discussions*, 1867–75, 4 vols.
MILLIOUD, M., *La Religion de M. Renan*, 1891.
MONOD, G., *Les Maîtres de l'histoire—Renan, Taine, Michelet*, 1894.
MORICE, H., *La Poésie de Sully Prudhomme*, 1920.
NÈVE, P., *La Philosophie de Taine*, 1908.
NOURRISSON, E., *Spinoza et le matérialisme contemporain*, 1866.
PARIS, G., *Penseurs et poètes*, 1896.
PARODI, D., *La Philosophie contemporaine en France*, 1919.
—— *Du positivisme à l'idéalisme—Études critiques*, 1930.
—— *Du positivisme à l'idéalisme—Philosophies d'hier*, 1930.
PERRY, R. B., *Philosophy of the Recent Past*, London, 1927.
PEYRE, H., *Louis Ménard (1822–1901)*, New Haven, 1932.
—— 'The Literature of the Second Empire—*La poésie*', *Symposium*, Syracuse, vol. vii, 1953, pp. 16–33.
POMMIER, J., *Renan, d'après des documents inédits*, 1923.
—— *La Pensée religieuse de Renan*, 1925.
—— *La Jeunesse cléricale de Renan*, 1933.
POPPER, K. R., *The Poverty of Historicism*, London, 1957.
PUTTER, I., *The Pessimism of Leconte de Lisle: Sources and Evolution*, Berkeley and Los Angeles, 1954.
RAVAISSON, F., *Rapport sur la philosophie en France au dix-neuvième siècle*, 5e éd., 1904.
RENAN, E., *L'Origine du langage*, 2e éd., 1858.
—— *Études d'histoire religieuse*, 3e éd., 1863.
—— *Essais de morale et de critique*, 10e éd., 1928.
—— *La Vie de Jésus*, 24e éd., 1895.
—— *Dialogues et fragments philosophiques*, 12e éd., 1925.
—— *Souvenirs d'enfance et de jeunesse*, s.d. (éd. Collection nouvelle, Calmann-Lévy).
—— *Nouvelles études d'histoire religieuse*, 1884.
—— *Discours et conférences*, 9e éd., 1928.
—— *Drames philosophiques*, 13e éd., 1928.
—— *L'Avenir de la science—Pensées de 1848*, 23e éd., 1929.

RENAN, E., *Feuilles détachées*, 17ᵉ éd., 1922.
—— 'Examen de conscience philosophique', *R.D.M.*, 15 août 1889, pp. 721–37.
—— et RENAN, H., *Lettres intimes (1842–1845), précédées de Ma Sœur Henriette par E. Renan*, s.d. (Nelson and Calmann-Lévy).
—— et BERTHELOT, M., *Correspondance, 1847–1892*, 1929.
RENOUVIER, C., *Essais de critique générale*, 1854–64, 4 vols.
—— *La Science de la morale*, 1869, 2 vols.
—— 'De la philosophie du dix-neuvième siècle en France', *L'Année philosophique—Première Année (1867)*, 1868, pp. 1–108.
REYNAUD, L., *L'Influence allemande en France au dix-huitième et au dix-neuvième siècles*, 1922.
—— *La Crise de notre littérature*, 1929.
RIBOT, T., *La Psychologie anglaise contemporaine*, 3ᵉ éd., 1896.
ROSCA, D. D., *L'Influence de Hegel sur Taine théoricien de la connaissance et de l'art*, 1928.
ROUDAUD, H., 'De Louise Ackermann aux révolutionnaires contemporaines', *Mercure de France*, t. 280, 1937, pp. 402–7.
ROUTH, H. V., *Towards the Twentieth Century—A Spiritual History of the Nineteenth Century*, Cambridge, 1937.
RUBOW, P. V., *Hippolyte Taine—Étapes de son œuvre*, Copenhagen and Paris, 1930.
RUGGIERO, G. DE, *Modern Philosophy*, translated Hannay and Collingwood, London, 1921.
SAINTE-BEUVE, C. A., *Nouveaux Lundis*, 1863–70, 13 vols.
SAMPSON, R. V., *Progress in the Age of Reason*, London, 1956.
SCHAFFER, A., *The Genres of Parnassian Poetry—A Study of the Parnassian Minors*, Baltimore, 1944.
SCHERER, E., *Mélanges de critique religieuse*, 1860.
—— *Mélanges d'histoire religieuse*, 2ᵉ éd., 1865.
—— *Études sur la littérature contemporaine*, 1863–95, 10 vols.
—— 'Hégel et l'hégélianisme', *R.D.M.*, 15 fév. 1861, pp. 812–56.
SCHWAB, R., *La Renaissance orientale*, 1950.
SÉAILLES, G., *Ernest Renan*, 1895.
—— 'Les Philosophies de la liberté', *R.M.M.* v, 1879, pp. 162–80.
SECRÉTAN, C., *La Philosophie de la liberté*, 2ᵉ éd., 1866.
SÉE, H., *Science et philosophie de l'histoire*, 1928.
SERTILLANGES, A. D., *La Philosophie de Claude Bernard*, 1944.
SIMPSON, W. J. S., *Religious Thought in France in the Nineteenth Century*, London, 1935.
SMITH, COLIN, 'The Fictionalist Element in Renan's Thought', *French Studies*, Oxford, ix, 1955, pp. 30–41.
SMITH, NINA, *L'Accord de la science et de la poésie dans la seconde moitié du dix-neuvième siècle*, Vienne, 1928.
SOURIAU, M., *Histoire du Parnasse*, 1929.
SPENCER, P., *Flaubert: A Biography*, London, 1953.
SPIESS, C., *Le Penseur chez Sully Prudhomme*, 1908.
STEBBING, L. S., *Pragmatism and French Voluntarism*, Cambridge, 1914.

SULLY PRUDHOMME, R. F. A., Œuvres—Poésies, 1925-6, 6 vols.
—— Œuvres—Prose, 1904-8, 2 vols.
—— La Vraie Religion selon Pascal, 1905.
—— Psychologie du libre arbitre, 1907.
—— Lettres à une amie (1865-80), 1911.
—— Journal intime: Lettres—Pensées, 1922.
—— Préface to C. Hémon, La Philosophie de Sully Prudhomme, 1907.
TAINE, H., Essai sur Tite-Live, 1856.
—— La Fontaine et ses fables, 26ᵉ éd., s.d. (Hachette).
—— Les Philosophes classiques du dix-neuvième siècle en France, 13ᵉ éd., s.d. (Hachette).
—— Essais de critique et d'histoire, 14ᵉ éd., 1923.
—— Le Positivisme anglais, étude sur Stuart Mill, 1864.
—— Histoire de la littérature anglaise, 18ᵉ éd., s.d. (Hachette), 5 vols.
—— De l'intelligence, 16ᵉ éd., s.d. (Hachette), 2 vols.
—— Philosophie de l'art, 21ᵉ éd., s.d. (Hachette), 2 vols.
—— Nouveaux essais de critique et d'histoire, 13ᵉ éd., s.d. (Hachette).
—— Derniers essais de critique et d'histoire, 6ᵉ éd., 1923.
—— Hippolyte Taine, sa vie et sa correspondance, 1902-7, 4 vols.
TAYLOR, A. C., Carlyle et la pensee latine, 1937.
THÉRIVE, A., Le Parnasse, 1929.
THIBAUDET, A., Gustave Flaubert, 1922.
—— Histoire de la littérature française de 1789 à nos jours, 1936.
TRONCHON, H., La Fortune intellectuelle de Herder en France, 1920.
VACHEROT, E., La Métaphysique et la science, 2ᵉ éd., 1863, 3 vols.
—— 'La Situation philosophique en France', R.D.M., 15 juin 1868, pp. 950-77.
VALLOIS, M., La Formation de l'influence kantienne en France, s.d.
VAN TIEGHEM, PH., Petite histoire des grandes doctrines littéraires en France, 1946.
—— Renan, 1948.
VÉRA, A., Introduction à la philosophie de Hegel, 1864.
WAHL, J., The Pluralist Philosophies of England and America, translated Rothwell, London, 1925. (Cf. original ed., 1920.)
—— Tableau de la philosophie française, 1946.
WEBER, A., Histoire de la philosophie européenne, 1914.
WEILER, M., La Pensée de Renan, 1945.
WEINBERG, B., French Realism—The Critical Reaction, New York, 1937.
WHITTAKER, T., Comte and Mill, London, 1908.
WILLEY, B., Nineteenth-Century Studies, London, 1949.
ZOLA, E., Mes Haines: Causeries littéraires et artistiques, 1880.
ZYROMSKI, E., Sully Prudhomme, 1907.

INDEX

Principal references are indicated by italicized numerals

PRINTED IN GREAT BRITAIN
AT THE UNIVERSITY PRESS, OXFORD
BY VIVIAN RIDLER
PRINTER TO THE UNIVERSITY